INVISIBLE REALITY

**New Visions in Native American
and Indigenous Studies**

SERIES EDITORS

Margaret D. Jacobs
Robert Miller

Invisible Reality

Storytellers, Storytakers, and the
Supernatural World of the Blackfeet

ROSALYN R. LAPIER

CO-PUBLISHED BY THE UNIVERSITY OF NEBRASKA PRESS

AND THE AMERICAN PHILOSOPHICAL SOCIETY

Names: LaPier, Rosalyn R., author.
Title: Invisible reality: storytellers, storytakers, and the
supernatural world of the Blackfeet / Rosalyn R. LaPier.
Description: Lincoln NE: University of Nebraska Press,
American Philosophical Society, [2017] | Series: New
visions in Native American and indigenous studies |
Includes bibliographical references and index.
Identifiers: LCCN 2017007891 (print)
LCCN 2017014913 (ebook)
ISBN 9781496201508 (cloth: alk. paper)
ISBN 9781496214775 (paper: alk. paper)
ISBN 9781496202383 (epub)
ISBN 9781496202390 (mobi)
ISBN 9781496202406 (pdf)
Subjects: LCSH: Piegan Indians—History. | Piegan Indians—
Folklore. | Piegan Indians—Religion. | LaPier, Rosalyn R.—Family. |
Blackfeet Tribe of the Blackfeet Indian Reservation of Montana—
History. | Blackfeet Tribe of the Blackfeet Indian Reservation of
Montana—Social life and customs. | Blackfeet Indian Reservation
(Mont.)—Biography. | Blackfeet Indian Reservation (Mont.)—
History. | Indians of North America—Montana—History.
Classification: LCC E99.P58 L345 2017 (ebook)
LCC E99.P58 (print)
DDC 978.004/97352—dc23
LC record available at https://lccn.loc.gov/2017007891

Set in Charis by Rachel Gould.
Designed by N. Putens.

For ancestors who believed in the power of stories

Robert Dumont Jr.

Darrell Robes Kipp

Thomas Little Plume

Bea Medicine

Theresa Still Smoking

and

Annie Mad Plume Wall

CONTENTS

ILLUSTRATIONS

MAPS

PHOTOGRAPHS

Writing about American Indian, Native American, or Indigenous peoples brings with it many distinct challenges and questions. However, if the author is also Native American, writing about Native peoples brings even more challenges and questions. Scholarship of Native peoples is always suspect in today's world. Scholars such as Vine Deloria Jr., Devon Mihesuah, Linda Tuhiwai Smith, Edward Said, and others question the validity of most scholarship written *about* Native people.[1] This assertion is especially true if the sources used for the scholarship are presumed to be from a non-Native perspective. Even the terminology used to describe Native people is questioned. For example, I use the terms "Native American" or "Native" to define the peoples of the northern Great Plains who were present before the arrival of Europeans and Americans and not "American Indian" or "Indigenous." I also use the phrase "old-time Indians" or "old-timers." I am not choosing these terms for academic, theoretical purposes or even political purposes but just because that is what people call themselves.

The beginning of a book is usually the place to provide basic information about a writer's methodology, what sources she will use, how she will interpret the sources, and how she will construct her own interpretation. However, because of these modern-day concerns regarding validity and authenticity I will begin by addressing questions such as, Am I really an "authentic" Native American? Am I someone who can speak for my ancestors? What data am I using? Where did the data come from? From outsiders? If so, are the data valid? Since I am writing about my own community, to what extent am I "using" my family for information? Am I exploiting Grandma? And am I revealing her sacred knowledge?

I will also address other questions that arise in more typical histories, including questions related to time, place, people, and interpretation. What historical time period will I cover? What place, area, or region did I research? What group will I research? This is a lot to address in a preface. However, it is necessary to address some of these questions (because they will arise with some readers, in particular, Native American readers) in order to be transparent about my intentions, my research, my interpretive conclusions, and my writing.

Authenticity

The Browning Mercantile was not far from my grandparents' house when I was growing up. My grandfather instituted an ingenious way of getting us kids to learn our Blackfeet heritage—he paid us money. (However, as this book reveals, perhaps his method was not so ingenious.) For a few pennies he would ask us to either sing a song, dance a dance, or recite our family tree. I was not so keen on the singing and dancing part, so I recited the family genealogy. With my newfound wealth I headed off to the Browning Merc to purchase what seemed like loads of penny candy. From this inauspicious beginning I learned the family tree. As an adult I also used the book *Blackfeet Heritage*, which is a census of the Blackfeet reservation conducted during allotment, as well as other census records and the research of C. C. Uhlenbeck.[2] I filled in this information by asking my grandmother about who was *really* related to whom. I can therefore unequivocally say that I know with whom I am related. Most readers will ask why this matters. All I can say is that it does! Most Native readers and scholars (and even some non-Native scholars) today want to know. They want to know if you are "authentic," if your experience is authentic, and if your voice is authentic. There's no getting around it; that is the way of the world today.

Authenticity within a Native community of course means more than just knowing your family tree. It also implies knowledge of tribal heritage, residence within a tribal homeland, and even participation in community activities. From community to community this authenticity can have different parameters, and these parameters can change over time and place. During my childhood, at least from my grandfather's perspective, encouraging his grandchildren to recite our genealogy was a basic yet essential component of Blackfeet knowledge.[3]

Níkso'kowaiksi—My Relatives

When I was growing up my grandparents taught me that the proper way to introduce myself was by introducing all four of my grandparents. In that way the person I was meeting for the first time or visiting with would easily know who I was related to and if they were related to me, without asking any intrusive questions. The purpose was to either establish a kinship tie, close or distant, or at the very least to know family relationships and connections. In the old days it was also proper to add the creek or river (which established band affiliation) to the introduction. So a person might say, "My grandfather is so and so from Blacktail Creek." Again the purpose was to address the question, "Am I related to you?" without ever having to ask the question.

My maternal grandparents are the late Francis Wall and Annie Mad Plume. However, for the most part neither of them went by either of those names. My grandfather went by the Blackfeet name Iòkimau, which is a shortened form of the word *ixtáiòkimau*, meaning "to make pemmican."[4] He was adopted as a young boy by Aimsback and Aimsback's second wife, Hollering in the Air. My grandfather's given name was Thomas Francis Wall, a nice Irish name, which is in reality what he was—Irish, and Blackfeet.[5] (Why an old-time Blackfeet would adopt a blond-headed Irish-Blackfeet boy is another story.) My grandmother went by both Annie Rattler and Annie Mad Plume. Earlier in her life her uncle, Rattler, took care of her siblings, so now half of her siblings go by Rattler and the other half by Mad Plume. However, she was raised by her grandmother, Not Real Beaver Woman (or Mary Spotted Bear) and great-grandmother, Big Tiger Woman, which is what everyone called her in English. (There really are not any tigers in Montana, just bad translators. The real translation should be Big Mountain Lion Woman.) On all of their official documents my grandparents' names were Francis Aimsback and Annie Mad Plume–Aimsback. I always thought it was rather progressive for the folks back in the day to give my grandmother a hyphenated name. But at some point my grandfather started using his birth name of Wall. And his documents evolve from using Aimsback, then Aimsback-Wall, and then Wall. On most of their documents my grandparents are listed as full-blood Blackfeet. However, the Blackfeet did not use blood quantum until 1962, when the tribe implemented the one-quarter blood rule; before 1962 the tribe based enrollment on descendancy.[6] With two full-blood grandparents (sort of) I had enough family blood to be enrolled as a Blackfeet tribal member.[7]

My genealogy gets a bit more complicated on the Métis side of the family. My paternal grandparents are the late Arthur Baptiste LaPierre and Louise LaFromboise. Both are from Montana, but both families originated in what is now Manitoba and were Red River Métis. Historians call the Métis a "new people" developed out of the North American fur trade of European men partnering with Native women, and within my family we seem to have always been French–Ojibwe Métis partnering with other French–Ojibwe Métis.[8] My father's Montana birth certificate states under "race" that he is a "breed" and that both of his parents are "breeds."[9] I can safely say that on my father's side of the family we have been Métis since the eighteenth century, my family participated in both Métis rebellions, the family owned Métis scrip, and we even play the fiddle. Scholars have written numerous books about the Red River Métis and there are even published genealogies, so I will not go into any greater detail except to say that some Métis moved to what is now Montana in the mid-nineteenth century and made Montana their home. The LaPierre family, now Americanized to LaPier, has been in Montana since the 1860s or perhaps earlier.[10] Despite this history my father was on the rolls with the Turtle Mountain Chippewa in North Dakota. (Again, that is another story.)

So am I authentic? I am half Blackfeet and half Métis. I am an enrolled member of the Blackfeet tribe. I was raised on the Blackfeet reservation and throughout the Pacific Northwest. I live on my own land on the reservation every summer. I have worked with community-based organizations on the reservation my entire adult life; that work included founding one organization myself. However, I also have a great-great-grandfather who was Irish. Unfortunately he was not royal.[11]

Why does this matter? And why do I care to share my family genealogy? Seems a bit narcissistic, some might say. I do so because in today's world, let's be honest, people lie. They lie about who they are, they lie about belonging to Native communities that they do not belong to, they change their tribal affiliation several times, they lie about who their families are or sometimes simply exaggerate, and they often just don't tell the whole story. People get academic jobs based on their fake "authentic" Native American identity. Because of such behavior in today's world some universities and scholars of Native peoples insist that people identify their social position. Personally I think that if someone states that they are Native, they should be prepared to prove it. I know that I can. I can recite my entire family tree. Pay me a few pennies and I will tell you.

Exploiting Grandma!

One question that scholars argue over is whether it is possible for a historian writing about her own community to remain objective. So am I studying my own community? The answer is both yes and no. I am writing about my own experiences learning about Blackfeet stories and history. I am also writing about the community of my grandmother and grandfather and their parents. Historians often quote the L. P. Hartley phrase, "The past is a foreign country: they do things differently there."[12] In this case I would argue that for my grandparents the past was a known country and the present became for them a foreign country. And for me the opposite is true. For me the Blackfeet past is a foreign country, a different world. When my grandparents grew up they spoke a different language, practiced a different religion, ate different foods, and had different customs than they had in the modern world. When I look at their past I am truly looking at a foreign place. So am I writing about my own community? I would argue that I am writing about the past of my community. And that past is a vastly different place than the present: "they do things differently there."

The histories and stories that I am recounting in this book I learned in five different ways. First, I have heard many of the stories throughout childhood and my lifetime. Most of these stories I heard from my grandmother, Annie, but some are from a variety of other relatives. Second, as an adult I participated in a process the Blackfeet refer to as "transferring" knowledge. As part of the process of transferring knowledge, the learner pays the knowledgeable person for their knowledge. I paid my grandmother, Annie, and my aunt, Theresa Still Smoking, each and every time I visited with them as that was the Blackfeet thing to do, since they were "transferring" their knowledge to me. It is much like paying to attend a university. The Blackfeet think of knowledge (both sacred and profane) as an investment, which can and should be bought and sold. Part of the historic Blackfeet economy was based on this exchange. The historian William Farr has described "transferring" or the buying and selling of religious knowledge as a "sacred economy."[13] Third, I acquired stories and history from working with Blackfeet elders at the Piegan Institute, in both structured and unstructured settings.[14] We worked on various research projects in which the Piegan Institute hired elders whom I interviewed regarding specific linguistic, historic, or cultural ways.[15] And because we worked together for more than a decade these elders often shared information about Blackfeet life with me while we were just visiting and having coffee. They are mentioned throughout the book. Fourth, I continue to ask elders within my own family to clarify questions I have about family or Blackfeet history. And I continue to pay them (yes, even as I drafted this book). And last, I researched and read both the unpublished and published stories collected by the early recorders of Blackfeet life at the turn of the last century.

So am I "using" or "exploiting" grandma? Revealing her "sacred knowledge?" The answer is no. And by buying this book you have just paid me to share my knowledge with you. And thus the Blackfeet knowledge economy continues.

Hey, You Spelled That Wrong!

The Blackfeet do not have an official orthography, that is, an official spelling system of the Blackfeet language. The spellings of the names of the Blackfoot Confederacy tribes change depending on who is doing the writing. There will be some who believe these spellings are incorrect. Perhaps they are. But without an official orthography of the Blackfeet I will rely on the various versions of the spelling of Blackfeet words created by the various recorders of Blackfeet life and the Blackfeet storytellers themselves. I hope that is not too confusing for the reader.

I worked for many years at the Piegan Institute on the Blackfeet reservation on Blackfeet language revitalization, and the institute never established its own orthography. We used the work of C. C. Uhlenbeck and R. H. Van Gulik—*An English-Blackfoot Vocabulary* and *A Blackfoot-English Dictionary* and Jack Holterman et al.'s *A Blackfoot Language Study*. The institute published the Holterman study. These works we viewed as the best language studies completed on the Amskapi Pikuni (South Piegan) dialect used on the Blackfeet reservation. Based on these works we created Blackfeet language lessons and materials for the classroom. However, we also relied on the elders who worked with the Piegan Institute to provide their own spellings of words.

What Is in a Name?

The question that most people ask in relation to a book like this is, What do you call "them," Blackfeet or Blackfoot? This common question has a relatively simple answer. The key word here is "relatively." Most scholars of the Blackfoot Confederacy use the term "Blackfoot" to describe the entire confederacy of four contemporary tribal groups: the Siksika (or Blackfoot), the Kainai (or Blood), the Apatohsi Pikuni (or North Peigan), and the Amskapi Pikuni (or South Piegan). To add a bit of confusion the North Peigan and the South Piegan spell their names differently: Peigan in Canada versus Piegan in the United States. Some scholars argue that these two contemporary groups were once one group, while others believe they were always two groups. For my purposes I treat them as two separate but related groups. Today the international boundary between what is now Canada and the United States splits these four tribes, with three tribes now in Canada and only one in the United States. In this book I write about the Amskapi Pikuni or Blackfeet who live in what is now the United States.

In the past the Blackfoot Confederacy divided themselves into even smaller groups that anthropologists called bands. Bands were autonomous groups of up to two hundred people usually but not necessarily related to each other. They were exogamous, which means they did not marry within their own band. Because of this practice a family could have relatives or kinship relationships with multiple bands. For example, my maternal grandparents were united in an arranged marriage, which was common in the old days. My grandfather's family were members of the Skunks band, and my grandmother's family were members of the Never Laughs band. And their parents were members of different bands. The early recorders of Blackfoot Confederacy life in the late nineteenth century documented between fifteen and twenty-five different bands in each of the four main tribal groups that made up the Blackfoot Confederacy.

Therefore although scholars usually spoke of the Blackfoot Confederacy as one monolithic group (as they still do today), in reality in the nineteenth century the confederacy represented between sixty and one hundred separate autonomous bands. These bands lived within Blackfoot Confederacy territory across the northern Great Plains. Viewed as bands, the Blackfoot Confederacy presents a much greater diversity of peoples than if the confederacy is viewed as one large group. It is easier for most scholars to oversimplify these dynamics of tribal relationships and band identification and just call everyone "Blackfoot." Since I am writing about only one group—the Amskapi Pikuni, now called the Blackfeet—and not all of the Blackfoot Confederacy, I center my terminology on just this one group.

When John C. Ewers was researching his book *The Blackfeet: Raiders on the Northwestern Plains* in the 1940s, he asked the tribal council which name he should use—Blackfeet or Piegan. Ewers noted that most of the tribal council members wanted to call themselves by their ancestral name, "Piegan." However, they concluded that since their new constitution stated that their official name was "Blackfeet," Ewers should use the name Blackfeet in the title of his book.[16] At that time the South Piegan had only recently voted to officially change their ancestral name to the Blackfeet with the passage of their Indian Reorganization Act constitution in 1935.

Still, the question remains: which name should be used, Blackfoot or

Blackfeet? I use the term "Blackfoot Confederacy" to describe the entire confederacy of all four tribal groups, and I use the individual tribal names when discussing each tribe. I use individual band names when discussing those bands. However, I primarily use "Blackfeet" to describe the reservation and its people within the United States.

Watch Your Phraseology

Some Native people and scholars are offended by the use of the terms "myth" or "legend" to describe their "oral traditions."[17] They sometimes view these words as condescending or even derogatory. The anthropologist Peter Nabokov commented that "one often hears Indian old-timers and intellectuals grumbling that characterizing their indigenous histories as 'mythology' or 'folklore' suggests fabrication or simple-mindedness, and furthers the stereotype that they had no sense of history or that they made things up."[18] The problem as Nabokov describes it occurs because some Native people believe their stories to be true whereas scholars (or those studying Native peoples) believe their stories to be metaphor or fiction.

What did the Blackfeet think of stories? The Blackfeet recognized that there were different types of stories. Clark Wissler and David Duvall observed early in the twentieth century that in addition to "mythology" there were also "historical, military, adventurous, ceremonial, and other forms of narratives."[19] But what distinguished what Wissler called "mythology" from other types of stories? Wissler and Duvall observed that

> the attitude of the Blackfoot people toward these [mythological] narratives is difficult to reduce to accurate statement, but one gets the impression that they are often valued more for their aesthetic factors than otherwise. Yet the active elements of this mythology seem to function in mythical characters so firmly fixed in folk-thought, *that each may be regarded as a reality.* One also gets the impression, after some familiarity with the serious life of these people, that mythical characters are generally accorded the same reality as pertains to a deceased friend.[20]

I use the term "story" and sometimes "history" to define narratives that most scholars would call "myth." Most of these stories would be considered "mythology" because they include supernatural elements. When Wissler explained that the Blackfeet viewed "mythical characters" as a "deceased friend," it becomes important to note what the Blackfeet believed about human death. The Blackfeet believed that human bodies die and decompose but the individual essence or soul of the human person lives on. Referring to a dead ancestor does not mean the person is "dead and gone"; it instead implies that the body is gone but the individual's essence lives on in another part of Blackfeet territory.[21] Therefore what did the Blackfeet believe about their stories? They believed they were true stories of life in this universe, and therefore I treat them as "true," as their version of what happened in the past. It may seem disconcerting to some historians for the author to (presumably) suspend critical analysis, but that is not what I intend to do. Similar to acknowledging a Christian's belief in the Holy Trinity without debunking their belief as "untrue," I write about Blackfeet stories in a similar vein, as both a part of their religious belief system and their historical record. It is their truth.

The other term I use is "religion." I do not use the currently popular word "spirituality" or the phrase "spiritual but not religious" to describe Blackfeet religious belief systems. These are twenty-first-century terms and have twenty-first-century meanings that the Blackfeet of the late nineteenth and early twentieth centuries would probably not recognize. Contemporary historians of religion and religious writers have a common definition (sort of) for what is and is not a religion.[22] And I believe (no pun intended) that the Blackfeet of the past most definitely had a religion.

One final comment regarding phraseology. Some scholars, such as A. Irving Hallowell, do not like to use the term "supernatural" but instead prefer phrases like "other than human persons."[23] I find the phrase "other than human persons" too cumbersome, and I believe it fails to describe what the Blackfeet meant when they described their worldview. Others, such as Father Emile Legal, frame reality using the terms "visible" and "invisible."[24] Whereas the Blackfeet used prefixes that translate as "real" and "not real," the true meaning is more complicated than the translations. In an effort to avoid too much confusion and because I like using these terms, in this history of stories about the natural world and the supernatural I will be using the words "story," "history," "natural," and "supernatural."

Reckoning Time

Time is an essential component in the field of history. However, time in Blackfeet society is a complex concept and different from the Western concept of time. This should not imply that the Blackfeet did not have a concept of the passage of time; they do.[25] However, histories written by historians are usually framed by a time period. There are essentially three "time periods" that this book addresses: one is my own lifetime, one is the time from about the 1880s to the 1910s, and the other is the time when the stories discussed in this book might have occurred.

The time period from the early 1880s to the 1910s could be considered the early reservation era for the Blackfeet. However, the press of American colonization began almost a century earlier, with the arrival of Americans after Lewis and Clark's Corps of Discovery, the ensuing fur trade, epidemics of disease, mining and resource extraction, and then homesteaders, settlers, and agriculture. It was the disappearance of the bison from the northern Great Plains in the early 1880s and then the corresponding "starvation winter" of 1883–84 that dealt a brutal blow to Blackfeet society. As a signpost of Blackfeet history the "starvation winter," as it was called, stands out as a critical moment. From that time on, with the loss of bison and loss of population, the Blackfeet would never be the same. At the other end of this time period is the 1910s. Although it roughly coincides with the Progressive Era, much of what occurred on the Blackfeet reservation for the typical tribal citizen is separate from elements of American history. Modern American history intersected with Blackfeet history in 1910 with the establishment of Glacier National Park. The park changed the Blackfeet reservation dramatically on several levels, including economically and culturally, and it marks the beginning of a new era of Blackfeet history.

The early recorders of Blackfeet life collected stories primarily from the 1880s to 1910s and again in the 1940s. They focused their attention in particular on one type of interviewee or collaborator—an individual who had lived most of his or her life during the days of the buffalo. Ewers called these individuals "buffalo Indians." These early recorders of Blackfeet life were not interested in recording the lives of individuals who were born and raised on the reservation, with no knowledge of a nomadic lifestyle. They wanted to know what life was like during the buffalo days and before. From the 1880s to the 1910s a variety of people came to the reservation to record Blackfeet experiences of the past. Even Ewers, who came in the early 1940s, interviewed only people he viewed as having that unique historic experience of life out on the northern Great Plains. Therefore, although the time period I am writing about is the 1880s into the 1910s, my interest is also the memories of a select group of individuals: those who came of age before the reservation era began and told their stories to the "storytakers" who came to visit them, as well as to their children—my family members—who are at the center of my historical narrative.

The third time period, and the most difficult to define, is the actual time when these stories told by the "buffalo Indians" may have occurred in the past. Most of these first-person narratives often do not speak of chronological time but speak instead of the ancient past or the ancient Blackfeet. These narratives include historical accounts, life histories, mythical stories, descriptions of daily life, and songs. On many occasions the collaborators were answering a specific question of the researcher. On other occasions they were just telling stories. It was not until the mid-twentieth century, with the ethnohistoric work of Ewers, that there was a sustained questioning of individual Blackfeet about a wide variety of topics. The religious scholar Howard Harrod, who first came to the Blackfeet reservation in the summer of 1963 to work on his dissertation, also struggled with this issue of time and evidence. In his last book, *The Animals Came Dancing*, Harrod commented that

these memories were recorded by anthropologists and other observers. . . . These memories sometimes connect to traditions that may be deeper than the time frame of this study. For example, those who were alive in 1910 and who were sixty years old were born in 1850. These people lived during the last stages of the buffalo days and learned the traditions of their parents, who, if they were thirty years old in 1850, would have been born in 1820. If the grandparents were alive in 1820 and they happened to be sixty years old or older, they would have been born in the 1750s or 1760s. It is evident that the chain of memory and transmission of oral traditions could be even older. . . . What is sedimented in the ethnographies of the late nineteenth and early twentieth centuries, then, are oral traditions that have been reduced to texts . . . mediated through the alien linguistic and interpretive frames of European observers. . . . Nevertheless, these early memories, captured in texts, provide a rich resource for reconstructing a portrait of past cultural meanings.[26]

For the most part the Blackfeet did not render their stories in chronological time, but that does not mean that they did not understand the passage of time and use it as a measurement to separate events or activities. There are many examples to choose from that express this idea. Beaver bundle owners kept a yearly calendar of wooden sticks decorated with notches, with each notch representing a day.[27] Prominent men kept a yearly record of their lives painted on buffalo robes called winter counts.[28] Within their documented narratives specific historic events also became guideposts for recalling when another event occurred. However, mythologies and other stories usually did not have specific historic time beyond stating that it was from the ancient past or that it was a story of the ancient Blackfeet. Harrod concluded in *Renewing the World: Plains Indian Religion and Morality* that "in the final analysis, however, we do not need to know with certainty the age or the evolutionary trajectory of the traditions which we confront in the mid-nineteenth century in order to appreciate their depth and symbolic power."[29]

Validation

The last question that almost invariably gets asked is, To what extent was the historical evidence used for this book valid? Was it created by "outsiders" or "insiders"? Did the "outsiders" exploit the "insiders"? Or did they somehow not allow the insiders' voices to be heard through the cascade of "colonial" translations of oral interviews collected at the turn of the last century? Was this information potentially tainted by "alien linguistic and interpretive frames," as Harrod suggests?[30] Did "outsiders" actually record the stories that the Blackfeet wanted "recorded"? Is it ever possible for an outsider to retell the story of an insider? Contemporary scholars often ask these questions of the ethnologists of the past. Some argue that it is the role of Native peoples to both "re-write" and "re-right" their community histories because these early ethnographers plain got it wrong.[31]

Scholars always struggle with the validity of their sources. What makes the Blackfeet different? I think the Blackfeet are distinct among other tribal groups because ethnologists recorded a significant amount of material during the early reservation period. It is not complete by any means, but it does provide scholars a foundation from which to begin to understand how the Blackfeet viewed their world. At the Piegan Institute on the Blackfeet reservation, where I worked for many years, one of its three founders, the late Darrell Robes Kipp, challenged the staff to "be experts on the Blackfeet." Because of my own personal interest and Darrell's call to arms, I have read almost everything worth reading—and the worthless stuff, too—about the Blackfeet. I have also conducted research and visited almost every archival repository and museum (with Blackfeet stuff) in the United States and Canada. I have also learned that many of the Blackfeet who were recorded were my own ancestors. That does not make me an expert, but I believe I can safely argue that the ethnohistoric data used in this book are not only valid but extremely useful to contemporary historians and Native communities. But you don't have to take my word. Why? Because the old-time Blackfeet told us many times that they wanted their voices and their stories "recorded for the record."[32]

The ethnographic materials shared and collected from the 1880s to the 1910s, as well as those collected in the early 1940s, have significant value. All of the storytellers recorded from the buffalo days told stories from their own experiences of their lives on the prairies. In addition to practical knowledge came a deeper understanding of the way they believed their world and the universe worked.

I was fortunate to have spent time with knowledgeable Blackfeet such as my grandmother Annie, as well as my aunt Theresa, the elders at the Piegan Institute, and others in the community. But I am equally fortunate to have spent many years learning about the Blackfeet from museum collections, archives, unpublished manuscripts, and published primary sources. Now, as a historian, I believe that combining these two types of sources—oral history and written history—is necessary to get a more nuanced and complete understanding of Blackfeet history.

When the "buffalo Indians" settled onto the reservation, their land base shrank and their lives became increasingly controlled by outside forces. However, these Blackfeet could control the information they left behind. They told the stories that they wanted recorded and that they viewed as important for future generations. Ewers noted of his collaborators, "I remember these kindly old people as good friends who were sincerely interested in describing tribal life in their youth as completely and accurately as their memories would permit."[33]

ACKNOWLEDGMENTS

At one time using the term "traditional" to describe a person brought with it a sense of honor and even reverence. In the past people did not use this word lightly or to describe themselves. Unfortunately in contemporary times it seems this word has lost its meaning in tribal communities. Now young people describe themselves as "traditional" if they attend powwows, and tribes give out embroidered "elder" jackets to tribal members over fifty. I rarely use the term "traditional" because it has evolved to either have no meaning or too many meanings for people to have a common understanding. However, I reserve using the word to describe individuals with a strong sense of their own individual identity that is grounded in their significant understanding of Native language, religious belief systems, tribal ecological knowledge, and community history. I dedicated this book to ancestors who have passed and who have been my mentors, my champions, those who have both empowered and inspired me to care and write about Native people.

Robert Dumont Jr. was one of the smartest people I have ever known. He thought deeply about the role of educated Native people in their own communities. He believed that being educated was both a privilege and a responsibility. Robert returned to the Fort Peck reservation in Montana after some years away, and he encouraged all educated Native people to go home.

Darrell Robes Kipp was a visionary thinker. He had a big personality and a big laugh. He inspired those around him to change themselves and their communities by telling crazy stories that made everyone laugh. He encouraged others to know more about their own community history than anyone else. He read everything about the Blackfeet, and we had weekly discussions about his new knowledge. His motto, "Don't ask permission, just do it," was meant as a challenge to act to create positive change in Native communities. And until his passing in 2013, Darrell read every word I ever wrote.

Thomas Little Plume was the most gentle of gentlemen. His patience, peaceful demeanor, traditional manners, and strong faith in God made him a quiet force of nature. He seemed to lower the blood pressure of all those who interacted with him. He did not go to Harvard University, like Robert and Darrell, but he was the most educated person I have known. He had an academic understanding of the Blackfeet language, which was his first language. It was typical to spend an entire afternoon translating and describing the complexity of one Blackfeet word. His knowledge of language was unparalleled.

Dr. Grandma Bea Medicine, as my children called her, was a power to be reckoned with. She spoke her mind at all times but carried herself with an old-fashioned dignity. She was a Lakota woman. She embodied the wisdom and knowledge of her ancestors. She encouraged Native people to get PhDs, become academics, and both research and write about their own communities.

Theresa (Wall) Still Smoking was the most traditional and toughest person I have known. She was my oldest aunt. As a young child I remember her hunting, butchering meat, gathering plants, and chopping wood for the woodstove. She had a large family with nine children. But she took the time to take care of the elders in our family, Ella and Louie Yellow Wolf, who never had children of their own. Her home was a refuge to many, and she always smiled when I came to visit her.

Annie (Mad Plume) Wall loved the past, and it seemed to me that she often lived in the past in her own mind. She was a true Blackfeet historian and storyteller extraordinaire. Sunday afternoons at her dinner table meant hours of reminiscing. She loved to visit, especially in

Blackfeet, and it was a difficult transition to speak only English with those around her. She was raised as a grandmother's grandchild, and she treated me the same.

There are many colleagues and scholars to thank for their encouragement and their careful reading of my writing, including Jeff Wiltse of the University of Montana's History Department, Patricia Albers of the University of Minnesota's Department of American Indian Studies, and Sarah Carter of the University of Alberta's History Department. Several others read different parts of this work; they include Frederick Hoxie, Dan Flores, William Farr, Wade Davies, and Trent Atkins. I visited with various scholars over the years about this book and Blackfeet history in general, including Dr. Hugh Dempsey, who in his own pithy way was always encouraging.

I would like to acknowledge the various people and organizations that helped fund my research for this book and my related publications on Blackfeet traditional ecological knowledge: the American Indian Program at the National Museum of Natural History, Smithsonian Institution, provided a predoctoral fellowship, a travel grant, and research associate status; the D'Arcy McNickle Center for the History of American Indians at the Newberry Library provided a Frances C. Allen fellowship and a graduate fellowship; Humanities Montana provided a research grant; and the University of Montana provided a university research grant, an international research grant, a President's Office research grant, and a Baldridge Book Subvention Fund from the College of Humanities and Sciences. I would also like to acknowledge the Women's Studies in Religion Program at the Harvard Divinity School, who provided me with a Research Associate position for 2016-17.

Final thanks go to my family on the Blackfeet reservation. David R. M. Beck, my life partner and husband, helped out tremendously by not only reading every word of this book but also carefully reading my footnotes and bibliography. Who does that? He encouraged me to continue telling my own story of Blackfeet history, to find my own voice. And for their neverending support of my ventures, our daughters, Abaki and Iko'tsimiskimaki Beck. They are both rock stars.

INTRODUCTION

Something Vital Was Missing

People often ask me how I became interested in plants. I sometimes jokingly reply, "I'm not sure if I am that interested in plants." I am asked this question because I give public talks throughout the Rocky Mountain West regarding historic Amskapi Pikuni or Blackfeet plant use, also called ethnobotany or traditional ecological knowledge.[1] I came to this knowledge in the old-fashioned way: I apprenticed with two old women for a very long time. *Oral tradition*

Well over two decades ago my oldest aunt, Theresa Still Smoking, told me in a matter-of-fact way that I needed to learn about plants. My aunt was not asking me if I was interested in learning about plants. She gently implied that it was my responsibility to learn. At the time I was living in Chicago and only returning home to the Blackfeet reservation in the summers and a few other times during the year. So I was not sure how this learning process was going to progress.

I come from a family of women who know about plants. My grandmother, Annie Mad Plume Wall, was well known for her medicinal plant knowledge. She was still going out to collect plants well into her nineties and providing doctoring to our family and others. She finally stopped going out into the field when an old ankle injury that she had sustained as a teenager came back to haunt her and made it too painful for her to walk on uneven ground. She relied instead on those of us who knew what she harvested. She learned about plants from her grandmother, Kitaiksísskstaki, or Not Real Beaver Woman, and her great-grandmother, Omahkataioaki, or Big Mountain Lion Woman, and they had probably learned from their grandmothers. The transmission of knowledge and stories from generation to generation, grandmother to granddaughter, aunt to niece, was a time-honored tradition in our family.

My aunt Theresa and grandmother Annie started sharing their knowledge and their stories about plants with me that summer. I took my aunt on long drives across the prairies and foothills of the Blackfeet reservation in Montana, up into the mountains of Glacier National Park, up into southern Alberta, and around ancestral Blackfeet territory. During these excursions I would get drive-by lessons on plant use, some that I knew very well, others that I had collected but did not know their uses, and yet others that were brand new to me. I also heard many stories from my grandmother. And my grandmother shared many of her recipes for medicinal remedies. The expectation was that I would just listen and not ask too many questions. At the time I remember thinking to myself, "I am never going to remember all this stuff." I started scribbling down notes after each trip. Being a nerd, I decided that if I was going to learn anything about these plants and their stories, then I had better start looking for some books to read.

I was in luck. On a family visit to the Head-Smashed-In Buffalo Jump Interpretive Centre in southern Alberta I purchased Alex Johnston's monograph *Plants and the Blackfoot*, published in 1987. "This is perfect," I thought. "I will not have to memorize all these plants after all; I can just read about them." However, even though Johnston included almost two hundred plants in his monograph, many of his descriptions did not provide sufficient detail about their uses. He did not discuss when certain plants were collected or how they were processed. He did not even include some of the plants that we collect on a regular basis, like *otahkoyitsi*, or blue sticks-root (*Comandra umbellata*). We collect bags and bags of this stuff every summer. I wondered how he could not list that one. Even more important was that he did not include stories about the Blackfeet and their understanding of the natural world. I asked myself, "Isn't this a book about plants and the Blackfoot? Well, so much for the easy way out." I concluded that I was going to have to rethink my approach. As I continued apprenticing with my aunt and my grandmother, I also continued looking for everything written about Blackfeet ethnobotany and stories about the Blackfeet relationship to the natural world.

I consulted Walter McClintock, an early recorder of Blackfeet life, who wrote the first study of Blackfeet ethnobotany when he published "Materia Medica of the Blackfeet" in 1909 with the Berlin Society for Anthropology, Ethnology, and History, based on research he conducted in the 1890s. He reprinted it in the appendix of his book *The Old North Trail; or, Life, Legends and Religion of the Blackfeet Indians* in 1910. In this book he relied on the knowledge of his female relatives from his adoptive Blackfeet family. McClintock used the term "botanists" for these women who had learned "the knowledge of herbs and wild plants" from an early age. McClintock sent the dried plant specimens he collected in the 1890s to the Carnegie Institute in Pittsburgh, and O. E. Jennings, the assistant curator of botany, identified them. Although McClintock's study listed only sixty-six plants, it was considered the most thorough review of Blackfeet plant use for most of the twentieth century.[2] The work of McClintock and others engendered my curiosity, and I began to think about scholars' understanding of Blackfeet concepts of the natural world compared to what I was learning from the women in my family.

I heard stories of Blackfeet life from a young age. When I was growing up my family used to go out to my great-great-aunt Agnes's house. Agnes and her husband, Albert, lived in the foothills of the Rocky Mountain Front just south of Badger Creek in a place on the reservation that butts up against what is now called the Badger–Two Medicine area.[3] My grandfather Iòkimau always called this area "God's country." In the winter they lived in a small house with minimal amenities in a thicket of aspen trees. Inside their house they had a woodstove, a small table with chairs, and a metal-framed bed that served as both their couch and bed. Agnes seemed to always have fresh bannock bread and tea ready for visitors. In the summer they lived mostly in the outdoors, and we sat outside under the shade of the aspens. My first memories of her were when she was in her sixties. She seemed ancient, but she was physically strong and agile. Whenever we visited Agnes told us old stories of the Blackfeet. When she told us these stories, the places on the reservation that we knew so well came alive. I remember how I could *see* the stories as she told them. I remember believing that animals could talk, the stars were living beings, and supernatural characters *lived* right here where I lived. I had learned that for the Blackfeet the purpose of stories is not to retell an event of the past but to make the event come alive in the present, so that it becomes part of our own present-day experience. Stories were not re-creations of the past but creations in the present. My earliest memories of learning Blackfeet history were from Aunt Agnes's vividly told stories.

As a teenager I read George Bird Grinnell's *Blackfoot Lodge Tales: The Story of a Prairie People*. This was the first book I ever read about the Blackfeet. Although it was originally published in 1892 (and was based on articles published in the 1880s), it is still considered one of the most authoritative books on Blackfeet life. I remember how flat these stories seemed, how one-dimensional, how unalive. Some of the stories were the same stories that Aunt Agnes told and that I had heard many times before. This was my first experience with reading something about the Blackfeet that did not *feel* quite right. Grinnell's stories were the same stories I had heard before. However, something seemed to be missing from Grinnell's stories.

The historian William Farr has observed that "the Blackfeet world possessed an extra dimension, for amid the visible world, was an invisible one, another magnitude, a spiritual one that is more powerful, more meaningful, more lasting. It was a universe alive."[4] It seemed to me that what Grinnell described was to a certain extent only the visible world and not the invisible one—the one I grew up hearing about and that my grandparents understood intimately. At that time in high school I was too young to truly differentiate these ideas.

My grandmother loved to sit and visit with people. One day when I was an adult my grandmother told me a story about Spotted Bear, her maternal great-grandfather. It was a story that I had heard many, many, many times before. I stress this point to show that I can be a slow learner. Spotted Bear was a great warrior, "one of the greatest," as she *always* emphasized. Her favorite stories of Spotted Bear were his adventures raiding the Crow. He always seemed to get into a predicament, and

Fig. 1. The author with her grandmother, Annie Mad Plume Wall. Photo courtesy of the author.

then of course he was able to get out of it. In this particular story about Spotted Bear versus the Crow my grandmother mentioned almost as an afterthought that Spotted Bear used his personal "medicine power" and changed the direction of the wind. "Whoa, wait one minute," I thought. "He changed the direction of the wind! How did he do that?" At that moment I realized that my grandmother and Spotted Bear's relationship to the natural world—and their concept of reality—was dramatically different from the one that the recorders of Blackfeet life often wrote about in their books. Until that moment it had not occurred to me that what I had learned and heard about the Blackfeet from my family was truly different than what had been written about the Blackfeet. These different versions of the same story intrigued me, and to a certain extent my interest in Blackfeet history sprang from those early experiences. This is where my journey began to explore and understand the different interpretations of Blackfeet stories and history.

The Blackfeet are one of the most studied and photographed tribal groups in the United States and Canada. This is probably because they appear to represent the iconic horse-riding, warbonnet-wearing Plains Indian. The historian Hugh Dempsey even published a bibliography containing thousands of entries on sources regarding the Blackfoot Confederacy.[5] Many of these histories reflect Ewers's sentiments that the Blackfeet were "a hardy, nomadic hunting people" who "enjoyed few luxuries" and "who wrested a living from the resources of their own country."[6] All my life I had heard different kinds of stories from my grandparents of how the Blackfeet altered nature, from stopping the wind from blowing, to controlling animal behavior, to creating a snowstorm so powerful it could freeze a person in midstep. Historians, like Ewers, often told of how the natural world shaped Blackfeet behavior, suggesting that the migration of the bison led the Blackfeet to follow the herds. However, my grandparents told stories of how the Blackfeet shaped the natural world. They made the bison come to them. As I thought about my grandmother's stories I began to recognize common threads that I had not truly noticed before—that the Blackfeet believed that they could change and control the natural world. And this belief gave them a certain level of confidence and authority. It occurred to me that although I had read a lot of books and articles on Blackfeet history, my grandmother's version was not present or even emphasized in these histories. I started rereading the same books again but with a new lens in place. The Blackfeet had a different view of reality.

For some time I had thought about the differences between oral history within a community and written history about a community, but it was not until I began formally learning about Blackfeet plant knowledge from my grandmother and aunt that I began to seriously understand these differences. This book reflects both a part of my own journey of learning knowledge and the stories of my family and my effort to interpret what other scholars and historians have recorded about the Blackfeet. Although historians have written a lot about the Blackfeet, I decided to begin my research at the time when my grandmother and grandfather first heard the stories that they shared with me and the rest of our family. They learned these stories beginning in the 1910s. I wanted to address the dichotomy between internal knowledge and external scholarship. Did Spotted Bear think he "wrested a living" from nature? Probably not. He had the power to change the direction of the wind. What did previous historians of Blackfeet life fail to interpret? <u>Something vital was missing.</u>

The Book

This book is my interpretation of Blackfeet life and their understanding of the natural world in the nineteenth and early twentieth century. It explores several interrelated overarching themes. First, I am interested in understanding the historic time period leading up to my grandparents' birth and childhood. From about 1880 to 1910 the Blackfeet reservation and its people endured dramatic changes in society and economy. It was during this time that the early recorders of Blackfeet life first came to the reservation to record stories of Blackfeet history. It is from these stories that we can begin to understand Blackfeet views of the natural world. Second, despite the hardships suffered by the Blackfeet their relationship with the natural world and their worldview provided them stability and continuity through privation and those changing times. And finally, the stories they told the early recorders of Blackfeet life reveal a fundamental philosophy of Blackfeet existence. The Blackfeet believed they could alter, change, and control nature to suit their needs, and they did this with the assistance of supernatural allies. <u>The Blackfeet did not believe they had to adapt to nature; they made nature adapt to them.</u> How do we know this? <u>Because they told us in their stories.</u>

As an academically trained historian I use different historical methods to tell these stories of the past, including researching archival documents, published primary sources, books, articles, and oral history. However, I also include first-person narrative and my own voice and journey to understand this history and address questions that I found unanswered in scholarship.

This book recounts some of the oral history of my family—stories narrated to me by my late maternal grandmother Annie, as well as my aunt Theresa, and many others. Some of these stories were recorded on an old tape recorder. Most were not. In the latter case I continued to ask elders in my family of their recollections of family stories, or I relied on my own memory to reconstruct those stories based on the many times I heard them. I tell these stories as I knew them and as I remember them.

Historians concern themselves with exploring different interpretations of historical events, people, places, or times. We are interested in new knowledge and new interpretations. Fortunately the Blackfeet are one of the most studied tribal groups in the United States, which means there is a lot of great stuff written about the Blackfeet. And unfortunately the Blackfeet are one of the most studied tribal groups in the United States, which means there is a lot of lousy stuff written about the Blackfeet. This means there is a lot to draw from when researching the past. There are numerous published and unpublished books and manuscripts and archival materials, from first contact to the present, to use as sources.[7] Historians continue to use these materials to write new histories of the Blackfoot Confederacy or to reinterpret what has already been written. I will be doing the same.

The Blackfeet began sharing stories of their history and their lifeways with outside visitors from first contact in the eighteenth century. However, their stories were not systematically recorded by outside scholars, ethnologists, and other early recorders of Blackfeet life until the late nineteenth and early twentieth centuries. I rely primarily on the stories collected at that time, the turn of the twentieth century. These stories were principally told in the Blackfeet language. The majority of these outside individuals relied on Blackfeet interpreters who either interviewed knowledgeable Blackfeet people or who were knowledgeable themselves. By the early 1900s the Blackfeet were suffering within a reservation system in which they did not control the economy, the political system, or the education of their own children. This book also examines the historical context of the Progressive Era and reservation life when the early recorders of Blackfeet life collected their information, as well as of the Blackfeet "storytellers" or collaborators and interpreters and the role of the "storytakers" or ethnographers in tribal communities. I include vignettes of family history and stories, of life during the beginning of the twentieth century, and of life on the reservation. And I also include

Fig. 2. Mary Spotted Bear and Annie Mad Plume Wall. Photo courtesy of the author.

my own personal narrative of my journey to understand the past of my own family and community.

The preface has addressed the variety of questions that are often asked by readers, scholars, and Native American communities regarding the history of family, community, and places. Native people will ask of any writer, Who are you? Who is your family? What is your experience? What gives you the right to write about "us"? For the typical historian these questions will seem out of place or even unnecessary in a history book. However, for Native American historians researching and writing Native American history, in their own community no less, these questions should be addressed because they reflect how history is not just about the past but is also an influence on contemporary Native life.

Chapter 1, "No Nothing: The Blackfeet Reservation in 1910," explores life on the reservation in 1910 as a tumultuous snapshot in time when "buffalo Indians" were transitioning to reservation society.[8] It is from within this time and place, just as the Blackfeet were learning to adapt to their new circumstances, that they told their stories to outside recorders of Blackfeet life. It was also the time when both of my grandparents were born and raised and when their families were adjusting to their new reality and new relationship with the natural world.

Chapter 2, "Invisible Reality: The Blackfeet Universe," explores the religious belief system of the Blackfeet. The Blackfeet believed that there existed three separate yet interconnected worlds, which they called the Above world, the Below world, and the Water world. Within these three worlds were both visible and invisible elements, or the natural and supernatural realms of existence. In addition to their practical knowledge came a deeper understanding of the way the universe worked. It is from within this system that the Blackfeet developed their ability to endure hardship and persevere in the visible realm.

Chapter 3, "Visible Reality: The Saokiotapi," explores the empirical knowledge about the landscape that the Blackfeet held. At one point in their history they called themselves the Saokiotapi, or the Prairie people, because they lived their lives on the northern Great Plains. The Blackfeet understanding of the world was drawn from this practical familiarity with the prairie. Their empirical knowledge of this vast territory informed their religious belief systems, and their belief systems determined how they interacted with their landscape.

Chapter 4, "Closed Season: The Blackfeet Winter," explores the Blackfeet perception of nature during the fall and winter. The Blackfeet divided the year into two seasons—Na-pos, or the "opened" season, and Sto-ye, or the "closed" season. This phraseology coincided with their religious belief system. In the fall the Blackfeet "closed" their major religious rituals and objects for the winter. The most important belief that the Blackfeet recorded with ethnographers was that they had an ancient relationship with nature, that nature gave them various gifts to live their lives, and that with supernatural help they could influence nature to accommodate their wants and desires.

Chapter 5, "Opened Season: The Blackfeet Summer," explores the Blackfeet perception of nature during the spring and summer. In the spring the sound of the first thunder signaled the time to "open" the religious season. The Blackfeet believed that the thunder controlled the rain and in turn the relative abundance of plant life. Many of the religious activities of the Blackfeet centered on reestablishing and strengthening their relationship to nature at the beginning of spring and summer.

Chapter 6, "Storytakers: Ethnographers Visit the Blackfeet," explores the role of outside recorders of Blackfeet life who came from the 1880s to 1910s and again in the 1940s. The story of recorders of Blackfeet life coming to a reservation is almost always told as a one-sided story, with the recorders of Blackfeet life being "takers" of local knowledge. To a certain extent this story is different with the Blackfeet. The Blackfeet wanted their history told, and they actively worked with ethnographers and sold them their stories, songs, and objects.

Chapter 7, "All That Remain: From the Prairies to the Atomic Age," reexamines Blackfeet life at the turn of the twentieth century by looking at the life of my great-grandfather, Aimsback, a "buffalo Indian." After living his life on the northern Great Plains Aimsback learned to be a farmer and agricultural leader, all the while remaining a religious leader of his community. Although transition to a new economy and sedentary life was difficult for the old Blackfeet, their religious belief systems provided stability and continuity.

It was almost twenty years ago that I gave my first public presentation on Native plants on the Blackfeet reservation at a women's wellness conference. The organizers had asked me to present because they knew that I had been learning from my grandmother and aunt. They held the conference at the Chewing Blackbones Tribal Park on the shores of Saint Mary Lake. The day before the conference I gathered live samples of all the plants I planned to discuss. The organizers set up the chairs in a circle out on the open field. Elders sat in the first row of chairs. As I spoke and passed around each plant sample the elders held them gently and breathed in their fragrance. Stories can be powerful. As I shared some of my grandmother's stories, the elder women did so as well. Some shared their memories of times long past, of their relationships with women in their families, of happy times picking berries and digging roots, of disruptions in their lives and relationships such as attending boarding school, of their disappointment that they lacked the knowledge of Native plants, but mostly many expressed pride in their own Blackfeet heritage, in knowing that Blackfeet women once knew the natural world so intimately.

As I complete the final words of this book I will again be giving a workshop on the Native plant uses of the Blackfeet at the annual summer Sobriety and Recovery Campout on the Blackfeet reservation. I will again bring plant samples for people to hold and smell. I will again share the stories of my grandmother and her grandmother. And although in the last few years both my grandmother Annie and my aunt Theresa have passed, I continue to gather and talk about Native plants with the women in my family, including my aunts Irene Old Chief, Rosalyn Azure, and Bernadette Wall, my mother, Angeline Wall, my cousins Debbie Comes at Night, Margaret Still Smoking, and Becky Dwarf, my daughters Abaki Beck and Iko'tsimiskimaki Beck, and now an increasing number of nieces.

As the years have passed I am still not sure if I am all that interested in plants. However, I am interested in the stories of elders, their view of the natural world, and their relationship with the supernatural. As the old-time Blackfeet lives became increasingly unpredictable and controlled by the outside forces, their work with the outside ethnographers provided them an element of control over the information that they recorded.

But this was nothing new. The Blackfeet believed that they always had control. It was fundamental to their basic belief system. And they found that creating a relationship with the supernatural and developing supernatural allies helped them make predictable the unpredictability of the natural world in which they lived. This is my effort to tell that story.

INVISIBLE REALITY

CHAPTER 1

No Nothing

The Blackfeet Reservation in 1910

My grandmother's mother, Minnie, was born in 1889, a year after the Blackfeet signed an executive agreement to sell the Sweet Grass Hills, the eastern portion of their original homelands, to the U.S. government.[1] This was the same year that Montana gained statehood. Unlike her ancestors and the previous generation Minnie grew up in a new land. Minnie grew up in America. Her family knew her only as Iko'tsimiskimaki.[2] She received her name from her grandfather Spotted Bear. He named her after one of the supernatural objects in his medicine bundle. However, she became known as Minnie to others.

Much like an immigrant to a new land Minnie learned about America at school. As a child Minnie attended the Methodist Willow Creek School on the reservation. She became a part of the first generation of Blackfeet children to learn to read, write, and speak English. At home, though, she continued to speak Blackfeet. At school she learned about life in America, patriotism, and Victorian values. She learned to celebrate the Fourth of July and George Washington's birthday.

She left the reservation to attend Fort Shaw Indian School for high school. There she learned a new set of skills to express her new American identity. She learned to garden and grow vegetables, to can fruit, and to cook new American foods like bread. She learned how to use a sewing machine to make her own clothing. She learned how to crochet and embroider. She looks young, confident, and contemporary, with her long hair upswept in a bun and wearing a crisp, sailor-inspired school uniform in her school photo taken just after the turn of the century.

The hope of her schoolteachers—for her to begin an American family after finishing school—grew to be her hope as well. Not long after she returned home from boarding school she married Elmer Mad Plume. Father J. B. Carroll officiated at the Holy Family Mission on the Two Medicine River.[3] Both of their large extended families lived on the south side of the reservation, where Elmer and his brothers were farmers. Together they embodied the new Blackfeet citizen: educated with American values and living the newly acquired American agrarian lifestyle. They were now part of the first generation of Blackfeet to begin using first names, Elmer and Minnie in their case, and a last name, Mad Plume. Within a few short years they started their family.

A cherished family photo taken around 1910 epitomized their transformation. Minnie, still confident, appeared en vogue in a flowing lace blouse, long wool skirt, and a stylish hairdo of the times. Next to her is her husband, Elmer, looking dapper in his modern suit, shirt, tie, and dress shoes. His hair was cut short and slicked back. Their two young children appear healthy and happy. Their daughter, Ella, was wearing a frilly dress with stockings and boots. She was holding a doll whose porcelain head had curly blond hair. Their son, Philip, with his hair cut short, was wearing another frilly dress, one of his sister's (as the family story goes) because he had soiled his suit. As their photo demonstrates, gone were any outward vestiges of a tribal heritage. By the early twentieth century the modern American world was calling, and many Blackfeet tried their best to adhere to that call.

Unfortunately tragedy struck: in 1915 Minnie died in childbirth. Her newborn son, Andrew, died soon after. She was only twenty-six years old. She left behind several young children that her husband Elmer would be unable to take care of. Various family members would adopt and raise her children. Elmer remarried not long after her death.

My grandmother's maternal grandmother, Not Real Beaver Woman, and her great-grandmother, Big Mountain Lion Woman, adopted her. She was only one and a half years old. Her two grandmothers' old-time Blackfeet ways replaced Minnie's modern American ways. In her grandmothers' home modernity was nowhere to be found. Her grandmothers wore handmade moccasins, modest calico dresses, thick leather belts from which hung various tools, wool shawls, and their long braids tied up and covered with colorful scarves. They rode horses. They lived in tents most of the year and spent most of their days outside. They hunted and gathered their food in the mountains in the summer. They processed and dried their provisions in the fall. They moved downriver after they had cut enough wood for the winter. They moved indoors, into a cabin without running water or electricity, during the cold months of the winter. They celebrated the beginning of the Blackfeet new year in the spring with the Thunder Pipe ceremony. Then they started the whole cycle again.

As my grandmother grew up she understood that the life of her mother Minnie and the lives of her grandmothers were dramatically different. Unlike her mother before her, my grandmother never fully made the transition to assuming American values or lifestyle. How could she? She was raised by two old women. But she did learn one thing: the Fourth of July was the biggest day of the year.

Fourth of July, 1910

By 1910 an entire generation of Blackfeet had been born, raised, and lived into adulthood on the reservation. It had been more than twenty-five years since any of the old men had gone bison hunting or since any of the old women had made objects from fresh bison hides. The older generation's transition to life on the reservation had not been easy. Adam White Man told John Ewers that "the Piegan were still buffalo hunters and the bands had not settled down" until after the demise of the bison herds and sale of the Sweet Grass Hills in the mid-1880s.[4] However, reservation life was the only life that their children knew. As the older Blackfeet settled into reservation life they learned that their lives would become increasingly controlled by outside forces.

In the 1910 issue of the *Indian Sentinel*, the annual periodical of the Bureau of Catholic Indian Missions, was an article by Father J. B. Carroll titled "The Fourth of July Dishonored," which was a scathing attack on the religious persistence of the Blackfeet people.[5] In his article Carroll described how the Blackfeet had co-opted the Fourth of July and incorporated within this patriotic celebration of "national greatness" the "darkest days of heathenism and bloodshed."[6] Carroll fervently wrote that the Blackfeet had been using the Fourth of July festivities as a way to also celebrate their outlawed annual O'kan, or Medicine Lodge ceremony.[7]

The O'kan was the Blackfeet's annual summer gathering that was both secular and religious. The Blackfeet had held it for generations in the late summer, usually in August or September.[8] However, this gathering and other religious activities had been controlled or curtailed by the U.S. government in the late nineteenth century and during the early reservation years. Blackfeet elders told the anthropologist Clark Wissler that in the past the O'kan was held "'when the service berries are ripe,' perhaps August, instead of Fourth-of-July week, as in recent years."[9] With the introduction of the Fourth of July as a national holiday sanctioned by the U.S. government the Blackfeet moved their annual gathering from the late summer to midsummer without risking significant governmental resistance. Carroll saw through this ruse. He angrily wrote that the Blackfeet "way of celebrating the Fourth of July [was] one of the greatest obstacles to Christianity and true civilization."[10] Instead of placing all the blame with the Blackfeet, however, Carroll believed that "the Government [was] greatly responsible" for allowing the situation to occur in the first place.[11] Carroll argued that the U.S. government, which was trying to "civilize" the Blackfeet, actually contributed to the perpetuation of their religious activities by not restricting their existence. Carroll also pointed out the two different institutional roles: the government was to civilize, and the Catholic Church was to convert. The local businesses made money during the celebration, so they had no desire to end it either.

The U.S. government did not introduce the Fourth of July to the Blackfeet until after the 1880s, when the Blackfeet stopped hunting bison in the summer. Beginning in 1882 the Blackfeet stayed put on the reservation, occasionally leaving to raid for horses, but the whole community never again left to hunt.[12] In the summer of 1880 the government agent used the Fourth of July holiday as a time to distribute rewards to individual Blackfeet for completing civilization projects such as building log cabins and starting small family gardens. However, even though there were efforts to stop the practice, the agent in 1880 also reported that the Blackfeet still conducted their O'kan in August.[13]

In 1910, though, the new town of Browning embraced the annual Fourth of July and the O'kan celebration because the traders enjoyed the economic boon it provided. Blackfeet from all across the reservation and their relatives in Canada came to town to partake in the celebration. Father Carroll even commented that "the town puts on a very lively appearance. The streets, stores, hotels, and other public places are alive."[14] The Browning Mercantile sold one hundred loaves of bread per day and dozens of cases of fresh fruit during the week of celebration.[15] With the businesspeople happy, including the railroad that was transporting goods from the west side of the mountains and Washington State, the U.S. government was not going to challenge the character of the celebration.

Father Carroll lamented the inability of the U.S. government to create cultural change within this economic boom. Ironically that same summer the U.S. government, through the Bureau of American Ethnology (BAE), a branch within the Smithsonian Institution, sent out a government-paid linguist to photograph and record the stories of the O'kan and to document the language of the Blackfeet. Dr. Truman Michelson arrived in Browning, the agency headquarters, in mid-June and stayed until mid-July.[16] His mission was to conduct for the BAE a survey of all the Algonquian languages within the United States. The Blackfeet represented one group within his survey. He hired a local interpreter and interviewed various old people, those who had lived when the bison still roamed the Great Plains. During his month of research he was able to collect a significant number of stories and songs.

Michelson, though, was not the only scientist or interested outsider to come that summer. As Carroll observed, "train loads of . . . white people . . . flow[ed] into Browning . . . to see the Indians dance."[17] Among those people were the Dutch linguist C. C. Uhlenbeck, who came for the entire summer of 1910 with his graduate student J. P. B. de Josselin de Jong, also to document the Blackfeet language.[18] The railroad tycoon Louis W. Hill sent Joseph Scheuerle, an artist from Chicago, to paint portraits of the pre-reservation Blackfeet and natural scenes from the newly created Glacier National Park for his "See America First" campaign for the Great Northern Railroad.[19] And the summer before, in 1909, the famed photographer Edward S. Curtis and anthropologist A. C. Haddon had come to photograph and interview the Blackfeet.[20] In the summer of 1910 the Blackfeet were fortunate to be able to relive the old days and sell their stories, songs, and portraits to this odd variety of people converging on the reservation.

Carroll viewed the O'kan as more than a tourist attraction. He saw its pernicious potential. He complained that the federal government did not stop the Blackfeet from "publicly parad[ing] their devilish idolatry and superstition for the admiration and amusement of a large audience of white people."[21] Looking back from the twenty-first century, one may view Carroll's commentary as ethnocentric or even racist, but his observations of Blackfeet life were essentially correct. Despite twenty-five years of reservation life and U.S. government control of Blackfeet affairs, church and government authorities were only beginning to change the inner life of the Blackfeet. Blackfeet religion was persistent.

And unlike these temporary sojourners into Blackfeet country it was Carroll, who lived with the Blackfeet every day for years, who better understood their character. Carroll had seen the O'kan practiced many times, and he knew that it served multiple purposes. In many ways the O'kan was like the Passion Play the Catholics performed. It was the reenactment of several stories that tell the larger history of the O'kan itself. These stories described the relationships and kinships between humans and supernatural deities. The Blackfeet told the ethnologist Clark Wissler, though, that the purpose for individual Blackfeet was "blessing the people."[22] They said that individuals or families gave offerings to the "sun priests," who in turn made "appeals to the sun," the greatest of Blackfeet deities, to "promote well-being."[23] Wissler pointed out correctly that "there was a feeling that an annual sun dance was, from a religious and ethical point of view, *necessary to the general welfare*" of the community.[24] Carroll saw it as usurping the Church's authority to "bless" people, an authority that carried the weight of God's favor.[25]

Ultimately Carroll tried to express that the O'kan did something else as well: it told a story of the past, when the Blackfeet with the help of the supernatural had control of their own destiny.

Threat to Catholic Church and Judeo-Christian religions

Creation of the Reservation

The U.S. government created the Blackfeet reservation in what is now Montana during the late nineteenth century with a series of executive orders. Prior to establishment of the reservation Blackfoot Confederacy territory included much of what is now Montana and the provinces of Alberta and Saskatchewan in Canada.[26] The United States recognized that the territory of the Blackfoot Confederacy extended from the North Saskatchewan River in the north to the Yellowstone River in the south and from the Rocky Mountains in the west to the confluence of the Missouri and Yellowstone Rivers in the east.[27] Within this vast territory emerged four distinct groups: the Siksika, Kainai, Pikuni, and the Inaksiks. They were affiliated by a common language, as well as political, social, and

Fig. 3. Willow Creek School. Image #77.0129, Joseph H. Sherburne Family Papers, Archives and Special Collections, Maureen and Mike Mansfield Library, University of Montana–Missoula.

religious practices.[28] No one knows for sure how long these groups existed individually before contact. Archaeologists argue that Native peoples have lived on the northern Great Plains for thousands of years.[29]

First contact with Europeans occurred in this region in the seventeenth century. However, significant demographic change and dislocation did not occur until the nineteenth century with the arrival of Americans. Throughout this time relationships with other tribal groups were just as detrimental as those with Europeans and Americans.[30] The most devastating was when the Crow tribe annihilated the Inaksiks during an intertribal war in 1846. The few Inaksiks who survived became incorporated into the other Blackfoot groups.[31] The Pikuni or Piegan also split into two separate groups, with one group settling in what is now Canada and the other in the United States. By the signing of the 1855 Lame Bull treaty the United States had recognized four distinct groups: the Siksika, Kainai, and North Peigan in Canada and the South Piegan in the United States.[32]

Fig. 4. Elmer, Minnie, Philip, and Ella Mad Plume. Photo courtesy of the author.

Fig. 5. Minnie Mad Plume, or Iko'tsimiskimaki. Photo courtesy of the author.

The 1855 Lame Bull treaty with the Blackfoot was not a treaty for land. It was primarily a treaty to define the boundaries or territories of tribes in what would become Montana, to negotiate peace between these groups, and to allow safe passage for American troops. The 1855 Lame Bull treaty defined Blackfeet land in the United States as being west to the Rocky Mountains, north of the Musselshell and Missouri Rivers, and up to the forty-ninth parallel.[33] However, after lines were drawn on paper the treaty provided the United States with an opportunity to begin to diminish Blackfeet territory and acquire land.

The territory defined in the 1855 treaty was a large expanse of land on the northern Great Plains that encompassed a wide variety of ecosystems, including dry and arid prairies, fertile river valleys, rich prairie oases like the Sweet Grass Hills or the Bear Paw Mountains, the foothills of the Rocky Mountains, and the alpine of the Rocky Mountains. In all of these places the Blackfeet acquired the animals, plants, and other natural elements they needed to live their lives. Unfortunately as the nineteenth century progressed and with each treaty and executive order the Blackfeet lost land within their traditional homelands. With the loss of land and corresponding rich natural resources the Blackfeet had to adjust to an ever-shrinking landscape and develop a new relationship with nature and the environment.

Not long after the signing of the Stevens treaties trespassing miners found gold in the "common hunting grounds," which treaties had set aside. This discovery precipitated a quick move toward Montana becoming a territory in 1864 and a rush of miners into the region. In 1865 the U.S. government negotiated a treaty with the Blackfoot Confederacy to acquire the lands in the "common hunting grounds." This treaty was never ratified. In 1868 the U.S. government again negotiated the same treaty for the same lands. And again the treaty was not ratified. By then the region included Montana Territory's three largest towns: Bannock, Helena, and Virginia City. Even though the United States did not ratify the treaties Americans nonetheless illegally occupied the land. But from their perspective the Blackfeet thought they had signed two treaties and they expected to be paid.[34]

Within the next few decades the Blackfeet lands continued to shrink.

And although the Blackfeet were never removed from their traditional homelands, their territory became smaller and smaller. The United States next reduced Blackfeet lands from the south with an act of Congress in 1874.[35] With this act the United States moved the reservation boundary north from the Musselshell and Missouri Rivers to Birch Creek and the Marias River. (The boundary had previously been moved to the Teton River in the 1860s with the two unratified treaties.) This change created the southern boundary of the current reservation. In 1877 the Canadian government signed Treaty 7 with the Canadian Blackfoot tribes. By 1878 only the "Southern" Piegan of the Blackfoot Confederacy were living in the United States.[36]

With the extinction of the wild bison on the northern Great Plains and the corresponding "starvation winter" of 1883 and 1884 the Blackfeet became confined to their shrunken land base in north-central Montana.[37] After the discovery of gold and the influx of illegal miners to the Sweet Grass Hills, in the winter of 1888 the United States returned to acquire the eastern portion of Blackfeet lands. The federal government moved the eastern reservation boundary from just east of the Sweet Grass Hills all the way west to Cut Bank Creek. Although the Blackfeet referred to themselves as the "Prairie people," they now lived pushed up against the Rocky Mountain Front.[38]

Finally in 1896 the United States returned to negotiate for the western portion of Blackfeet lands, again believing that they would find gold and minerals in the mountains. (Part of this land eventually became Glacier National Park.) With this last agreement the United States fixed the modern-day external boundaries of the reservation when the government moved the boundary from the continental divide east to the foothills of the mountains. Although the external boundaries of the reservation would remain the same throughout the twentieth century, the United States reduced the communally held lands again with the allotment of farm and ranch lands to individual tribal members from 1907 to 1912.[39]

It was no coincidence that the government negotiated settlements removing land from Blackfeet ownership roughly ten years apart from the 1850s to the 1910s. Each agreement (except allotment) included a stipulation that the United States would pay the Blackfeet over a ten-year time schedule. The government paid the Blackfeet each year for ten years with goods and services for the land they ceded. But with each successive agreement, from the 1850s to 1860s to 1870s to 1880s and finally in the 1890s, the economic self-sufficiency and stability of the Blackfeet became more precarious. They needed the annual payments provided in exchange for the sale of their lands simply to survive.

New Economy

Beginning with the 1855 Stevens treaty the United States agreed to pay the Blackfoot each year for ten years for peace on the prairies. The government did not pay the Blackfoot with money. They instead paid with goods, such as fabric or blankets, or with services, such as a teacher for the children. These were called annuity payments because the U.S. government paid them on an annual basis. After the 1855 treaty the U.S. government began to make annuity payments on the Missouri River at the mouth of the Judith River.[40] That change constituted one of the first disruptions to the seasonal cycle of the Blackfeet. Instead of being out hunting or gathering in preparation for winter they now had to stop at Judith Landing in the fall of each year to pick up their payment. In the 1860s the United States made annuity payments at Fort Benton, farther up the Missouri River. And by the 1870s the United States was making annuity payments at reservation agency headquarters, first on the Teton River and then on Badger Creek.

Initially members of all four Blackfoot groups came for their share of the payment. The Blackfeet leader Three Calf described to Ewers, the ethnohistorian, that these payments were not given out to individuals; instead they were "issued to the band chiefs and they gave it out to the heads of families."[41] James Willard Schultz estimated that there were forty-eight bands in the nineteenth century.[42] The early annuity payments consisted of American food items such as flour, rice, sugar, and coffee. They also included household objects and weapons, including blankets, calico, flannel, knives, axes, guns, and the most coveted item of all, tobacco.[43] Many Blackfeet took their American food items, which they did not eat but which they knew had value, and traded them at the trading post in Fort Benton.[44] Three Calf told Ewers that the Blackfeet also bartered their food items to the "white men who married into the tribe" in exchange for food they would acquire in the future.[45] Beginning with the 1855 Stevens treaty the collection of the yearly annuity payment became a time when all of the Blackfoot gathered together in one place that was not for their annual O'kan. The receipt of annuity payments in the fall and then trading or bartering some of the goods to traders or white relatives developed into a new economy for the Blackfeet.

Transition to the Reservation

In 1875 the U.S. government moved its Blackfeet agency headquarters from the Teton River north to Badger Creek. The purpose of the agency was to provide oversight of Blackfeet resources, to provide protection from outside influences, and to issue annuity payments. By 1875 the government agent was reporting that only 50 percent of the subsistence economy came from hunting; the other 50 percent came from collecting annuities.[46] With their annuity money the Blackfeet paid for the majority of the services that the U.S. government provided, including the salary of the federal agent. When the agency moved from the Teton River to Badger Creek a completely new structure had to be built. The Blackfeet paid for the wood to build the agency and even provided the workers. Blackfeet women helped build the agency headquarters because men deemed it improper that they do such manual labor themselves.[47]

The local federal agent decided how to distribute the Blackfeet monies. One way he adopted was to distribute "tickets" to families to be exchanged for their annuities. However, even though the Blackfeet owned the annuities and the annuities were supposed to be distributed to each member of the tribe, that was not what happened. Those families that were physically able were forced to work for their tickets. Those who were infirm were not required to work, but there was an expectation that someone in their family should work for their tickets. This system of working for something that they already owned became a sore spot for many Blackfeet leaders. As food became scarce on the northern Great Plains these annuity "tickets" became worth more than money, and the Blackfeet began to sell, trade, and barter the tickets among themselves.[48]

The Blackfeet went on their last communal buffalo hunt to the Judith

Basin in 1879.[49] After this hunt they retreated to what was left of their lands to the west, and the Blackfeet began to settle along its creeks and rivers. Living along the Rocky Mountain Front consistently throughout the year was new to the Blackfeet. For the next few years only small groups of individual men went out east to find what was left of the wild buffalo. The last buffalo hide tipi was made in 1881, and it required fourteen hides.[50] The Blackfeet killed their last four wild buffalo in the Sweet Grass Hills in 1884.[51]

In the fall of 1883 the Blackfeet leader Three Suns warned the federal government of their impending doom: "You see how poor we are; there [are] no buffalo; we are on the verge of starvation."[52] Three Suns was correct. As the winter of 1883 began the only food that reached the reservation agency was sugar.[53] At the beginning of the winter the government agent John Young issued a mere one and a half pounds of beef per person per week from the tribally owned cattle herd. By midwinter he had cut that ration to a quarter of a pound per person per week.[54] Cut off from their traditional sources of food and resources and with inadequate provisions from the U.S. government, death from starvation and disease followed. Not all families were affected in the same way. The fortunate families—those who maintained a subsistence lifestyle—survived on small game, roots, and berries. Some survived by "stripp[ing] the bark from the saplings that gr[ew] along the creeks and [eating] the inner portions to appease their gnawing hunger."[55] My grandmother's father, Elmer Mad Plume, was only eight years old at the time, and his entire family survived.[56] However, for some families the impact was greater. In some families two-thirds of the people died.[57] One Blackfeet leader, Almost-a-Dog, kept a record of Blackfeet deaths by putting a notch in a willow stick; he recorded 555 deaths that winter.[58] The historian Paul Rosier has described the aftermath of the "starvation winter" as one of "the most rapid demographic declines of full-blood Indians on the Great Plains."[59] This extermination by hunger not only precipitated a loss of tribal leadership but also began to break apart the band system. Life would never be the same again for the Blackfeet. The reservation era began, and it began inauspiciously with widespread starvation and disease.

In terms of daily survival the next few years were probably the most difficult in Blackfeet history. Starvation, malnutrition, and disease continued to create social turmoil. Bands and families had to regroup, choosing new leadership and adopting orphans. It was a time, elders said, that bands began to get "mixed up" or reorganize because of the loss of members.[60] Religious leaders also had to reorganize and restructure the membership of religious societies. Living in close quarters allowed for communicable diseases, including smallpox, to break out on a regular basis, further weakening Blackfeet families. Diseases not only affected humans but also their horses and cattle. An epidemic of mange infected Blackfeet horses and many died. Families began to travel to the agency headquarters with dog travois instead of horse travois to collect their weekly rations.[61]

One of the government agent's primary roles was to oversee the management of Blackfeet resources and distribute the funds derived from those resources. In those early reservation years the main natural resources were grass, timber, and minerals. However, the government agent struggled to maintain control over the vast reservation. People began to illegally mine in the Bear Paw, Little Rockies, and the Sweet Grass Hills in 1885, even though all of these places were on the Blackfeet reservation. Several companies were illegally cutting timber and selling it off-reservation, and the operators of large ranches were illegally bringing their cattle to graze on the reservation prairies.[62] Incompetent agents with limited administrative skills became the norm on the Blackfeet reservation. Outside businesses knew that they could take advantage of the situation and did.

By the winter of 1887 the Blackfeet had become desperate. Commissioners from Washington DC arrived in "sub-zero weather" in February to negotiate the sale of the eastern portion of the reservation in exchange for ten more years of payments for food and services. The Blackfeet monies were going to be used to purchase "livestock, agricultural implements, clothes, subsistence, and education" plus "Agency buildings, medical care, mechanical shops."[63] Unfortunately the Blackfeet were not able to purchase an honest agent.

The Blackfeet leader White Calf charged that their agent took their annuity goods and sold them to the local white population for a profit and also sold their annuity payments back to them for furs. White Calf noted, "If he [the agent] should remain, before that time elapsed he will steal us blind and starve us to death."[64] Although the agent's role was to purchase goods with Blackfeet money for their welfare, the agent often purchased lower quality merchandise and livestock and sometimes did not even distribute what was purchased. When the agent did not give the Blackfeet the horses they purchased after the mange epidemic and lied to them, Eagle Flag commented, "See this reservation how big it is, but Old Tomorrow [the agent] has filled it with lies."[65]

Because the various agents, traders, and businesses all seemed to be profiting from the resources on the reservation a group of Blackfeet leaders went to Washington DC to protest in 1891. They were especially upset that the Great Northern Railroad was cutting hay and timber on the reservation and taking land for its depots without compensating the tribe. White Calf facetiously asked the commissioner of Indian affairs, "We wish you would give us some key there to lock up the reservation."[66] Bear Chief added, "We wish to keep our ground" but also indicated that the big off-reservation cattle ranchers kept "steal[ing] the grass." Little Plume also protested that the agents made the Blackfeet work for their own annuities, which were part of their payment for the Sweet Grass Hills.[67] Protesting usually resulted in the hiring of a new agent and not a solution to their problems.

The headquarters of the Blackfeet agency moved permanently to Willow Creek and the new town of Browning in 1895.[68] Local residents and officials commented that moving the agency headquarters even farther north to one of the most "dreadful locations" on the reservation was a mistake. The inspector for the Indian office reported that "a more dreary, bleak, desolate spot would be hard to find. The buildings stand in the prairie, in a valley, where wind sweeps with great power to and from the mountains about 9 days in the week. There is no grass, no shade, 'no nothing.'"[69]

What the Blackfeet did not fully appreciate, despite their continued protests, was that the United States gave the agents significant control over their lives. For example, in 1883, the same year that the Blackfeet suffered through the starvation winter, the U.S. secretary of interior approved new regulations to engender greater social change. The secretary

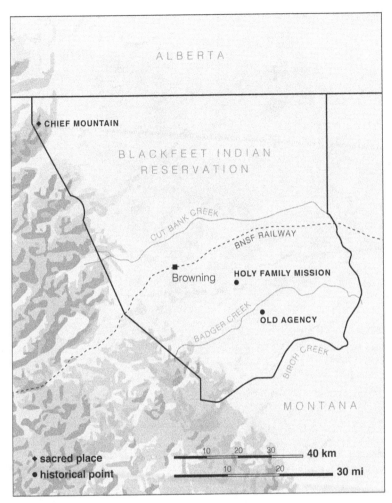

Map 1. Blackfeet reservation. Map courtesy Lucien Liz-Lepiorz.

of interior gave the reservation agents permission to enforce "punishment by withholding of rations, fine, imprisonment, or hard work for [the offense of] . . . participating in [a] sun dance . . . plural marriages, [and] practice of the medicine man."[70] One agent even threatened to imprison women who did beadwork.[71] This precedent set a new low of punishing the Blackfeet by withholding their own money.

As the end of the ten-year cycle of annuity payments was approaching,

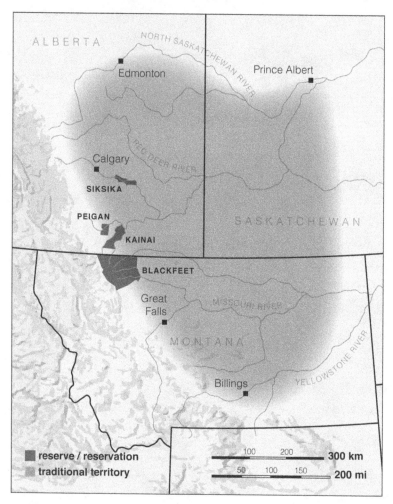

Map 2. Traditional territory, with reservations and reserves. Map courtesy Lucien Liz-Lepiorz.

the U.S. government returned in 1895 with a final request for land. Local businesspeople believed that there was mineral wealth in the mountains, and they wanted to mine the region. The Blackfeet wanted a guarantee that they would receive enough money to pay for their transition into the American economy. Little Dog contended that "those mountains will never disappear. We will see them as long as we live; our children will see them all their lives, and when we are all dead they will still be there. . . . Those mountains will last forever; the money will not."[72] Little Bear Chief restated their previous protests that "the money we received from the last treaty has been wasted."[73] (In the end the Blackfeet received only half of what they asked and the U.S. government took twice as much land as the Blackfeet were willing to negotiate.) White Calf and the other Blackfeet leaders reluctantly agreed out of economic necessity. For twenty years White Calf "complained of the encroachments of whites, and the taking away of the fairest portion of their reservation," to no avail.[74] In 1895 White Calf declared, "In the future we don't want the Great Father to ask for anything more."[75] The government no longer asked; they just took charge.

A New Citizenship

In his 1902 annual report the reservation agent James Monteith reported that there were two populations on the reservation: those born on the reservation and those born before the reservation. Monteith reported for the first time that a new citizenship was emerging. Those born and raised on the reservation were different than those born and raised on the prairies. There were the obvious physical and visible differences. He noted that the majority of the younger Blackfeet had short hair and wore Western clothing. The older men were another matter. They all wore their hair long and in braids. Monteith noted that it was "inadvisable" to "get after" the older men to cut their hair. His solution was to wait for them to pass away, and with them their Blackfeet habits.[76] It seemed to be a common sentiment. Only a few years earlier the agent had stated that "as long as the present generation lives" they will continue to practice their beliefs and use the "native medicine men."[77] Thus at the beginning of the twentieth century the government agent recognized two different groups; one had no intention of changing.

One ancient custom that agent Monteith did attempt to change caused great community upheaval. The new commissioner of Indian affairs, W. A. Jones, acting on national policy, believed that rations promoted dependency, and he ordered the local agent Monteith to stop them. The Blackfeet protested. The *Great Falls Tribune* reported that Monteith threatened the elderly leader of the Blackfeet, White Calf, with jail if he could not control his angry tribal members. The *Tribune* aptly described the situation with the headline, "Piegans are in Open Revolt."[78] Little Dog replied, "If you dare to arrest White Calf, his people will bind you [Agent Monteith] with ropes and throw you ahead of the next passing train."[79] Monteith did not arrest White Calf, and he partially acquiesced to the Blackfeet leader and continued rations for the elderly, infirm, and families with young children. The Blackfeet viewed the weekly rations in a different way. On the one hand the Blackfeet leaders reminded Monteith that "our rations are not a gratuity—they are bought with our own money."[80] The weekly rations reflected to the older generation a time when the band leaders provided for the community from the fruits of their labors. In this case it was redistributing weekly rations "bought with our own money" that they negotiated from land exchanges.

One year later, in 1903, White Calf returned to Washington DC to protest the inefficiency of the local agent and the poor conditions on the reservation.[81] He became ill and went to the hospital. White Calf knew that he was dying. He sang his own death song while he was in the hospital just before he passed away. He had been the leader of the Skunks band, and he was considered the last true leader from the buffalo days. Twenty years before White Calf died Father Peter Prando had converted him to Catholicism and had given him a pipe as a gesture of friendship between the Jesuit fathers and the Blackfeet.[82] After his death officials took White Calf's pipe and pipe bag to the Bureau of American Ethnology at the Smithsonian.[83] The ethnohistorian John C. Ewers argued that the death of White Calf marked a transition from "traditional leadership" to a new kind of governance on the reservation.[84]

Final Say

The older generation of Blackfeet had grown into adulthood on a large expanse of land. In the latter half of the nineteenth century the Blackfeet lost the majority of their territory to the U.S. government. The destruction of the bison in the 1880s, also by outside forces, destroyed the Blackfeet economy and dealt them a devastating blow. With the loss of land and the loss of bison the Blackfeet could no longer gather the rich resources of the prairies. Their longtime economy changed permanently, and a new economy emerged. It included collecting an annual payment for their sold lands, and that payment eventually turned into a weekly redistribution for the most needy.

Unbeknown to the Blackfeet the U.S. government would ultimately control how all the Blackfeet monies were spent. The United States used the Blackfeet money to build their own government buildings, to hire farmers to teach the Blackfeet about agriculture, to build schools, and to hire teachers to teach Blackfeet children. In 1895 the U.S. government set up their new (and what would become the final) headquarters in the town of Browning to manage the affairs of the Blackfeet. The old-time tribal leadership struggled to maintain a sense of control over their own affairs during the early years of the reservation. There were numerous battles, mostly over how the U.S. government spent Blackfeet monies. It was a battle that the Blackfeet lost again and again. A final blow came to the Blackfeet when one of their last old-time leaders, White Calf, died from an illness while in Washington DC in 1903 protesting yet again the mismanagement of tribal funds.

Joseph Tatsey, a Blackfeet translator, lamented to the linguist C. C. Uhlenbeck in the summer of 1910 that "when the buffalo were gone, the whites drove us up here. They began to feed us with beef, bacon, coffee and sugar, flour. They gave us blankets, (and) clothing, too. In the first place we did not like these kinds of food and clothing, and we could not do anything. The buffalo were gone. We had no place to go to, we became stationary."[85] The Blackfeet would never gain control over their own economy in the early twentieth century. Attempting to maintain control over their cultural life was another matter.

In the summer of 1910 when Father Carroll wrote his scathing report on Blackfeet religious persistence, Father A. Soer, a representative of the Catholic Church, also expressed the Church's continued frustration at its inability to completely convert the Blackfeet to Christianity. Blackfeet homes, he wrote, still contained "sweet incense burning in honor of the sun" and "medicine bags, otter-tails, bear-paws, medicine pipes . . . pack[ed] away with herbs in ornamental sacks in a place of honor."[86] It was discouraging to the Church that the Blackfeet whom they initially thought they had converted then developed a new syncretic belief in both "the Holy Church and the medicine-man."[87] Somehow the Church did not recognize that just as the Blackfeet had incorporated the Fourth of July into their annual summer festivities, they had also incorporated the Holy Church into their worldview. In the Catholic worldview there was simply not room for both.

The summer of 1910 witnessed an odd variety of scholars and tourists who came to experience and record the last days of the Blackfeet and their ancient celebration, the O'kan. The linguist Truman Michelson hoped to record the Blackfeet language as an academic exercise for the use of future scholars. In the process he was able to record in his writings and in his audio documentation the voices of many different Blackfeet people who all had a common story to tell. Instead of expressing dissatisfaction with their economic situation—the job of the band leaders to carry out in Washington DC—they instead told stories that they wanted recorded for future generations. A common theme emerges from these stories. They attempted to explain to America how they experienced the world. The Blackfeet believed that they had a distinct relationship with the natural world that was both practical and divine. Based on their ancient experiences they had control and say in the final outcome of their lives.

CHAPTER 2

Invisible Reality

The Blackfeet Universe

My grandmother told me many stories of her own life and the adventures of her two grandmothers and their husbands. It was rare when she told a story of sorrow or suffering. Many stories were of daily life, of moving from place to place, hunting, berry picking, looking for medicine, and cooking and eating. She told a lot of stories about cooking and eating. "Oh, happy times," she would say.

But interwoven within these stories of daily life were different stories about people, animals, and beings that the Blackfeet shared space with and often encountered. For example, when she talked about picking berries along the Badger–Two Medicine she would often talk about the supernatural horses that lived in the small mountain lakes. These horses lived underwater and they swam underwater between lakes. Some of these horses she said swam from the small lakes on the east side of the mountains underwater and under the mountains to the west side and Flathead Lake.

Other times she told stories of her family's interactions with the supernatural. Once her grandfather Spotted Bear was near a creek, and he stopped to water his horse. He saw a beaver and her children. But he recognized immediately that these were unlike normal animal beavers; they were supernatural beavers. The mother beaver was standing on her hind legs like a human on the bank of the creek and singing a song. Her children were doing the same, and they were dancing in the sand. Spotted Bear watched them for a while until the mother beaver saw him. Suddenly the beaver threw her children into the water, and they swam away.

This type of interaction happened on an occasional basis in the past. The

Blackfeet felt blessed to observe the lives of the supernatural. And they often named people as a memory of the experience. Later in life Spotted Bear named several of his relatives based on this one encounter. He named his granddaughter Not Real Beaver Woman after the mother beaver, and my grandmother named me Not Real Beaver Woman after her mother (Spotted Bear's granddaughter). My grandmother told a lot of stories like this, of the benign observation of the lives of supernatural entities.

But she had other stories that were not so benign, stories in which the supernatural actively pursued human interaction. In one story she told about an incident that occurred with one of my grandfather's ancestors. It was about a young man who went out hunting alone. While he was out he was captured by a supernatural eagle. The eagle took him way up high in the mountains to his nest, where he left the young man. Once there, my grandmother said, if the young man squinted his eyes he could see his village far below in the prairies. He knew that no one would look for him because he had headed out alone. The eagle then started bringing him food to eat. "How nice," the young man thought. The eagle brought rabbits and deer. He had more meat now than if he had gone hunting himself.

Finally the young man realized that the eagle intended to eat him—after he had fattened up. The young man realized he had better start planning his escape. He waited for the right opportunity to attack and kill the eagle. He dismembered the eagle but saved all its body parts. Using one of the deer skins he fashioned himself a flying cape with the various parts of the eagle. Its wings were attached to his arms and tailfeathers in the back. He then jumped off the mountain. When he landed he untied the eagle's wings, its tailfeathers, and head. He wrapped them all up in the deer hide and made a bundle. He then walked back to camp. At the end of this story my grandmother would exclaim, "That was really true about those old-time Indians, a real story. You can write it down."

"Real stories" to her were about the supernatural. I began to realize that when I asked her to tell a story; to her that meant "a real story," a story about the supernatural and not just one of daily life. Once a group of researchers from the University of Lethbridge came to interview my grandmother. On the phone they told her that they wanted to hear stories of the old days. But when they arrived they asked her about life on the reservation (and they asked in chronological order; tell us about the 1920s, tell us about the 1930s, tell us about the 1940s, etc.). At the end of the session my grandmother was exasperated, and she asked, "I thought they wanted to hear real stories?"

"Old-timers" like my grandmother saw a distinction between the "real" world that was full of supernatural beings, animals, rocks, trees, and other elements and the one of our daily existence. The old-time Blackfeet lived in a multilayered reality where the extraordinary experiences of the Blackfeet with the supernatural were interwoven with the natural.

"Real Stories"

The vast majority of stories collected by the early recorders of Blackfeet life were what my grandmother would call "real stories," or stories that told of the relationship between the Blackfeet and the supernatural. In his attempts to understand the North Peigan in the late nineteenth century Father Emile Legal reflected that it was a "natural instinct in all of us to believe in the existence of invisible realities."[1] He recognized that at the essence of Blackfeet life was the belief that "the visible [was] really only a manifestation of the invisible."[2] From their earliest recordings the Blackfeet told others about their unique view of the history of their people. They emphasized that the Blackfeet believed that the invisible dimension *was* the real world and that the visible dimension was a partial expression of this world. The Blackfeet believed that the visible dimension was only a small part of their total reality, "the tip of the iceberg," to use a modern-day metaphor. Most of their reality lay within the invisible dimension, unseen but known. The Blackfeet told James Willard Schultz, Walter McClintock, George Bird Grinnell, Clark Wissler, David Duvall, John C. Ewers, and other recorders of Blackfeet life hundreds of stories of what Father Legal described as the "invisible reality" of the Blackfeet.

It was no surprise then that the first publications on the Blackfeet included a significant number of "real stories," among them the early articles by Schultz in *Field and Stream*, Grinnell's *Blackfoot Lodge Tales*, and Wissler and Duvall's *Mythology of the Blackfoot Indians*. Wissler and Duvall learned that the stories they collected fell into "four groups, — Tales of the Old Man, Star Myths, Ritualistic Origin, and Cultural or other Origins."[3] Grinnell found a similar division. Wissler and Duvall recognized that the majority of stories they collected were from the last category. These stories described the origins of just about every relationship the Blackfeet had with the supernatural. They also described why things were the way they were in the visible world of the Blackfeet. These early recorders of Blackfeet life, like the recorders from the University of Lethbridge who came to interview my grandmother, learned that "real stories," or stories of supernatural relationships, formed the basis of Blackfeet history—their distinct version of history—which included both the seen and unseen.

Worldview

The Blackfeet told the recorders of Blackfeet life that they divided the universe into three dimensions, which they called the Above world, the Below world, and the Water world.[4] The Blackfeet believed that these three dimensions were parallel dimensions, existing side by side and separate. But they were also interconnected and permeable. The Blackfeet understood that within the earth, the water, and the sky reside a great variety of natural and supernatural beings. Within the Blackfeet universe lived not only the Niitsitapi, the original people, but also the Ksahkomitapi, or earth beings, the Soyiitapi, or underwater beings, and the Spomitapi, or sky beings.

The Above world consisted of all the celestial bodies, stars, and constellations, including what the Blackfeet consider their holy trinity: Naató'si, the Sun, and his wife Ko'komíki'somm, the Moon, and their son Iipisówaahs, the Morning Star or Early Riser, that is, the planet Venus.[5] The Above world was considered a separate dimension where beings lived out their lives in their own homes and where animals and plants also lived. It included forces of nature such as Thunder, who controlled thunder, lightning, and rain. Other Above world supernatural beings included the Raven, who lived in the mountains, or Spider Man, who lived in the Sky world east of the North Star and used his web to help people travel between the Above world and the earth. There are also animals such as eagles or geese who lived here on earth but were considered part of the Above dimension. There were of course restrictions for humans against eating animals from the Above realm.

The Water world consisted of the Soyiitapi, or underwater beings. Similar to those in the Above world, the beings who lived in the Water world also had their own villages, homes, animals, and plants. Supernatural beings such as the underwater bison, underwater bears, underwater dogs, and underwater horses also lived in villages among their own people within the Water world. It included forces of nature such as Wind Maker, who lived under the water in upper Saint Mary Lake in present-day Glacier National Park and who controlled the wind. There were also underwater monsters, as well as animals such as beavers, otters, fish, and turtles who lived here on earth but were considered part of the Water dimension. There were of course restrictions for humans against eating animals from the Water realm.

The Below world consisted of the Niitsitapi, the original people or humans. Similar to the Above world and Water world, the Below world consisted of humans who lived in villages and homes with animals and plants. There also existed the Ksahkomitapi, the supernatural earth beings, which include giants and little people and certain animals, plants, insects, rocks, shells, and fossils. There were monsters, lots of monsters, and of course forces of nature such as Cold Maker, who lived to the north and controlled snow, ice, and winter.

Some of the supernaturals found in the three worlds have numerous stories told about them, while others have only a few. Some have notorious reputations, while others were considered more benevolent. There were no all good or all evil supernaturals. Their personalities represent all the variations found within humankind.

In addition to the distinct natural and supernatural beings, deities, and forces in each of the three dimensions there are some who transcend these worlds, such as Napiwa, Katoyissa, and Paie. Napiwa, or Old Man, is a supernatural being who as far as was known has lived forever. He was foolish, petty, and greedy. He lived life in the extreme, always wanting too much and thinking too little. Katoyissa, or Blood Clot, was a superhero who traveled the Below world, ridding it of monsters to make it safer for the Niitsitapi, or humans. And Paie, or Scar Face, played a similar role in the Above world. He became a superhero for his role in traveling the Above world, ridding it of evil beings to make it safe for the beings in the Above world.

If one were to look at these three worlds in the Blackfeet universe and assume a hierarchy, the Above world would contain beings, deities, and forces with the most supernatural power, the Water world would be a close second, and the Below world would contain the least amount of supernatural power. Within this hierarchy human beings did not have any supernatural power of and by themselves. Instead they needed to seek out supernatural power from those beings who had it. The Blackfeet believed that humans had to create alliances with the supernatural to live life to the fullest. The Blackfeet told the early recorders of Blackfeet life about these relationships and how it was rare for a Blackfeet *not* to have an alliance with a supernatural entity. An essential part of being Blackfeet was having a relationship with the supernatural world.

Creating Alliances

The Blackfeet told the early recorders of Blackfeet life that there were three ways to acquire supernatural power or supernatural allies. The first was for a supernatural entity to seek out an individual, speak to that person, and transfer some of its supernatural power to him or her, thereby creating an alliance. Wissler, whose work was based on that of Duvall, noted that

> the Blackfoot theory is that there functions in the universe a force (natoji = Sun power) most manifest in the Sun but pervading the entire world, a power (natoji) that may communicate with individuals making itself manifest in and through any object. . . . Such manifestation is through speech . . . at the moment of speaking the object becomes for the time being "as a person." . . . The being conferring power . . . formally transfer[s] it to the recipient. . . . This is regarded as a compact between the recipient and the being. [The relationship therefore is] . . . solely between one individual and the being who gave it.[6]

In one story a Blackfeet man explained to Duvall and Wissler that his horse talked to him and told him that the horse would give him some of his supernatural power. The man then pointed out a distinction. He stated to Duvall and Wissler that "this story is not an account of a dream, but a statement of things that really happened."[7]

The Blackfeet differentiated between interacting with a supernatural in the visible realm and interacting with a supernatural in a "dream" state. The second way to acquire an alliance was for a human to go out and search for supernatural assistance, through a dream. It was often through or within dreams that the Blackfeet interacted with the supernatural. George Bird Grinnell observed that the Blackfeet "were firm believers in dreams. These, they say, are sent by the Sun to enable [them] to look ahead, to tell what is going to happen. A dream, especially if it is a strong one,—that is, if the dream is very clear and vivid,—is almost always obeyed."[8] The early recorders of Blackfeet life wondered if the Blackfeet really differentiated between reality and dreams or the visible and invisible dimensions. Walter McClintock stated it this way: "The old generation . . . lived in a sort of dream world of myth and legends and ceremonies."[9] Clark Wissler stated it more bluntly in a letter to the anthropologist Franz Boas: "Psychologically these people are 'dream mad.'"[10]

The third and easiest way to create an alliance with the supernatural was to "purchase" supernatural power from another human who had already acquired it through any of the three methods. With this last way a human could "purchase" all or part of the supernatural power, and the human (the "seller") would transfer knowledge and ability to the "buyer."[11] This method was probably the most common way to create an alliance with the supernatural; Wissler published the more than two hundred pages of Duvall's field notes in *Ceremonial Bundles of the Blackfoot Indians*, which explained in great detail how the Blackfeet "bought" and "sold" supernatural power.[12]

Overarching this system of individual Blackfeet developing alliances with the supernatural was a larger understanding of the history of the relationship between humans and the supernatural. Most of this history was public knowledge, but some of it was known only to a few. The Blackfeet, though, had limited written accounts of their history.[13] Instead the Blackfeet surrounded themselves with and relied on objects that served as mnemonic devices to remind them of their stories. Their landscape was one such narrative or ancient manuscript. Each place they traveled reminded them of their history, and at each place they retold the stories of the adventures of the various supernatural beings in their three worlds. They also carried with them devices or objects, such as a quill blanket band, that reminded them of the stories of these supernatural beings and the relationships that humans formed with them.

Fig. 6. Albert Mad Plume, Heart Butte, 1944. Photo courtesy Jessie Wilber Papers, MS 2252, Merrill G. Burlingame Special Collections, Montana State University, image #ORH 86.

Niitóyis

Tipis were one public place where the Blackfeet wrote their history for all to see. Painted on the outside of these "real dwellings" was a story that not only told the Blackfeet history of the universe but also of their relationship with the supernatural.[14] As they traveled around they took their stories with them. Their account placed humans and nonhumans, natural beings and supernatural beings, in interconnecting and often kinship relationships. For the Blackfeet this narrative functioned as a framework for a distinctive Blackfeet experience of the world; their stories and their symbols were a part of their everyday lives, predictable and regular, painted on their *niitóyis* for all to see, know, remember, and tell.

The Blackfeet told the early recorders of Blackfeet life of the stories painted on the sides of their tipis and the mnemonic methods they used to remember these stories. Some of the recorders of Blackfeet life published the information they learned from the Blackfeet, including George Bird Grinnell, Clark Wissler and David Duvall, C. C. Uhlenbeck, S. A. Barrett, and Walter McClintock, among others.[15] In most published manuscripts, articles, or books the recorders of Blackfeet life muted the identity of the individual Blackfeet they interviewed. However, the majority of these recorders left behind field notes or unpublished records that identify the Blackfeet they collaborated with or interviewed. With these notes it is sometimes possible to reconstruct and find the voices of Blackfeet storytellers.

The Blackfeet told the recorders of Blackfeet life that they painted the top of a tipi black, representing the night sky or the Sky world. On the back facing west and left unpainted or white was the shape of a Maltese cross, which was Iipisówaahs, Morning Star, the son of Naató'si, the Sun, and Ko'komíki'somm, the Moon. On the northern smoke flap were six circles, left unpainted or white, representing the constellation of Mióhpokoiksi, the Lost Children (Pleiades). And on the southern smoke flap were seven circles, also left unpainted or white, representing the constellation Ihkitsíkammiksi, the Seven Brothers (Ursa Major).[16]

They said they usually painted the bottom of the tipi red, representing the earth or the Below world, with either rounded forms, representing the prairies, or triangular forms, representing the mountains, extended around the tipi base. Within this red area were circles left unpainted or white, representing Kakató'si, a star child who fell to earth. This design was considered the basic universal design that Blackfeet could paint on their tipis.[17] This design was the communal history of the Blackfeet and the supernatural.

In addition to the universal design sometimes a tipi also had a supernatural being, animal, or object painted on its sides, representing the individual tipi owner's own personal relationship with a supernatural entity. If so, the owner would paint a representation of the animal or entity on both sides of the tipi. Both images would be painted facing east toward the door and the rising sun: the male representation painted on the north side and the female representation painted on the south side.

My grandfather's parents, Aimsback and Hollering in the Air, had a unique tipi design called the "Big Rock" tipi.[18] Instead of having two separate images for male and female, this tipi design had two large, round figures painted on the front and back of the tipi. The two images of the "Big Rock" embodied the male and female essence of the rock lodge of a supernatural entity. The Blackfeet told Grinnell that "the paintings on the lodges represent sacred animals or objects which possess protective power . . . to insure good fortune. . . . The paintings thus require no special explanation and need be accounted for by no elaborate theory."[19] The Blackfeet told Duvall and Wissler that the individual tipi designs were the sole property of the owner. Thus it was up to owners to decide if they wanted to share the story with others.

The universal design, however, consisted of communally held stories that everyone knew. My grandmother told these stories to me throughout her life. The characters of these stories were well-known members of their community. The Blackfeet told Duvall and Wissler that "mythological characters [were] so firmly fixed in folk-thought, that each may be regarded as a reality."[20] The Blackfeet had limited restrictions as to whom or when these publicly held stories could be told. The Blackfeet told Duvall and Wissler that there were "no restrictions" as to who could tell stories.[21] (This was not the case with individually owned stories of a person's own interaction with the supernatural.) Because anyone could

Fig. 7. Heart Butte, 1944, property of Albert Mad Plume. Photo courtesy Jessie Wilber Papers, MS 2252, Merrill G. Burlingame Special Collections, Montana State University, image #ORH 176.

tell these stories the early recorders of Blackfeet life recorded multiple versions of the same story, and they worried about the accuracy of the stories they collected. One Kainai man told Duvall and Wissler that stories were like plant life: "The parts of this weed all branch off from the stem. They go different ways, but all come from the same root. So it is with the different versions of a myth."[22] The universal design painted on a tipi represented several public stories of Blackfeet history that were altered (but not changed) with each storyteller, because this history was known by all and could be retold by anyone. I am going to retell them too, but I will focus on the versions told by the Blackfeet from the turn of the twentieth century.

The Story of Morning Star and Mistaken Morning Star atop the Tipi

The Blackfeet painted a representation of Morning Star (the planet Venus) on the back or west side of their tipis. Venus appears brightest on the eastern horizon in the early morning. The Blackfeet painted it in the shape of a Maltese cross. Although there are multiple stories about Morning Star, the one that is most associated with its place on a tipi is the story of his friendship with a human named Paie, or Scar Face.[23] This first story that is part of the universal tipi design of the Blackfeet describes a close friendship that develops between Morning Star, a being from the Sky world, and Paie, a human, and also the relationship that developed between Morning Star's parents, the Sun and Moon, and Paie.

The story of Morning Star and Paie is long and complex, with multiple sections that will not be recounted here. However, the basic story line tells of Paie, a poor young man, traveling east to ask the Sun to remove an unsightly scar from his face. Paie has many adventures as he travels east across the prairies, over the mountains, and finally to a big lake. Across the lake and up in the Sky is the Sun's lodge. Along the way Paie befriends Morning Star, the son of the Sun and the Moon.

Morning Star brings Paie home to meet his mother while his father is away. At night the Sun returns from his travel across the sky, and he notices upon reaching the door of the lodge the smell of a human, which is disagreeable to the Sun. The Sun asked the Moon to make a smudge with *siiksinoko*, or juniper (*Juniperus spp.*), to cleanse the lodge. Humans learned in this story and others the process of smudging to purify a person, place, or object before interacting with a supernatural, such as the Sun.[24]

The Sun welcomed Paie to the Sky world and told Paie that he could go anywhere but warned him to avoid the west, as it was dangerous. Ignoring this advice (of course it would not be a myth if the young hero actually heeded the advice of an elder), Paie set off to see the far west. He immediately encountered the wicked cranes (*Grus canadenis*). Morning Star also warned Paie and reminded him that these were the cranes who had killed all but one of the children of the Sun and Moon: Morning Star. Paie balked at the potential danger, took his spear, and fought the cranes to the death, killing all seven of them one by one.

The Sun and Moon were overjoyed at the destruction of the cranes, and in gratitude the Sun transferred some of his supernatural power via various objects to Paie, who in turn gave them to the humans in the Below world. (This part of the story used to be told and acted out as part of a ten-day ceremony.) The Sun also performed a ritual to remove the scar from Paie's face. The Sun did this by performing four sweat lodges in a row. With each sweat Paie's scar began to fade. By the last sweat the scar was removed and the Sun made Paie look like Morning Star, so much so that the Moon actually mistook Paie for her own son. Thereafter the Blackfeet knew Paie or Scar Face as the Mistaken Morning Star. The Sun then instructed Paie on how to best communicate with the Sun: "When you return to your people and wish to make an offering to me, you must first build a sweathouse and there make your offerings. Then I will hear your prayers and accept them."[25]

At the end of his adventure up in the Sky world, including ridding the Sky world of the evil cranes and other creatures, Paie returned to the Below world with the help of Spider Man. Paie brought back the knowledge of a great many things that he taught to the humans below. He also gained status as a deity. His symbolic representation was added to all Blackfeet iconography, along with the Sun, Moon, and Morning Star. Morning Star was honored for his friendship with a human who made the Sky world safe with his representation of the Blackfeet tipi. It was Morning Star's friendships and relationships with humans that created a lasting bond between supernaturals in the Sky world and humans in the Below world.

The Story of the Star Child at the Bottom of the Tipi

On the bottom of their tipis the Blackfeet painted white circles that represented the Star Child, a star who came to earth. The Blackfeet told the early recorders of Blackfeet life the story of Soatsaki, or Feather Woman, a human who married a Sky person, Iipisówaahs, the Morning Star, and their son, the Star Child.[26] In this story a human married a Sky person and they had a child who returned to the Sky world as a star, thereby creating an everlasting kinship relationship between humans and the Sky world. Both as a star and as its physical earthly representative the Star Child in turn provided assistance to humans.

This story began when two young women decided to sleep outside of their lodge on a hot summer night. They woke up before dawn and looked up to see the stars in the sky. One of the girls, Soatsaki, looked up and proclaimed upon observing Iipisówaahs, the Morning Star or Early Riser as he was also known, that she would like to marry him because he was the brightest star. As it would happen, of course, she forgets that she made this statement.

Later when Soatsaki was alone collecting wood away from camp Iipisówaahs appeared in human form and stopped her from returning to the camp. Soatsaki did not recognize him, and she did not like his intrusion. She asked him why he was stopping her. He replied that he was Iipisówaahs and she had pledged to be his wife. After a moment she remembered, acquiesced, and agreed to go with him to the Sky world.

His parents, Naatósi, the Sun, and Ko'komíki'somm, the Moon, were happy with his human wife. The Sky world was similar to the Below world but with different landscapes, animals and plants, and other types of natural life. After she had been there awhile Ko'komíki'somm provided her daughter-in-law with a root digger and instructed her on how to dig roots. Ko'komíki'somm told her daughter-in-law that she could go anywhere in the Sky world, but Ko'komíki'somm warned her daughter-in-law not to dig up the forbidden prairie turnip.

Time passed and Soatsaki continued to live in the Sky world. Eventually she and Morning Star had a child. However, she never overcame her curiosity about the forbidden prairie turnip. One day she decided to dig it up, believing that no one would find out. She immediately learned that when she removed the prairie turnip it opened a hole in the Sky world through which she could see the earth below. She saw her village, her friends, and family, and she became very lonesome for her old life. When she returned to her lodge Iipisówaahs knew by her sad demeanor what she had done.

He knew that she would never be happy in the Sky world again. And so he instructed her to return to the Below world with the Spider Man's web. She brought along her son and her new digging stick. Blackfeet women claim that they learned to dig roots from Soatsaki, who learned how from the Moon. Iipisówaahs warned his wife about not letting their son touch the earth. Soatsaki abided by this warning until one day when she allowed an old grandmother to watch the Star Child while she did her chores. The old woman did not understand the severity of the prohibition and allowed the Star Child to get off the bed. When Soatsaki returned, she discovered that the Star Child had turned into a puffball fungus. Later that night she looked up into the sky, and there was a new star in the hole left by the turnip. The Star Child had turned into the North Star (Polaris).[27]

The Blackfeet called the North Star and the prairie puffball by the same name, Kakató'si. The North Star was an important star to the Blackfeet for several reasons. The North Star helped the ancient Blackfeet travel across the northern Great Plains. The Blackfeet also used the movements of the constellation Ihkitsíkammiksi, the Seven Brothers (Ursa Major), to tell time with the North Star. They watched the Seven Brothers as they moved around the North Star during the night.[28] The Blackfeet also calculated the seasons by the nightly movement of these stars. For the Blackfeet the North Star remained an important supernatural being, half human and half Sky person, a distant relative who helped them tell time and move across the landscape. The Star Child's earthly representative was the prairie puffball, which provided medicine and tinder. The Star Child was painted on the base of their tipis as a daily reminder of the kinship relationship between the Sky world and the Below world.

The Story of the Lost Children atop the Tipi

The Blackfeet painted six white circles representing the constellation Mióhpokoiksi, the Lost Children (Pleiades), on the north smoke flap of their tipis. The story of the Lost Children began during the spring, when the Blackfeet first went out to hunt bison.[29] At that time the Blackfeet were still using *pishkun*, or buffalo jumps.[30] In this particular season a group of poor children asked the bison hunters for the fresh yellow hides of the young bison calves so that they could make themselves new robes. However, the men said they were too busy, and they ignored the children's pleas for help. Year after year these poor children asked the hunters for new robes. And year after year the hunters ignored their pleas.

Finally the children grew tired of the neglect and decided to leave camp and set out on their own. But then they argued about what to do and where to go. One said, "We have nowhere to go." Another said, "Where can we go?" The oldest among them knew what to do. He told the others that they should go join the Sky people. "They will take pity on us and take care of us," he said. The oldest then took the hairs of a weasel and sprinkled them on each of the children. And he took some of the weasel hair in his mouth and rubbed it on his hands. He blew the weasel hair up into the sky, and the children arrived in the Sky world.[31]

The next they knew they were at the home of the Moon and the Sun. They told the Moon and Sun their pitiful story of misfortune and rejection. The Moon immediately took pity on them and took them in. However, the children also wanted to seek their revenge on their former camp, which they could do only with the Sun's help.

The children asked the Moon to ask the Sun to dry up all the water on the earth for seven days. It took some coaxing, but the Sun finally acquiesced to the Moon's request. The humans down on earth began to suffer from this retaliation. They asked their dogs to help them find water. The dogs went out to the dry riverbed and dug for freshwater springs. When this was not enough, the dogs dug for more. Eventually even the dogs were tired of the drought. On the seventh day the dogs prayed to the Moon (they howled) to bring back the water. On the eighth day the water returned with a great rainstorm.

The Moon told the children to remain in the Sky world, and they became the constellation known as the Lost Children, or Pleiades. The Sky world became a refuge for humans when other humans were not behaving in an acceptable way. And humans suffered the wrath of other humans' anger via a supernatural being. The Lost Children are best seen in the night sky from October to February. The Lost Children disappear from the sky each spring to remind the Blackfeet of their uncharitable behavior just when it is time to hunt bison again. Although the majority of Blackfeet stories do not have a "moral to the story"–type purpose, some stories encourage the Blackfeet to behave in socially appropriate ways. The Blackfeet painted the constellation called the Lost Children on their tipis as a reminder of their moral duty to take care of the least within their society, especially children, and of the continuing relationship between the Sky world and Below world.

The Story of the Seven Brothers atop the Tipi

The Blackfeet painted seven white circles representing the constellation Ihkitsíkammiksi, the Seven Brothers (Ursa Major), on the south smoke flap of their tipis. The story of the Big Dipper is a long, complex story of an evil woman with supernatural power and her impact on her family.[32] It began with two women: an older sister and a younger sister. The elder sister had been taking evening walks, during which she met a bear who became her secret lover. Her mother was worried about where her daughter went in the evening. She asked the younger sister to follow the older sister to uncover the truth. When the younger sister revealed the situation to her family, their father got together a group of the men from the camp to kill the bear.

After the bear was killed the elder sister convinced the younger to go retrieve a piece of the bear's body. Unbeknown to the younger sister the bear was supernatural. The younger sister got one of the bear's paws and returned it to the older sister. (It is well known in Blackfeet stories that supernatural beings can be regenerated with the smallest bit of their flesh. To kill a supernatural, a person would need to completely incinerate the being or learn its secret weakness.) With this one bear paw the elder sister acquired the supernatural power to turn herself into a bear. She then sought revenge on those who had attacked her lover and headed to camp to kill the villagers. Her younger sister pledged to be her eternal servant if she spared her life.

Meanwhile the sister's seven brothers returned from a hunting trip to find everyone in the village killed. They found the younger sister, who explained the whole sordid situation. The seven brothers then asked the younger sister to find out the secret of how to kill the elder sister. Feigning concern for the older sister's safety, the younger sister tricked the sister-bear into telling the younger sister her weakness—the sister-bear could be killed with an awl. The seven brothers then scoured the camp for awls. The younger sister scattered these outside of their lodge. One evening the younger sister tempted the elder sister into chasing her outside of the lodge, where the sister-bear stepped on an awl. Her powers became weakened, and the seven brothers jumped on her, killed her, and set her on fire. Unbeknown to them a small piece of her finger blew away, and she was able to resurrect herself.

The elder sister grew into a large and angry supernatural bear. She was set on killing her seven brothers and younger sister when the middle brother took out a feather with supernatural ability. He blew the feather up into the Sky world, and with the feather's assistance the seven brothers and sister escaped. Once there they turned into the stars. The younger sister carried her youngest brother and placed herself nearest to the North Star. The eldest brother moved next to her. These two stars form a line that points toward the North Star. The other siblings then spread out from oldest to youngest to form the Seven Brothers, or the Big Dipper.

Once again the Sky world provided refuge for humans leaving the Below world. In this case they sought safety from an evil Below world supernatural being who killed their entire village, pursued them, and tried to kill them. The humans were fortunate that they escaped and found sanctuary in the Sky world. The Blackfeet painted the Big Dipper on their tipis for several reasons. First, it provided the Blackfeet with powerful evidence that the universe in which they lived was endowed with supernatural power, especially at times when it seemed that they had no control over it. However, in the end they could acquire either the knowledge or the power to overcome the natural or supernatural

Fig. 8. Rainbow lodge. Image #638.145, Joseph H. Sherburne Family Papers, Archives and Special Collections, Maureen and Mike Mansfield Library, University of Montana–Missoula.

Fig. 9. Big Boulder lodge. Image #638.150, Joseph H. Sherburne Family Papers, Archives and Special Collections, Maureen and Mike Mansfield Library, University of Montana–Missoula.

entities and live a good life. Second, it provided assistance to the Blackfeet because the Big Dipper along with the North Star could be used to tell time during the night, to tell the seasons of the year, and to help them navigate their way across the prairies.

Distinct Reality

The early recorders of Blackfeet life interviewed dozens of people at the turn of the twentieth century in an attempt to understand Blackfeet life and lifeways. All of these individuals told similar stories; the Blackfeet had a distinct view of the universe that included having well-established relationships with the supernatural. They created alliances with the supernatural and accessed supernatural power for a variety of purposes. The supernatural provided a place for friendships, kinship, and even sanctuary. The Blackfeet told the recorders of Blackfeet life that the "invisible" realm was not only real to them but omnipresent. It structured not only their views of the universe but much of their social behavior. It permeated their daily lives, and they created mnemonic devices to remember and share their stories about it. Duvall and Wissler noted that "mythical characters are . . . regarded as having made at least some important contribution to the welfare of the people."[33]

The Star Child covered the hole in the sky left after his mother, Feather Woman, dug up the forbidden turnip. He then became the North Star, which created a visible reminder of the kinship between the Sky world and the Below world. Every night he was there for all to see. And every day his earthly representation, the puffball fungus, or the circle painted on the bottom of the tipi, was also there for all to see.

The visible symbolic representations served as reminders to the Blackfeet of the role of their own history, stories, family, and community and of the humble place of humans in the larger unseen universe. But it also represented who they could contact when they needed assistance to alter the natural world. For the Blackfeet the unseen was just as real or even at times more real than what they saw in everyday life. Father Legal recognized this from his first interactions with the Blackfeet. He observed that the Blackfeet believed in an invisible dimension that took on "a completely distinct reality."[34] It defined their existence.

CHAPTER 3

Visible Reality

The Saokiotapi

My grandmother's maternal great-grandmother, Big Mountain Lion Woman, was born sometime in the 1850s. At the time Fort Benton was the center of life in the northern reaches of a vast territory extending across the Great Plains, which was claimed but not yet organized by the United States. In her late sixties and seventies she helped raise my grandmother. She entertained my grandmother with exciting stories of her youth on the northern Great Plains. She married a man named Spotted Bear, and many of her stories were of their life together. And others were of his supernatural ability to transcend the natural world. Big Mountain Lion Woman told my grandmother of happy times traveling to Fort Benton to trade, picking roots and plants along the Missouri River, and using the ferry (instead of fording) to cross the river to go south to raid the Crow. There were unhappy memories as well, like the "starvation winter," when her husband, Spotted Bear, traveled for miles off the newly created reservation to trade for food to feed his family.

My grandmother's great-grandparents were accustomed to a lifestyle that included significant travel. Similar to other Blackfeet they were also accustomed to living in various places throughout their historic territory. The reservation changed that. After 1875, when the U.S. government set up a permanent head-quarters within reservation boundaries, the government officials expected and demanded that the Blackfeet follow suit. My grandmother's great-grandparents, Spotted Bear and Big Mountain Lion Woman, moved onto the reservation and set up a permanent home on Little Badger Creek on the south side of the reservation along with other members of their band, the Never Laughs band.

They attempted to continue their previous lifestyle, moving on and off the reservation to get the resources they needed to live. But they also learned to move within the reservation. In the summer they would move up to the mountains and live in tents or tipis while they gathered roots and berries and hunted. Sometimes they even worked as hunting guides for non-Blackfeet adventurers. They returned downstream to their log cabins for the winter, bringing their dried provisions. When my grandmother came to live with them, this became her life as well. Although they were essentially restricted to the reservation, this movement back and forth between mountain and river valley in summer and winter became a part of their new lives. My grandmother remembers caching their supplies in a pit at the end of each summer season in the mountains. They returned the next spring to dig up their supplies, picking up where they left off. Her grandmothers allowed her great freedom. Riding her horse in the foothills along the Rocky Mountain Front, as well as in an area now known as the Badger–Two Medicine, became my grandmother's favorite pastime and memory.

The Blackfeet, though, continued to view places off the reservation as part of their territory. My grandmother's family taught her about these places even though she would never see most of them. They remembered the places where they used to go hunting. They remembered the places where they had collected bitterroot, prairie turnips, berries, and medicines. They remembered the places where they forded rivers. They remembered sacred sites and religious areas.

Despite the changes in their lifestyle, memory of the past was something they could maintain and teach to their grandchildren. They remembered the uses and environmental knowledge of these places. And they shared that knowledge with my grandmother. My grandmother said one of the things her grandparents missed the most on a day-to-day basis was the plants they used for both food and medicine. Some of the plants they were accustomed to using could now be found only far off the reservation. They were now restricted from returning to some of these places. Others were too far to travel to without spending several days camping. And with new American settlers to contend with they could not camp in their usual places.

My grandfather's family shared a similar experience. My grandfather's father, Aimsback, and his grandfather, Calf Looking, also moved onto the reservation and set up a permanent home on Blacktail Creek on the south side of the reservation. Adjusting to this smaller landscape took time. However, like my grandmother's family, hunting for deer and elk (instead of bison) was a less difficult transition than trying to find all the plants they used. One time my grandfather's parents, Aimsback and Hollering in the Air, took the train more than five hundred miles east to Fort Berthold, North Dakota, for a community celebration. They traveled with a group of other Blackfeet families. While they were at Fort Berthold the women took advantage of the opportunity to collect a large quantity of prairie turnips, which could be found in abundance on the central plains but not near the mountains. They returned home with bags of turnips to dry for future use.

My grandparents' families did not always have to travel that far to gather plants. Their days of traveling to Fort Benton and the Missouri River were pretty much over once they settled on the reservation. However, my grandfather's mother used to also travel one hundred miles south down to the Sun River near Fort Shaw to gather plants such as yucca, which they valued for its medicinal qualities. These and other plants became more highly prized as they became more difficult to acquire. And now these women added these plants to the items they traded with each other.

Both of my grandparents' families thought of themselves as fortunate. In the early reservation years the Blackfeet lost control of their mobility. However, my family continued to travel to some of the places off the reservation where they could gather the plants and other resources important to their lives. These excursions provided the women with happy memories of returning to a place they had once frequented and of a time when they had freedom of choice. After thousands of years living on the prairies they were beginning to learn how to live in a new place close to the mountains. Despite their loss of mobility my grandparents' families continued to tell their grandchildren (my grandparents) stories of the past, of their prairie life, and of their freedom to do as they chose. These stories gave my grandparents the strength and the knowledge to shape their own lives.

Story of a Prairie People

Unfortunately in contemporary America most people forget that reservations are usually the remnants of once larger homelands of Native American tribes and that their earliest residents had to make significant adjustments to live within them. Many younger tribal members themselves forget this as well and believe that their ancestral homelands and sacred sites are confined within reservation boundaries. One name the Blackfeet once called themselves was the Saokiotapi, or the Prairie people. Their ancient name signifies their recognition of their place on the northern Great Plains. The early recorders of Blackfeet life noted this in their writings. George Bird Grinnell, for example, subtitled his 1892 book *Blackfoot Lodge Tales: The Story of a Prairie People*.[1] Nearly ten years earlier James Willard Schultz wrote that "the Blackfeet are pre-eminently a prairie people," stressing that "on the prairie . . . from the Saskatchewan to the Yellowstone, there is not a streamlet or slough by which they have not pitched their lodges."[2] Blackfeet understanding of and relationship to nature and the environment emanated from their empirical knowledge of this place in North America.

However, what we know of their ancient knowledge also emerged from a particular time period within global history known as the Little Ice Age.[3] During that time the Blackfeet drew on many different ecosystems within the northern Great Plains to gather the resources necessary for daily life.[4] Because of their use of numerous ecosystems, recorders of Blackfeet life sometimes made heavy-handed assumptions about the nomadic lifestyle of the Blackfeet, believing that the Blackfeet "roamed" from place to place without any ecological or environmental awareness. Others state the opposite.[5] One reason we know that the Blackfeet did not randomly roam across the landscape is because they told us in their stories.

Kainaikoan was one such storyteller. Kainaikoan told his stories of Blackfeet life and his family's history to the linguist C. C. Uhlenbeck.[6] In his published writings Uhlenbeck did not provide his collaborator's complete English name, but he was Jim Blood, a Blackfeet born in the 1850s.[7] Joseph Tatsey, also known as Istχkyáχtso, served as Kainaikoan's interpreter. Tatsey was a Blackfeet who was about the same age as Kainaikoan.

It is difficult to calculate the age of stories that the various Blackfeet individuals told Uhlenbeck. We do know that for the most part individuals learned history and stories from their families. Contemporary scholars such as the late Howard Harrod tried to figure out the age of such stories, as mentioned earlier. According to Harrod's methodology, if Kainaikoan was born in the 1850s, his father in the 1820s, his grandfather in the 1790s, and his great-grandfather in the 1760s, then Kainaikoan's oral historical knowledge stretches back to the mid-eighteenth century. This would be about the time the Blackfeet first acquired horses.

The story that Kainaikoan told Uhlenbeck, titled "How the Ancient Piegan Lived," probably described the story of his grandfather's band, the Aápaitapì, and it was probably a life that Kainaikoan experienced along with his family when he was a child and young man.[8] Jim Blood's grandfather was Nínaistako, or Chief-Mountain (now called Mountain Chief), one of the leaders of Aápaitapì, or Blood-people band of the South Piegan, and a knowledgeable, longtime leader.[9]

Kainaikoan's story is significant because it documented the annual movements of one Blackfeet band for one year on the northern Great Plains. Unbeknown to Uhlenbeck, no scholar had ever documented this process even though it was a well-known aspect of Blackfeet life. This story provides contemporary scholars with insights into the "visible" world of the Blackfeet, their empirical knowledge about land, and the use of its natural resources during the late eighteenth and nineteenth centuries. Retracing the steps of Kainaikoan and the Aápaitapì band will give us a better understanding of the life of a Blackfeet band over the course of one year.

Social Organization

The Blackfeet, similar to the other prairie peoples, organized themselves into what Kainaikoan called kaiyok'kowŏmmostïijaw, or bands, which consisted of several related families living and traveling together.[10] Soon after first contact Europeans and Americans recognized that the Blackfeet and the other groups of the Blackfoot Confederacy organized themselves into these smaller units. No visitors documented the total number of bands within the Blackfoot Confederacy until the late nineteenth century, after the bison were gone and the early reservation years had arrived. It is possible and probably likely that there were more bands before this time. In 1883 James Willard Schultz documented twenty-one Piegan bands, fifteen Kainai bands, and twelve Siksika bands (forty-eight total).[11] A few years later the ethnographer George Bird Grinnell documented twenty-four Piegan bands, thirteen Kainai bands, and eight Siksika bands (forty-five total).[12] These numbers do not, however, include the Inaksiks (or Small Robes) who were almost annihilated by the Crow in 1846. Despite this gap in the data contemporary scholars have regarded these numbers as representative of the number of bands in earlier historic and even ancient times.[13] However, we do not know what community life was like on the Great Plains before the horse. Therefore we can only extrapolate and use information gathered during the reservation period.[14]

Fig. 10. Tipis, camp, and mountains. Image #638.143, Joseph H. Sherburne Family Papers, Archives and Special Collections, Maureen and Mike Mansfield Library, University of Montana–Missoula.

Historically the Blackfeet tribe divided itself into numerous bands of related families. If Schultz enumerated twenty-one bands and Grinnell, twenty-four bands, by the end of the nineteenth century we can safely assume there were around two dozen bands in the mid-nineteenth century. Although scholars often described the Blackfeet as nomadic, the travels throughout their territory were not haphazard but strategic. They usually did not follow animals; instead they went to places where they knew animals to be or to places they created by altering the landscape. They hunted large game such as bison, elk, and deer and gathered berries and fruit, plants, roots, and other natural resources at these specific places.[15] The only agriculture that the Blackfeet practiced was the raising of tobacco. The Blackfeet chose a particular site to grow tobacco, which they sanctified, and they returned to it throughout its growing season.[16]

With the help of Blackfeet elders the ethnohistorian John Ewers estimated that Blackfeet bands, after the advent of horses, usually consisted of twenty to thirty lodges with one family living in each lodge. Such a band would consist of about 120 to 180 people.[17] In addition elders told Ewers that the Blackfeet had as many as ten horses per lodge, with some families having more.[18] On average each band traveled with two hundred to three hundred horses.[19] Each band lived separately and traveled separately within Blackfeet territory. Their territory included prairies, grasslands, and wetlands, and they sometimes went into the mountains. They moved to known places to acquire specific resources. Elders told Ewers that during the winter individual Blackfeet bands settled in designated river valleys. In the spring they moved to specific sites to hunt and gather berries or roots. Late in the summer all the Blackfeet bands traveled to a specific location for the annual gathering, the O'kan.[20] It was the only time during the year when all the bands of the Blackfeet came together, until annuity payments began. In the fall the bands separated and moved to continue hunting and gathering to prepare for winter. As winter approached they would return to the river valley designated as their own.

Before Moving

Historically the Blackfeet divided their year into two seasons—winter and summer.[21] During the winter a band typically stayed in one place for about six months, and throughout the summer they traveled to gather the resources they used. Kainaikoan recounted that the Aápaitapì band moved fourteen times in one year. They began and ended their year in the same place, called Itsipútsimaup, or Battle Coulee, on the Kyúiesisɑχtaii, or Bear River (now called the Marias River), a tributary to the Missouri River in what is now central Montana.[22]

Most Blackfeet bands did the same, and many wintered in this same area along the Marias River.[23] In the winter of 1875 an agency employee wrote, "When I made a visit to Marias this last winter [1874] I found the Indians camped along the river for 38 miles on either side."[24] John Ewers reported that "elderly Piegan informants recalled the Marias valley as a favorite winter location. They said the several bands were spread out, at distances of several miles apart, from near the junction of Cut Bank and Two Medicine Creeks forming the Marias to the big bend of the Marias."[25] If there were approximately twenty-four different Piegan

Fig. 11. Little Badger. Photo courtesy Jessie Wilber Papers, MS 2252, Merrill G. Burlingame Special Collections, Montana State University, image #ORH 10.

bands, as Grinnell recorded, then there would have been anywhere from 480 to 720 lodges, 2,880 to 4,320 people, and 4,800 to 7,200 horses wintering along the Marias River.

Kainaikoan tells us that the Aápaitapì stayed at the place called Battle Coulee on the Marias until the end of the Blackfeet winter (late spring), after their horses were fattened up and had finished shedding their winter hair.[26] At this point they were ready to make the summer journey. If there were twenty-four different bands of the Blackfeet, as Grinnell calculated, and they all moved fourteen times in the summer, as Kainaikoan remembered, that would mean the Blackfeet moved to 336 different places during their summer on the northern Great Plains. These 336 places and the places in between represent a vast understanding and knowledge of the landscape of this region.

Moving Camp in the Summertime

At the end of the Blackfeet winter (end of spring and the beginning of summer), Kainaikoan said, the Aápaitapì made their first move north to the Katoyísiks, or Sweet Pine Hills, now known as the Sweet Grass Hills, near the U.S. border with present-day Alberta, Canada. Weasel Head, an elder who told John Ewers stories in the 1940s, said that each time a band moved "it was a noisy time, horses whinnying, dogs yelping, people shouting."[27] With more than a hundred people and horses all moving at the same time it could seem like mass chaos. However, Cecile Black Boy, another elder who spoke with John Ewers, said that moving was an orderly activity in which "people could tell which way camp was to move by watching the extended back pole of the tripod on which the medicine pipe bundle rested. This back leg of the tripod pointed in the direction of the day's march."[28] This kind of march marked the beginning of the fourteen moves the Aápaitapì would make in a summer.

Kainaikoan told Uhlenbeck that the Aápaitapì stopped first at the Sweet Pine Hills to hunt buffalo bulls. However, in ancient times the Blackfeet did not always hunt first; instead they planted tobacco before going after bison. The Blackfeet leader White Calf told George Bird Grinnell about the ancient tobacco ceremony that by 1897 had become inactive. White Calf described an elaborate process in which women worked together to clear a site using fire alongside a fertile riverbed or creekbed. In the freshly cleared and fertilized area the men mixed animal dung with dried serviceberries (*Amelanchier alnifolia*) and the tobacco (*Nicotiana quadrivalvis*) seeds and proceeded to plant the mixture with a root-digging stick.[29] White Calf explained that everyone in the community—men, women, and even children—were expected to work, even though Blackfeet religious leaders oversaw the planting, which they regarded as a ceremonial activity. White Calf explained to Grinnell, "After seed has been planted. They leave it and go off after buffalo!"[30] Kainaikoan did not list tobacco planting as part of his family's yearly activities, probably because this ceremony had fallen into disuse by the end of the nineteenth century, when the Blackfeet began to purchase commercial tobacco.[31]

Going to the Sweet Pine Hills to hunt bison was an activity that the Blackfeet probably engaged in for millennia.[32] It is also something many different tribes did during the spring. Like all northern Plains tribes the Blackfeet hunted bison of different genders, different ages, at different times of year, and for different purposes. It was a complex process. Clark Wissler noted that the Blackfeet told him that "buffalo bulls were regarded in the best condition at about June of our calendar."[33] Bison bulls were used for fresh food after a long winter of eating primarily dried meat and other dried foods. The Blackfeet also used bison bulls for a wide variety of other purposes. For example, one Blackfeet man told David Duvall that they used the scrotum of bulls to cover their stirrups.[34] They used a bison bull's thick hide for objects such as war shields, which they had been using for centuries.[35]

Weasel Head told Ewers that there were strict community standards that everyone followed regarding communal bison hunting. Weasel Head said when a band moved its camp near the Sweet Pine Hills and herds of buffalo were sighted, "the chief sent the herald through camp announcing 'We don't want anybody to go off hunting buffalo until we are all ready to go.' Anyone who breaks this rule and goes out alone and kills a buffalo, will be followed by the soldiers. They would take the buffalo from him, also his weapons and tear up his clothes."[36] Weasel Head said that public humiliation and losing property were sanctions sufficient to keep most people from breaking this rule.

Their next stop was farther north at Aiiχ'kímmikuyì, or the Cypress Hills, which is now within the present-day provinces of Alberta and Saskatchewan, to hunt for more bison bulls. Kainaikoan said that at the Cypress Hills the Aápaitapì band dried their meat and made new parfleche containers out of the thick hides of the bulls.[37] It is not surprising that they would stop to make new parfleche first. They used the parfleche containers, shaped like rectangular boxes, to hold all of the supplies that they would gather in the next few months. They used these containers for their winter camp supplies and throughout the year.[38] One of the most important food items that the Blackfeet made and processed for winter use was pemmican, a mixture of dried meat, berries, and fat. Wissler wrote that to make pemmican "the best cuts of buffalo were dried in the usual manner. Then they were pounded on a stone until fine. . . . Marrow and other fats were heated and mixed with the pounded meats, after which crushed wild cherries were worked into the mess. Often, a few leaves from the peppermint plant were added in order to give flavor to it. The whole was then packed into parfleche."[39] Pemmican was a major food source for the Blackfeet, and the surplus was used as an item to trade with other tribes. Three Calf told John Ewers how in the old days the Blackfeet prepared meat for long-term use:

> Uncooked strips of dry meat were spread out inside parfleches and packed with a layer of uncooked [bison] back fat in strips over that; then wild peppermint sprinkled over it; then berries; then a final layer of dry meat. When the parfleche was full it was tied up and put away in back of the beds. In time the grease soaks through the parfleches. The contents of these parfleches often served for lunches when camp was on the move. The parfleches were untied from the pack horses, opened and given to the people without cooking. The dried meat and backfat was eaten uncooked, with water to top off the meal.[40]

These parfleche "lunch" packs could last for months without being opened, and the Blackfeet often used them throughout the winter months. The peppermint served as a preservative to prevent the food from spoiling.

From the Cypress Hills they moved south to Paχkå'χkeyi, or Pakoki Lake, which is now within present-day southern Alberta. Pakoki Lake is a large, shallow lake halfway between the Sweet Pine Hills and the Cypress Hills. The area is out in the wide open prairie with tall prairie grass and no trees. Kainaikoan said that the band hunted bison in this area and used the bison skins to make tipi lodge covers. Wissler wrote, "Formerly, tipis were covered with buffalo skins, soft dressed without the hair. Twelve to fourteen skins were regarded as necessary to the making of a tipi cover, though the number varied with the size of the tipi."[41] If the band's size was, as Ewers claims, from twenty to thirty lodges and if each family needed a new tipi covering, they would have needed between 280 and 420 new bison hides.

After hunting bison, Kainaikoan said, they moved next to a place called Akaií'niskuyì, or Many Berries, out on the open prairie along a tributary leading into Pakoki Lake. At Many Berries, Kainaikoan said, they gathered a wide variety of berries, including serviceberries (*Amelanchier alnifolia*), gooseberries (*Ribes hirtellum*), and red willow berries (*Cornus sericea*). They dried the berries for winter use and to add to the pemmican. Kainaikoan said that they also used this place to start processing their bison hides into lodge covers. Wissler wrote, "During the berry season, the Blackfoot camps were shifted to favorable localities where the women and girls worked industriously gathering the fruit into rectangular rawhide bags."[42] Part of the processing that occurred was to dry the mass quantities of berries to use throughout the year. By moving to a location in the middle of the plains without trees, exposed to the sun, and with high winds, they could process the berries at a quicker rate. Green Grass Bull also told John Ewers that the Blackfeet used serviceberry wood (*Amelanchier alnifolia*) to make ceremonial pipestems, "because we pray over these willow berries in ceremonies. . . . Men sometimes swore to tell the truth by saying they would talk straight as a willow pipe stem. They put the stem in a smudge, saying 'Now you tell nothing but the truth. If you don't tell the truth your life will be taken.'"[43]

Kainaikoan said that from there they moved north to Einiótokå'nisi, or Buffalo Bull's Head, to pick chokecherries (*Prunus virginiana*). Buffalo Bull's Head is a hill shaped like a bison head on the western side of the Cypress Hills. Kainaikoan said the band both picked and processed the chokecherries here for winter use.[44] The Blackfeet told Wissler that chokecherries were "gathered when ripe and pounded on a stone until the fruit with its pits was reduced to a thick paste. This was dried and packed away in bags or used to make pemmican."[45] The Blackfeet also used chokecherry for its wood. Chokecherry is a hard wood, so the Blackfeet used it for a variety of tools. Stakes made from chokecherry wood were used to hold down the edges of tipis.[46] The Blackfeet also used chokecherry wood in making their water buckets. The Blackfeet stretched a bison rawhide around a wooden hoop, and this became their portable water bucket. The Blackfeet made different sizes of buckets, with large ones holding as much as five gallons of water.[47]

Kainaikoan said that after completing their gathering of berries for the winter they moved farther north to Iχ'kitsíkitapìiks, or Seven Persons, to hunt for elk and to process the hides. The Blackfeet used elk hides, horns, and teeth for a variety of purposes. Blackfeet women used elk hides to make women's dresses because the hide was thinner than that of bison.[48] Oftentimes the Blackfeet used bison and beaver fur for their winter clothing, and hides such as elk without fur were used in the summer. Elk clothing was eventually replaced by trade cotton cloth and wool robes.[49] They also used elk teeth to decorate both girls' and women's dresses.[50] The Blackfeet men used elk horns for making parts of their saddles and quirts.[51] They used elk rawhide for their quivers.[52]

The Blackfeet of course also used elk meat for food and boiled down the bones and marrow to collect the fat. After the fat was collected it was stored in parfleche bags for future use.[53] However, the hunting and use of elk had an added dimension in Blackfeet society. The Blackfeet told Wissler that "the dressing of skins was an important household industry. . . . [A woman's] worth and virtue were estimated by her output."[54]

Kainaikoan said that after they finished at Seven Persons they moved back south to Aiiχ'kímmikuyì, or the Cypress Hills, to cut new poles for their tipis from lodgepole pines (*Pinus contorta*). Out on the relatively treeless and dry prairies the Cypress Hills are an oasis and one of the few places to find lodgepole pine. The Blackfeet used lodgepole pines for both their tipis and travois.[55] The Blackfeet told Wissler that "as the tipi is made and owned by the woman, it is she who cuts the poles and prepares them." The women "carefully selected, cut and hauled home [timbers] from the foothills of the mountains, then peeled off their bark, set up as a frame for a tipi and left to season." The Blackfeet told Wissler that, similar to work that women put into elk hides, "a set of well-seasoned poles is looked upon as a valuable asset and is not to be parted with for trifles."[56]

The Aápaitapì band was now halfway through its seasonal stops. Kainaikoan said they moved west to Inokímists, or Long Lake, but he did not describe the activities that they conducted at this place.[57] It is possible that they participated in religious activities. One other reason that they may have stopped in this location was to care for their horses. Weasel Head told Ewers that

> in warm weather (ie. not winter camp)—in late afternoon or early evening herds were driven to water and then to some place away from camp, a valley or coulee, then one horse taken home and tied in front of the tipi by a tie around legs. That horse was used to go

after the horse herd next morning. In morning the person caring for the horses would go after them early, water them, then drive them to a place where there was good grass, watch them a while and then return home. About noon the horses were watered again. The horses were watered again. The horses were watered 3 times a day in all. There was no all day herding. For watering they were driven to a nearby lake or stream. If a man had a family the liveliest of the boys would care for the horses.[58]

Short Face added that boys were often hired by the owner to watch their horses because of predators. Depending on where the Blackfeet were in their journey, wolves, bears, or mountain lions might kill colts and horses.[59]

After their stay at Long Lake, Kainaikoan said, the Aápaitapì band headed to Mátokeks omɑ'nis tàmoai otsítskitaχpiau, or Women's Society Left Their Lodge Pole, to hunt stray bison bulls. Usually at this point in the year the bison separated into smaller groups that were easier to hunt on an individual basis. The band moved next to Å'χkomonoàsiu, or Green Lake, to process the hides. The women made more parfleche containers, rawhide for their travois, string from the sinew, and rope from the hair on the buffalo's head.[60] A lot needed to be completed, as this was one of the last opportunities to prepare for winter.

From there the Aápaitapì band headed south to A'isinaiχpì, or Writing on Stone, on the Milk River. They collected their last chokecherries along the Milk River and dried them for winter use. One other resource they found along the Milk River was cottonwood trees. Cottonwood was used for a wide variety of purposes, including making bowls and plates. It was also used for horse gear. Weasel Head stated that "stirrups were made in late summer. At that time of year cottonwood could be easily bent into stirrups without breaking, or heating or anything else."[61]

Kainaikoan said that the Aápaitapì band then moved west up along the Milk River to A'kekoksistakskuyì, or Women's Point, to hunt antelope. The Blackfeet used antelope hides to make a wide variety of clothing and a lot of different useful objects. One of the reasons the Blackfeet liked using tanned antelope hides was because they were thin and soft.[62]

Men's shirts were made out of two uncut antelope hides, and women's leggings were often made of antelope.[63] The Blackfeet used the neck hide of a young antelope to create tobacco bags in which men could carry their tobacco and pipes, and they made bags out of the feet, with the dewclaws attached, for women.[64] My grandmother made these types of bags throughout her life and well into her eighties. These last couple of stops in their summer travels reflect the organized preparation required to make new objects and repair old ones before winter.

They next moved farther west up the Milk River close to the mouth of Ponákiksi, or Cut Bank Creek, in what is now Glacier National Park. They moved up into the mountains to cut more lodgepole pines for their tipis and to complete the sewing of their buffalo lodge covers for winter use. It was now fall, and they made their final preparations for their winter camp. Kainaikoan said they stayed in the mountains until the first light snow.[65] It is possible that they also used this time to collect stone for making pipes and other objects. Lazy Boy told John Ewers that "in his youth they only got pipestone from the bank on the Two Medicine River above the mouth of the Badger Creek. He called the site Pipestone Cliff. He said the Piegan often passed that way en route down the Marias from near the Mtns. There was a well worn trail to the Pipestone Cliff."[66]

With the first snow the Aápaitapì band followed Cut Bank Creek downriver to the point where it flowed into the Two Medicine River to become the Kyúiesisaχtaii, or Bear River. They returned to the same area of their previous winter camp and set up their winter camp again.[67] Tom Spotted Eagle said the area of the Marias from near its source (by the junction of Cut Bank and Birch Creeks) and Willow Round, an area of steep sides and a narrow, canyonlike valley, was known to the Blackfeet as Bottom Trunk. That section was not used for winter village sites. Willow Round was the first broad valley on the Marias below this Bottom Trunk section that the Blackfeet used for winter camp.[68] The various Blackfeet bands then made winter camp from that area down to the Missouri River.

The Marias (Bear) River valley was a favorite place to winter horses. Weasel Tail stated that "in the fall of the year the men looked for localities to feed horses where grass was still green."[69] Three Calf added that the Blackfeet chose the Marias (or Bear River) because there were several types of grass that they could find there that their horses liked to eat. Three Calf said, "On [the] side hills on the Marias in fall the Indians would find what they called, 'jingle grass.' ([It] had little seeds on it that made noise when shaken.) [The] horses loved it. [There was] another grass, white but looked like sage, [it was] called 'weasel grass,' [it] grew down on [the] Marias. [It was] especially good for horses. [There was] another grass, called 'blue stick.' [The] horses liked it very much. . . . Also on the Marias (below Shelby and down river) was a sort of white clay streaked with yellow which horses loved."[70] Because of the Blackfeet's reliance on horses by the nineteenth century, there is limited written information and oral history on Blackfeet winter village sites before they acquired horses.

Kainaikoan reported that once the Aápaitapì had set up their winter lodges, they built a corral for their horses and continued to hunt the local bison near the river valley. At this time of year they preferred to hunt two- to four-year-old bison. They dried this meat for winter use and made winter robes for their families. When they could they augmented their preserved berries and meat with foods they found locally, which were usually collected in late autumn and included things such as cottonwood tree (*Populus deltoides*) cambium, roots, black alkali, rosehips from a wild rose (*Rosa woodsii*), silverberries (*Elaeagnus commutata*), and bull berries (*Shepherdia argentea*).[71]

After the first big snow the women would collect all their winter wood. The women preferred the old dry cottonwood found along river valleys. Andre Dusold, the agency detective, stated in 1875 that the Blackfeet "only use small dry sticks and brush" for firewood. He added that "there were no adequate supplys [*sic*] of firewood on any streams between Teton and Marias and Birch Creek for winter fuel—so Indians didn't camp there in winter."[72] Jim Walters stated that his grandmother told him that "they did not worry about cold so long as they had plenty of fuel and meat. They did not suffer from cold in their tipis."[73]

Once the Aápaitapì had all of their provisions for the winter, their horses corralled, meat, berries, and other plant foods preserved, and wood collected, the leaders allowed the men to return to the prairies to hunt bison for robes and other animal fur to trade.[74] The families set up time for family fun. David Duvall collected examples of the great variety of

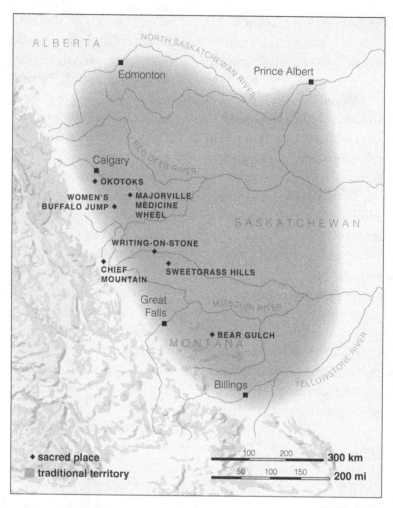

ALBERTA
NORTH SASKATCHEWAN RIVER
Edmonton
Prince Albert
RED DEER RIVER
Calgary
◆ OKOTOKS
WOMEN'S ◆ MAJORVILLE
BUFFALO JUMP ◆ MEDICINE
WHEEL
SASKATCHEWAN
◆ WRITING-ON-STONE
◆
CHIEF ◆
MOUNTAIN SWEETGRASS HILLS
Great
Falls
MISSOURI RIVER
◆ BEAR GULCH
MONTANA
YELLOWSTONE RIVER
Billings

◆ sacred place   100   200   **300 km**
▪ traditional territory   50   100   150 **200 mi**

Map 3. Traditional territory. Map courtesy Lucien Liz-Lepiorz.

children's toys and adult gambling games that the Blackfeet used for fun, which he provided to Clark Wissler and the American Museum of Natural History.[75] For example, in the winter the boys and girls made sleds out of the large rib bones of bison.[76] Kainaikoan's story of the life of the Aápaitapì reveals that the fur trade played a minimal role in this band's society and that the band leaders did not allow hunting for trade items until the band was fully provisioned and had returned to the permanent winter camp.

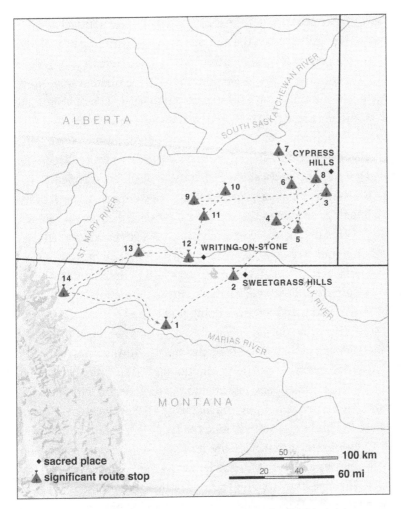

Map 4. Kainaikoan's seasonal route. Map courtesy Lucien Liz-Lepiorz.

End of the Story, End of a Way of Life

I was fortunate to have spent the summer of 2004 driving the entire route of the Aápaitapì band with Shirlee Crow Shoe, a North Peigan community member and Blackfeet language teacher.[77] Using Kainaikoan's story as our guide, I read the story out loud in Blackfeet while she attempted to understand my bad pronunciation and American accent. We drove on both gravel and paved roads throughout northern Montana and southern

Alberta, with two separate gazetteers. We tried our best to travel as close to the sites as possible, given the fact that we were traveling by car, and ended up going down several incorrect roads. I was able to photograph each site (or what we thought was the site). These photographs along with my notes of Kainaikoan's story were put together in a presentation for the Montana Historical Society annual history conference, and that talk was later published online by the Glenbow Museum's *Niitsitapiis-inni: Our Way of Life* website.[78] Throughout the drive we realized how huge and varying the landscape was that these Blackfeet traveled. Some places were as dry as a moonscape, while others were a rich, green oasis. We also imagined the magnitude of work done each year by the women and men of this one band. Essentially these Blackfeet went northeast for the summer, then zigzagged around the region, then moved west to the mountains before winter, and returned south to their winter village. With each stop these Blackfeet carried more and more food and objects for winter. We had a difficult time doing it in a car.

The story "How the Ancient Peigans Lived" stands out regarding Blackfeet understanding of their own life on the prairies. It was unintentionally recorded in the summer of 1911 by the linguist C. C. Uhlenbeck. That summer Professor Uhlenbeck returned to the reservation with his wife, Willy, to continue documenting the language of the Blackfeet. He had been there the previous summer. Like the recorders before him he was primarily interested in interviewing individuals with pre-reservation linguistic abilities and societal knowledge. As the linguist recorded the Blackfeet language, they told him stories of their life on the prairies in their own language. He recorded these stories and later translated them into English. Although he initially set out to conduct an academic linguistic study, the by-product of his work was that he recorded a substantial history of pre-reservation Blackfeet life. Even though Uhlenbeck recorded these stories during the early reservation years, contemporary scholars use them to help them understand the lifeways of ancient prairie peoples.[79]

Kainaikoan's story of the Aápaitapì along with David Duvall, Clark Wissler, and John Ewer's collected stories provide us with important images of life for one Blackfeet band in the late nineteenth century. It is representative of the thousands of different places that the Blackfeet,

North Peigan, Kainai and Siksika, and other allied bands traveled to each year and knew intimately. In addition to telling us where they were, this story also tells us where they were not. Often in the past the Blackfeet did not physically go to sacred sites but left them alone since they were the homes of supernatural entities.[80] Despite their loss of territory in the late nineteenth century the Blackfeet, especially the "buffalo Indians," continued to have extensive knowledge of their old territory. And some, like my great-grandparents, even continued to use these places. "In later years," Adam White Man said, "his band (Lone Eater's) went down to the Marias River only for berry picking."[81] Once the reservation was established the Aápaitapì settled on the far south side of the reservation near Birch Creek. After the Sweet Grass Hills were sold with an executive order in 1888 the various bands on the reservation began to reorder themselves. The Aápaitapì who initially lived near Birch Creek moved closer to Heart Butte and then they split. Some of their group moved north to Cut Bank Creek while the remainder stayed near Heart Butte.[82] It was common during that time for bands to separate and move to different areas of the reservation.

Today most Americans, including many Blackfeet themselves, believe that the Blackfeet have always lived near the mountains and on the reservation. However, it was not until the late nineteenth century that the Americans concentrated the Blackfeet into this far western edge of their ancestral territory. Kainaikoan's story of the Aápaitapì reminds us that the Blackfeet of the early reservation years remembered their time on the prairies, where their knowledge of the natural world formed. They could not always use that knowledge near the mountains on the reservation. In addition to telling stories about the "invisible" realm they could also tell stories about their understanding of the visible realm to the early recorders of Blackfeet life. Doing so kept alive their relationship with their surrounding environment, even in absentia.

CHAPTER 4

Closed Season

The Blackfeet Winter

My grandmother along with her sisters and brothers attended Holy Family Mission, the on-reservation Catholic boarding school. Holy Family Mission was located on the Two Medicine River just east of the main road running north and south across the reservation (now Highway 89). It stood pretty much at the geographic center of the reservation. The Catholic Church acquired the land from White Calf, a convert, who gave his own land along the Two Medicine River to the Church. The Holy Family Mission boarding school existed from 1890 to 1940, but the church building is still there today.

Many of the children who attended Holy Family lived at the mission year round. Others, like my grandmother, were there only during the academic year. Catholic holidays during the school year, such as Easter, provided an opportunity for families to come together and see their children. When my grandmother was growing up the Catholic Church held a weeklong Easter celebration at the Holy Family Mission. Holy Week began on Palm Sunday and lasted until Easter Sunday. It commemorated the Resurrection of Christ Jesus and his ascent into heaven. People from around the reservation would travel by wagon to the mission to set up tents nearby and along the Two Medicine River valley for the entire week. The church allowed the children to camp with their families. My grandmother remembered getting small presents from her grandmothers, including new ribbons for her long hair, at their Easter camp. She also remembered that it often snowed, as the final snowstorms of the year frequently occurred during Holy Week. She remembered the nuns hiding eggs in the snow for the children and how odd this seemed to her grandmothers.

However, at the same time that the Blackfeet were celebrating Easter with the Catholic Church they were also gathering for another purpose. The Blackfeet celebrated their own sort of holy week. For generations the Blackfeet celebrated the end of winter with numerous religious rituals to renew their relationships with their supernatural allies. In my grandmother's childhood the community came together to conduct these rituals at the same time as the Easter Holy Week at Holy Family Mission. In their tent villages the community "opened" their bundles and pipes and prayed to their own holy trinity—the Sun, Moon, and Morning Star. As David Duvall explained, "The Blackfoot expect[ed] long life, health and happiness" if they properly maintained their supernatural relationships.[1] The Blackfeet learned to incorporate their end-of-winter rituals within the Catholic Church's Holy Week celebrations, much like they incorporated the O'kan within the Fourth of July celebrations.

Christianity celebrates Easter near the vernal equinox.[2] This was close enough for the Blackfeet to adjust their rituals to coincide with the Catholic Holy Week. The Blackfeet historically held the Thunder Pipe rituals at the sound of the first thunder of the spring, which signaled the return of the Thunder from the south to the north. They historically held the Beaver bundle rituals after the ice on the rivers melted, which signaled the safe return of the beavers to open waters. And other rituals had similar seasonal triggers. My grandmother remembered singing and praying occurring in the tents often with snow all around.

In the early twentieth century many people on the reservation lived along rivers and creeks with their band relations (although the band system was beginning to be dismantled). The Easter gathering was often the first time since the previous summer that extended families got together. Their first gathering of the year centered on renewing relationships with the supernatural, as well as renewing relationships with family. My grandmother remembered these gatherings as a happy and carefree time with all the generations of her family together.

Two Seasons

The Blackfeet divided their year into two seasons: winter and summer, or Sto-ye and Na-pos.[3] In the winter the numerous Blackfeet bands camped along river valleys, with each band usually camped in the same place every year. In the summer they traveled to a dozen or more places, also usually returning to the same places year after year. The Blackfeet typically divided their seasons evenly, spending about six months in their winter village and six months living on the northern Great Plains.

Although scholars often describe the Blackfeet as "nomadic," they lived a semisedentary lifestyle. The story "How the Ancient Piegan Lived" that Kainaikoan told C. C. Uhlenbeck in the summer of 1911 described this lifestyle for one band of the Blackfeet.

Not surprisingly the Blackfeet viewed their religious life as having two seasons, one "open" and one "closed." This terminology referred to the status of their religious "bundles," which they "opened" and "closed" during the change of seasons. A "bundle" was the material object that contained the Blackfeet's religious iconography, which formed the basis of a religious ritual. David Duvall and Clark Wissler began using the term "bundle" to describe these religious objects, large or small, of the Blackfeet. They explained, "We have used the term bundle for all objects associated with rituals because . . . the owner keeps them wrapped up in various pieces of cloth."[4] The Blackfeet also used this word in their own description of religious objects, such as the Beaver bundle, which they called "beaver-bundled-up."[5]

After the Blackfeet settled into their winter villages they "closed" their religious bundles for the season. "Opening" and "closing" of course were metaphors. Each time there was a religious ritual the bundle, large or small, was physically opened (unwrapped) and then closed (rewrapped). The Blackfeet used the terms "opened" and "closed" to imply that the relationship with the supernatural power(s) changed during these two religious seasons.

Super Natural

The Blackfeet believed that they possessed two types of knowledge: material or empirical knowledge learned from longtime experience or observation of the environment and immaterial knowledge gained from developing a relationship with a supernatural ally. The "real stories" told by the Blackfeet to the early recorders of Blackfeet life reflected their understanding of immaterial knowledge. The story of Kainaikoan provided one example of material or environmental knowledge of the Blackfeet landscape. The Blackfeet used these two types of knowledge together in their everyday life. The Blackfeet considered it unwise or even foolish to live life with only one type of knowledge. The Siksika

Fig. 12. Bear Chief's feast. Image #638.190, Joseph H. Sherburne Family Papers, Archives and Special Collections, Maureen and Mike Mansfield Library, University of Montana–Missoula.

elder Crooked Meat Strings told the anthropologist Jane Hanks in 1938 that only the "poor go to war without holy protection [they go] with own bravery."[6] Going it alone was not a part of the Blackfeet philosophy.

The Blackfeet learned the environmental knowledge of their landscape over generations of time.[7] However, this knowledge came from a deeper past. The Blackfeet descended from Indigenous people who had lived on the northern Great Plains and learned its intricacies for millennia.[8] The Blackfeet learned the ethnobotany of plants on the northern Great Plains. They relied on this knowledge for daily health needs, food, shelter, and fuel. The Blackfeet also learned "bison ecology" and the complexities of bison behavior so as to be able to hunt year round.[9] The Blackfeet learned how to live in a dry and arid environment.[10] However, for the Blackfeet, learning about and understanding their environment and the natural world was only half of the equation. The Blackfeet understood that not everything in their environment was "natural"; some of it was "super natural." In their complex universe and worldview using their age-old environmental knowledge would not solve all the problems that arose. The Blackfeet believed that with the assistance of supernatural allies they could resolve important concerns. Their biggest issue was what to do when "nature" did not behave the way they wanted.

Power of the Waters

Academically trained recorders of Blackfeet life such as Clark Wissler and Truman Michelson asked David Duvall to carry out a particular process when gathering stories from the Blackfeet people. First Duvall interviewed everyone in the Blackfeet language. He wrote down most of their stories in Blackfeet. He then wrote out a literal, word-for-word translation of these stories into English. Wissler asked Duvall to write out as well a free translation into English before returning it to Wissler. However, in the case of Michelson at least, Michelson wrote out a free translation from Duvall's translation into standard English. The result was that they often ended up with three versions of a single story. Finally, to make sure that the stories were correct Duvall read the English texts back to the Blackfeet storyteller in the Blackfeet language. Duvall thereby retranslated his own interviews, from Blackfeet to English and then back to Blackfeet. Duvall then made corrections for the final draft of their texts. It was a tedious process to get the stories right, and it often took months.[11]

One set of stories that every recorder of Blackfeet life collected consisted of the stories of Beaver "medicine" in the Water world. Duvall and Wissler wrote that the Blackfeet used the word "*saam*, which we have translated as medicine," to describe objects with supernatural affinity.[12] The early recorders of Blackfeet life collected the Beaver "medicine" stories because the Blackfeet believed they were the "oldest ritual" from which all other Blackfeet religious rituals emanated.[13] There are multiple versions and numerous stories surrounding Beaver medicine within the four different tribes and the dozens of different bands of the Blackfoot Confederacy. Duvall and Wissler published four different versions of the basic Beaver medicine story, one from each of the tribes of the Blackfoot Confederacy, in *Mythology of the Blackfoot Indians*.

The story of Beaver medicine begins in winter, during Sto-ye, the closed season. The many versions of this story have a common pattern, but each storyteller had a particular version.[14] As The Boy told Duvall before recording his version, "There are many ways of telling the story of the beaver medicine, but this is the way it came to me."[15] The basic story line featured an interaction between a human and the most powerful being in the Water world: Kitaiksísskstaki, the Not Real Beaver.[16]

In the basic story line a beaver and his family invite a human to live an entire winter in their lodge. In most versions this situation arose because the human was shamed by his or her community and left, while in others it was by pure happenstance. During that winter the beaver taught the human a great deal of new knowledge and introduced him or her to new natural elements such as the tobacco plant. And when the human returned to the Below world the following spring the beaver "transferred" this supernatural knowledge and material objects to the human, who in turn shared them with other humans. Duvall and Wissler outlined this process: "The being . . . offers or consents upon request to give power [to a human]. . . . The being conferring power . . . transfers it to the recipient. . . . This is regarded as a compact between the recipient and the being . . . and each is expected to fulfill faithfully his own obligations. The compact is a continuous relationship."[17] Duvall and Wissler pointed out that although the supernatural power being transferred may benefit an entire community, the ownership and transfer of the power would be "in every case still a matter solely between one individual and the being."[18] The principal ability the Kitaiksísskstaki, the Not Real Beaver, transferred to that human was the "power of the waters."[19]

Beaver Medicine

The first person to be considered a "Beaver man" was the person who came back from a winter spent with the beavers.[20] His first obligation was to build a Beaver "bundle" of objects that represented the lessons and knowledge he had learned from the beaver. Some people say that the first bundle included the hides of all the animals and skins of all the birds (kind of like a Noah's Ark, except in this case one hide per creature). It also included all of the creatures' corresponding songs and movements.[21]

That original human then transferred the "title" of ownership of the original Beaver bundle to a married couple and the succeeding generations.[22] The Blackfeet understood that each "title" transfer, from couple to couple, represented the original transfer from supernatural to human. In essence each transfer was not from human to human but a transfer of supernatural power from the original supernatural to the new humans. Duvall and Wissler explained that "the ritual, to the Blackfoot[,] is in reality an assumed faithful reproduction of the original transfer."[23]

Inside of any "bundle" were the various material objects used in a ritual. These varied from a few objects to dozens contained in one or more wrappings. Duvall and Wissler explained that the objects in a bundle "symbolize[d] some concept of power."[24] Each object represented the power of a living or nonliving (to Western minds, that is) entity. For example, the skin of a loon represented the supernatural power of a living loon. Duvall and Wissler said that rituals included "a narrative, one or more songs, an object and accessories, and in many cases, certain requirements [or protocols of behavior] of the person concerned."[25] The Blackfeet used these objects much as they did the designs on the outside of a tipi — as mnemonic devices to remember the narrative, songs, and movements in a ritual.

The Blackfeet saw a difference between the material object within a bundle and the supernatural power it represented. The Blackfeet believed that the supernatural power existed apart from the object. Cecile Black Boy explained to John Ewers that a religious object could be remade if it were lost or destroyed.[26] Black Boy explained that "to the Indian it was unimportant if the object had been remade or not, so long as the person who remade it possessed the 'power.'" Ewers wrote, "For the Indian the 'religious power' of the article is of primary importance, for the white it is . . . the material object itself."[27] Ultimately what was important to the Blackfeet was the relationship between the human and his or her supernatural ally that the object represented. The object could be replaced or remade when necessary. (Selling or transferring the supernatural power was another matter altogether.)

The Beaver bundle was considered the oldest, largest, and most expensive bundle of all of the medicine bundles owned by the Blackfeet. Besides the personal expense of purchasing the "title" to the bundle, acquiring it also came with numerous protocols (taboos) that restricted daily

Fig. 13. Heart Butte stick game, 1944. Photo courtesy Jessie Wilber Papers, MS 2252, Merrill G. Burlingame Special Collections, Montana State University, image #ORH 48.

behavior and were time consuming. If purchasing the bundle seemed too expensive, sometimes the new owners would ask others to invest in one part of the bundle.[28] The new owners, the husband and wife, then had to learn hundreds of songs, prayers, and movements (hand movements and dances) related to each of the objects within the bundle. There was no expectation that the new owners would learn the songs immediately. They usually continued to pay the former owners for song lessons. Twice a year the new owners also paid for a large community feast to correspond with the "opening" or "closing" of their bundle.[29] With a bundle this expensive it would seem that most people would not want to own one, and they didn't. But those who did viewed it as an investment—one that provided many benefits.

Seeds of Change

In the various stories of Beaver medicine that the Blackfeet told, the supernatural beavers spent their winter with their human guest teaching him how to plant, cultivate, harvest, and process *pisstááhkaan,* or tobacco

(*Nicotiana quadrivalvis*). The beavers also taught their guest how to conduct the rituals related to growing tobacco. At the end of the winter the beavers gave the human a small container of tobacco seeds to bring to the Below world from the Water world, along with the knowledge to cultivate it, and they transferred the rituals used in the tobacco planting ritual.

Tobacco was the only plant that the Blackfeet cultivated in a garden before the reservation period. Despite their significant travels in the summer the Blackfeet took the time to plant, cultivate, and harvest tobacco. However, by the time the early recorders of Blackfeet life came to the reservation the Blackfeet no longer planted tobacco. White Calf, the elderly leader of the Blackfeet, told George Bird Grinnell in 1897 that he had seen tobacco planted once in his life, but he had never seen it grow.[30] The stories about tobacco recorded at the turn of the century were what the Blackfeet remembered or had heard about growing tobacco and did not report firsthand experiences. By the turn of the century the Blackfeet used commercial tobacco (*Nicotiana tabacum*), originally from South America, for all of their rituals and social activities.[31] Many medicine bundles continued to hold seeds of the tobacco that was a species native to the west coast of North America (*Nicotiana quadrivalvis*), but the bundle holders did not plant these. The seeds were kept as religious relics. The story of tobacco's introduction to the Blackfeet through the beavers, though, was well known by all.[32]

Two of the roles the Beaver bundle owners had within the community were to store tobacco seeds and leaves from season to season and to direct the community's planting and harvesting efforts.[33] Both White Calf, who spoke with Grinnell in 1897, and Three Bears, who spoke with Duvall in 1910, gave similar accounts of the tobacco planting ritual. At the beginning of winter and the "closing" of the Beaver bundle, the Blackfeet placed the next season's seeds and their supply of dried tobacco leaves into the bundle. The Beaver bundle owners left the tobacco seeds and leaves in the bundle throughout the winter, and the tobacco remained consecrated there.[34] The Blackfeet viewed everything surrounding tobacco—from storing it, planting it, cultivating it, harvesting it, to finally using it—as religious activities.

White Calf told Grinnell that in the springtime, after the ice on the rivers began to melt and the last snowstorm had passed, the owners of a Beaver bundle held a feast to announce their intentions of planting tobacco. Planting tobacco was a community-wide activity and they needed everyone.[35] The Beaver bundle owners selected a particular place for planting the new tobacco field along a river valley near cottonwood trees.[36] Three Bears told Duvall that "to prepare the ground . . . a lot of brush is gathered by every man, woman and child," and then "at the four corners of this place a fire is started." After they burned the field "each and everyone make a little brush broom and sweeps the place off clean."[37]

The Beaver men combined the tobacco seeds with pulverized animal dung, serviceberries, and water. Three Bears said that they then divided the field into sections, one for each Beaver bundle owner. All men of the community, not just the owners, were expected to help plant the tobacco. The Blackfeet viewed this process as a religious activity. They used long, sharp sticks to punch individual holes into the ground and drop in the seed mixture. White Calf said that each time they put one small ball of seed mixture into the ground they sang a song. The Blackfoot Confederacy were reported to have had 230 different tobacco planting songs.[38] After they planted the tobacco they held a feast, and the community was free to leave. The tobacco field was then left alone all summer, without fencing and without any daily oversight by the Blackfeet.

One of the benefits of being a Beaver bundle owner was the important supernatural allies that came to your aid. Growing tobacco was one of those activities that the Blackfeet did not leave to "nature." The Blackfeet viewed tobacco as a sanctified plant from the Water world that required special attention. After the manual labor provided by the humans to plant the tobacco the actual cultivation of tobacco was left up to the supernatural world.

The Beaver bundle owners did not need to watch their fields because the Ni-wax-saxs (the little people) did this for them.[39] The Blackfeet believed that there were little people who were about one foot tall who guarded and protected their tobacco fields.[40] The little people were benign supernatural beings who were part of the Below world. The little people came to aid the Beaver bundle owners, if the owners asked for their assistance and if they were given gifts for their help. At the end of the tobacco planting ritual Blackfeet women made little moccasins, little shirts, digging sticks, and small bags of food. They left these in the field before they departed for the summer.[41]

The little people worked tirelessly on behalf of the Blackfeet to maintain the tobacco crop. Periodically throughout the summer the Beaver men gathered together in their camps to sing songs for the tobacco. As they sang their songs the men hit the ground with their planting sticks, symbolically killing insects, grasshoppers, and worms. Meanwhile the little people simultaneously killed the insects in the field.[42] This symbiotic supernatural relationship allowed the Blackfeet to travel throughout the summer to a dozen or more places on the prairies without returning to fields.

However, throughout the summer at least one Beaver man returned to the tobacco crop to see how the fields were doing. If the Beaver man did not feel that there had been sufficient rain for the tobacco, he did something to change the situation. Another major benefit to being a Beaver man was that he had access to supernatural power that would change different aspects of "nature" on his behalf. If there had not been enough rain the Beaver man went to his bundle and asked the otter for his assistance and his power over water. The Beaver man took the otter skin from the Beaver bundle and sang the individual otter's song: "Water is my medicine. Rain is my medicine." Three Bears said, "Shortly after the singing is done a heavy rain storm follows and soaks the ground and especially the tobacco crops."[43] The Blackfeet believed that they did not need to rely on the natural world for their crops to succeed. Instead the Blackfeet relied on their supernatural allies to help them manage their crops and even change the weather, if needed.

White Calf said that at the end of the summer the community returned to the tobacco field to harvest their tobacco crop, hold a thanksgiving feast, and sing and pray again before they collected their seeds for the next season. But before they did this, they took a little bit of the tobacco, with a new set of little moccasins and digging sticks, and left them in the center of camp for the little people, just the way the beavers told them to.[44]

Both Grinnell and Duvall recorded several Blackfeet who told stories about the tobacco planting ceremony, which the Blackfeet no longer practiced by the twentieth century. The Blackfeet told them stories about a relationship with their supernatural allies and their ability to help the Blackfeet. These relationships were complex. Similarly complex was the Blackfeet's knowledge of horticulture on the northern Great Plains. The ability to cultivate a plant in a dry, arid landscape required intimate knowledge of the environment and the climate. Tobacco was not a plant that had edible or medicinal properties. It was used primarily for smoking. It was not necessary for their physical survival. However, the Blackfeet believed they had an obligation to the supernatural to cultivate tobacco. The quid pro quo was that tobacco would help provide what the Blackfeet wanted: control over the rest of nature.

Holy Smoke

Before the introduction of commercial tobacco (*Nicotiana tabacum*) the Blackfeet grew and used their own tobacco (*Nicotiana quadrivalvis*). Historically the Blackfeet used tobacco in all their rituals, large or small, and in daily prayer. In the past when the Blackfeet smoked for pleasure they often smoked other plants, such as *kakahsiin* (*Arctostaphylos uva-ursi*) and *omahksi-kakahsiin* (*Chimaphila umbellata*), and not true tobacco.[45] The Blackfeet viewed smoking true tobacco as something that was done to communicate with the supernatural when seeking aid.

The Blackfeet smoked, burned as incense, or offered dried tobacco leaves to the Sun and other supernatural beings at each religious ritual.[46] They also treated tobacco seeds and sometimes the ashes after smoking with great care and reverence.[47] Tobacco brought all three worlds together. Tobacco came from the Water world when the supernatural Beavers transferred it to the Below world. Humans utilized it as a method to communicate with the Above world. Using tobacco either created new relationships or cemented old ones between humans and the supernatural. Tobacco served as a key ingredient that the Blackfeet utilized to communicate with other supernatural entities.

However, by the time the early recorders of Blackfeet life were interviewing the Blackfeet beginning in the 1880s everyone was using commercial tobacco and had probably used commercial tobacco for decades. Ewers noted that since the late eighteenth century the Blackfoot

Confederacy leaders had conducted "a long and tedious ritual" of smoking each time they traded with Europeans.[48] However, Ewers noted, by 1858 the Blackfeet had asked the U.S. government to purchase 2,660 pounds of tobacco as part of their annuity payment.[49] And by the time that Kainaikoan recounted his story of "ancient" Blackfeet life they were already purchasing tobacco from American traders at the cost of one bison robe for four plugs of tobacco.[50] Contemporary scientists tell us that *N. quadrivalvis* (native tobacco) has the lowest nicotine content of any domesticated tobacco.[51] By comparison commercial tobacco (*N. tabacum*, the same used today) has a highly addictive level of nicotine. It is impossible to know how much native tobacco the Blackfeet used before contact, but it is easy to see how they became addicted to commercial tobacco.

Previous to the introduction of commercial tobacco the Blackfeet used their own native tobacco for specific purposes. Although the Beaver bundle owners oversaw the planting and cultivating of tobacco (and held the tobacco and tobacco seeds throughout the winter), the entire community benefited from its cultivation. At the end of winter the Beaver bundle owners divided the tobacco up within the community for their use throughout the Blackfeet summer.

The Blackfeet used tobacco not only for religious purposes but also as a method of social control. Duvall and Wissler wrote that if people in the community believed that someone was lying, they would challenge them to smoke: "The sun is called upon . . . when a man tells an improbable story he may be asked if he will smoke upon its truth."[52] The community used the same method if someone was behaving badly, such as trying to hurt or even kill someone. They would ask that person to make an "oath" or "pledge" to change their behavior and then smoke, which the Blackfeet considered a "binding" contract.[53] The contract was not between the community and the person. The contract was between the Sun or other supernatural entity and the human person. If the person did not modify or alter his or her behavior the supernatural entity would mete out appropriate punishment for the broken contract. This method of social control also provided a buffer within the community among humans engaging in inappropriate judgment or punishment, and social relationships could be maintained.[54]

Got Bison?

James Willard Schultz was the first to write about how the Blackfeet divided animals into three "classes": "First, Spŭhts'-ah-pēk-sēks or 'above animals,' including everything which flies; second, Sō-ōhts'uh-pēks-sēks or 'beyond animals,' including all strictly land animals; third, Kse-ōhts-uh-pēk-sēks or 'under animals,' including fishes, lizards, crabs, 'pollywogs,' turtles and the beavers and otters."[55] Schultz did not entirely explain in his 1883 article that these divisions represented the three worlds of the Blackfeet universe or that the Blackfeet recognized that there was a hierarchy of supernatural power and strength for these three worlds and the animals within them. He was explaining Blackfeet life as he understood their stories. The Blackfeet had heard stories about these levels of power their entire lives.

The supernatural Beaver, from the Water world, told the humans that they could have power over the bison, from the Below world.[56] The Beaver assured the Blackfeet that they would never go hungry in times of need because they could use the power of the Beaver to change and control bison behavior. Japy Takes Gun on Top told Duvall that "when Buffalo have drifted far away and in the winter and the snow being very deep and people cant [sic] very well get to the Buffalo, the people call on the beaver bundle owners to get back the buffalo."[57] They did this with a religious ritual. Rituals were one sure way of communication with the supernatural.

In the ritual to call the bison the Beaver bundle holders invite "old men and women" to attend and sing songs to the various supernatural entities. It was an intricate process that required communication with the various supernatural beings of all three worlds. They first sang songs to the Blackfeet holy trinity—the Sun, Moon, and Morning Star. Next they sang about the bison and their lives out in nature. Next they sang songs to the birds, including the Raven, asking its assistance in locating the bison. They then sang songs for the people in attendance. Japy added, "Now these songs which come next are the Beaver bundle men's most powerful and greatest songs and are used to handle the buffalo as they wish to. . . . These songs are called Charming the Buffalo songs."[58]

At this point in his narrative Japy Takes Gun on Top clarified that "charming" the bison was something that was done only on rare occasions. The Blackfeet took their power seriously and did not use it on trifles. The Beaver men did not sing these songs on a daily basis or even when they held their regular bundle opening or closing rituals. The Blackfeet sang the "Charming the Buffalo songs" only when they were "very hard up and are about starving, when very much in need of food."[59] The next set of seven songs included one imploring the wind to help find the bison. It was only with the help of the weather that the bison would change their position. Japy said, "When this is done the wind will come from the one direction in which the Buffalo are, and a very cold snow storm will come with the wind, which will drive the buffalo towards the camps."[60] The last set of seven songs directed the bison to their village. As the snowstorm pushed the bison to the Blackfeet village, the Beaver medicine pulled the bison as well. Once the bison arrived the Beaver man's final act was to change the weather "into a warm chinook which melts all the snow and making it more comfortable for the butchers."[61]

The Blackfeet were able to attain much of what they needed based on their knowledge of the natural environment. But in difficult circumstances, or to make life easier, they could call upon supernatural allies to provide them with control over aspects of the natural world such as weather or animal behavior. They needed to temporarily change nature to ensure the communities survived or to increase their wealth.

Winter Time

The Blackfeet tell us that they recorded time in their own way. They recorded time from night to night, new moon to new moon, and winter to winter. Big Brave told Duvall that in prayer the Blackfeet included the phrase, "We are looking at the snow," which implied that "they will all live to see the next winter."[62] According to the Beaver medicine stories the beavers introduced counting or keeping track of time to the Blackfeet during the winter that the human spent with them. Within the community the duty of keeping track of time and monitoring the weather fell to the Beaver men.

The supernatural beavers gave the humans counting sticks to keep

Fig. 14. Heart Butte giveaway, 1945. Photo courtesy Jessie Wilber Papers, MS 2252, Merrill G. Burlingame Special Collections, Montana State University, image #ORH 81.

track of time. Counting the new year started at the beginning of each winter, when the Beaver bundle owners "closed" their bundles for the year. Duvall and Wissler argued that since the Beaver men kept track of time, and since the number seven was sacred to them, they recorded that each winter lasted seven months and the summer, five.[63] The Beaver men kept these counting sticks with their Beaver bundle, and they included sticks for days, months, and sometimes years. To keep track within one day, "the time of day was noted by the sun and the night by the position of Ursa major, the Seven Stars."[64]

Tom Kiyo told Duvall that the Beaver men "are credited with good memories (perhaps because the [Beaver] ritual is so long) and formerly kept count of the days and months. For this purpose sets of sticks were kept in bags. They claim twenty-six days for a moon and four days during which the moon is invisible (dies, or covers itself) making a period of thirty days. It is the duty of each bundle owner to keep tally of the days, also to note signs [of the moon] for forecasting."[65] Watching the sky each night, counting each day, and observing each new moon afforded the Beaver men significant knowledge of the seasons. Not everyone in the community had this knowledge, but the supernatural beavers assigned this duty to a small number of people in the community: the Beaver men.

Related to their duty to keep track of time was their duty to keep track of and ultimately predict the weather. Three Bears told Duvall that the "Beaver men are noted for forecasting the weather." Three Bears added that "they keep track of each day of the year and can tell when a storm is to come on and when good weather can be expected. They have good memory and by using their counting sticks can easily tell each day and month of the year." Instead of looking at a calendar the members of the band just went to the Beaver men to ask what day of the month it was or even when spring would be coming. They accomplished this by daily observation. Three Bears added, "The Beaver men usually take good notice of the new moon in winter." The Blackfeet believed that understanding the variations of the nightly moon and especially the new moon helped them predict coming weather patterns, particularly winter storms.[66]

However, forecasting the weather was not the same as changing or controlling the weather. Their knowledge of weather patterns based on daily observation over long periods of time informed their ability to help make community decisions. They knew that the weather would give them a sense of control in the material world. The Blackfeet went to the Beaver men to ask about potential weather concerns before embarking on community activities such as hunting or gathering plant foods. On a daily basis the Beaver men did not alter the weather, but there were occasions, such as when the bison were scarce, when they used their supernatural powers to make the weather change (not always for the better) to assist them.

Satisfaction

The Blackfeet believed the Beaver bundle owners had a direct connection to the Water world and to the powerful supernatural beavers and related beings who could and would change nature to improve the human condition (if asked correctly). The Blackfeet believed that the connection between the original human and Kitaiksísskstaki, the Not

Real Beaver, remained unbroken over time and just the ownership "title" transferred. The Blackfeet told Duvall that "they do regard a bundle as a good investment because of its absolute indestructible nature."[67] The Blackfeet believed that even if a bundle was lost, stolen, or even sold to a museum, the owners could rebuild it piece by piece. What was important to the Blackfeet was not the material object but the "relation, or rapport, between the supernatural source and a single individual."[68]

The primary benefit of owning a Beaver bundle was that it worked. Japy Takes Gun on Top told Duvall that "a man owning a [Beaver] bundle generally has good luck, raises his children up to manhood or womanhood. It brings him in clothen [sic], food and horses. [If] he follows the rules of the bundle and prays frequently to it."[69] It also benefited the community. The beavers introduced the tobacco, which was necessary for humans to communicate with their supernatural allies. Japy added that "the Beaver bundle is considered as great medicine and very holey [sic] and when one prayes [sic] to it for help generally gets some satisfaction."[70]

The Blackfeet believed that humans learned a great deal from the beavers during that one fateful winter during Sto-ye, the "closed" season. With their great ally and the "power of the waters," humans were now able to change and control the natural world, the behavior of animals, and the weather. The Blackfeet used these powers only when necessary and not on a daily basis. But with their power the Blackfeet learned that they did not need to suffer. They could change nature whenever they needed to with the help of a supernatural ally.

CHAPTER 5

Opened Season

The Blackfeet Summer

My uncle Gilbert enlisted in the Marines during his junior year of high school at Flandreau Indian School, a boarding school operated by the federal government in Flandreau, South Dakota. He entered the Marines in August 1966. He completed two tours of duty in Vietnam, both in combat. The worst part of the war did not come until his second tour of duty. Gilbert served as a forward observer.

In early 1968 the North Vietnamese began an artillery barrage that continued for several weeks at Khe Sanh when two divisions of North Vietnamese soldiers surrounded the Americans. The Marines were trapped on a hill and resupplied entirely by air. They engaged in some of the most difficult hand-to-hand combat of the entire war. In an infamous ambush on February 25, 1968, the Vietnamese almost wiped out an entire Marine platoon. On that day Gilbert successfully directed mortar fire at the enemy and administered first aid to other soldiers, and when his platoon leader was fatally wounded Gilbert carried him several hundred yards to a defensive position instead of leaving him behind. He received the Bronze Star with Valor for his actions. He came home one of the most decorated Vietnam veterans from Montana, having earned two Purple Hearts and many other medals. (I did not hear this story about Khe Sanh from him. I read about it in books.[1])

Gilbert rarely spoke of his experiences of the war to his family except on the rare occasion when he pulled out his slides of the photos he had taken. All of his slides were from combat positions and included dozens of pictures of his friends. Most died in the war. He knew every one of their life stories. Each time he told their stories they grew to be old family friends. His "war stories" were of his friendships and the exotic places they came from: New York City, Texas, and California.

At this time in my life I was living with my grandparents. They lived in a two-room tar paper lean-to; one room was the kitchen and living room and the other was the bedroom. We used a woodstove, water from the creek or well, and an outhouse. Every morning before dawn my grandfather made a fire and then sang old Blackfeet songs for Gilbert's success and safe return. He sang what the Blackfeet called "going to war" and "return to camp" songs. My grandfather also made for my uncle Gilbert small reel-to-reel tape recordings of these same songs and mailed them to Vietnam for Gilbert to play every day.

After Gilbert went to war my grandmother sought out old Tom Many Guns.[2] She wanted to buy his father's name—Aakainaamahk, or Many Guns.[3] The Blackfeet view names as personal property. The name "Many Guns" gave him supernatural power to overcome his enemies, to survive, and to live well into old age. (This is why everyone eventually called him "Old Man" Many Guns.) By acquiring this name my grandmother hoped that Gilbert would also acquire the same supernatural powers. She believed that Gilbert would die in the war if he did not have supernatural protection with him.

When my mother was a child her paternal grandmother, Hollering in the Air, blessed her grandchildren every day. She did this by smoking her pipe and asking the supernatural to allow them to have healthy and long lives. Some people called these "women's pipes" because they were for daily use and not associated with ritual uses. Each day she undertook the same routine. Before she smoked her pipe she blew smoke into her hands and "washed" each of her grandchildren with the smoke. She then "washed" herself. Then as she smoked she spoke to the supernatural. The tobacco smoke both purified and blessed my mother and her siblings.

The old-time Blackfeet believed that creating an alliance with the supernatural gave a person protection and control over their destiny. My grandparents believed that their children grew up blessed because my grandfather's mother purified them and asked the supernatural for blessings each day. When my uncle Gilbert went to war and was in a situation of real danger he brought these blessings with him, along with my grandfather's songs and the name of Many Guns. The old-time Blackfeet believed that daily prayers, songs, and names provided supernatural connection and power. They had power to protect a person from harm. They had power over a person's enemies. They had power to provide a person a safe journey home. They had power to give a person long life. The old-time Blackfeet believed that supernatural power was necessary for everyday life.

Weathering Changes

The historian Theodore Binnema has described the northern Great Plains as a place that had a "fierce climate of violent contrasts."[4] The summers could be exceptionally hot and dry, and the winters fluctuated from arctic freezes to the occasional reprieve of a chinook. Binnema summarized that "the nearly ceaseless wind [made] the climate of the northwestern plains what it is, subjecting the region to the most sudden weather changes on the globe."[5] Looking back from the twenty-first century one would suppose that the ancient Blackfeet lived a life of uncertainty and that the intense and unpredictable weather of the plains directed their lives. However, despite the fluctuations of the weather James Willard Schultz learned that the Blackfeet divided their year into only two seasons: winter and summer. Kainaikoan reported that in the winter they stayed in one place, creating semipermanent villages along sheltered river valleys. In the summer they moved a dozen times or more across the northern Great Plains, replenishing their supplies and renewing their relationship with the supernatural. Each year seemed to have been a predictable pattern of settlement, movement, hunting, gathering, trading, and ceremony.

The "sudden weather changes" of the plains did not appear to have affected the Blackfeet the way that it seems they should have. That is probably because the Blackfeet believed that the weather was not a "natural" phenomenon but "supernatural." The Blackfeet viewed different kinds of meteorological conditions as stemming from different supernatural entities. Because of this the Blackfeet did not believe that they needed to adapt to or endure the weather. They believed they could transform or change the weather and other elements of their environment when they pleased with the help of supernatural power.

The early recorders of Blackfeet life learned of a few of the names for the weather. The Blackfeet told George Bird Grinnell about "Wind Maker," a supernatural entity who lived underneath upper Saint Mary Lake, within what is now Glacier National Park. The Blackfeet told Grinnell that the Wind Maker created the wind from underneath the water. The Wind Maker then pushed the wind up from underneath the water and onto the earth's surface. This is the reason, the Blackfeet said, that the wind blew mostly from the mountains out onto the prairies.[6] The Blackfeet told Walter McClintock that the Wind Maker was a large bull elk that lived under the water at Saint Mary Lake and that when it moved its large head and antlers the wind blew.[7] The Blackfeet believed that the Wind Maker created wind as a deliberate action; it was not accidental. Because of this, Schultz explained that instead of saying the wind was blowing from the west, the Blackfeet would say the wind was blowing toward the east.[8] They believed that the Wind Maker created the wind and that it was being directed somewhere on purpose.

The Blackfeet told Grinnell that "Cold Maker" lived in the north country, where everything was white. Similar to the Wind Maker, his actions were deliberate. He sent winter storms down from the north toward the south without mercy.[9] Mad Wolf told McClintock about the Cold Maker's home, the "Snow Tipi." In Mad Wolf's story an individual named Sacred Otter created an alliance with the Cold Maker to stop blizzards temporarily when the Blackfeet thought it was necessary.[10] In his story Cold Maker reminded the Blackfeet, "It is I who bring the cold storms, the whirling snow and the biting winds from the north, and I control them at my will."[11]

The Blackfeet did not view weather as being part of the natural environment. They believed that the weather comprised supernatural entities that intentionally challenged the Blackfeet. When the Blackfeet spoke with the early recorders of Blackfeet life about these forces, they often spoke of their reverence. McClintock explained that "the presence of the mysterious Cold Maker . . . filled everyone with awe and dread of His Power."[12] The Blackfeet did not view weather as a benign presence but as something that they should try to both change and control, or they would live at its mercy. One of the most powerful forces that the Blackfeet respected was the "Thunder Maker." Thunder ruled over the summer.

Thunder Maker

The Blackfeet told Grinnell that "Thunder is one of the most important [deities]. . . . He brings the rain. He is represented sometimes as a bird, or, more vaguely, as in one of the stories, merely as a fearful person."[13]

Fig. 15. Sun dance lodge, 1944. Photo courtesy Jessie Wilber Papers, MS 2252, Merrill G. Burlingame Special Collections, Montana State University, image #ORH 17.

The Blackfeet also told Grinnell that "Thunder Maker" lived on Chief Mountain, at what is now the current U.S.-Canadian border, and controlled several natural phenomena, including thunder, lightning, hail, and rain. When Thunder Maker left in the fall for his home in the south, he took the thunder, lightning, hail, and rain with him. The sound of the first thunder in the early spring marked his return and the beginning of summer.[14] Na-pos, the open season, began with the return of Thunder.

The Blackfeet believed that the Thunder controlled one of the key factors of summertime weather—the rain. In the arid to semiarid northern Great Plains annual rainfall determined much of life. Binnema stated that the arid climate "determined primarily by the ratio of precipitation to evaporation" defined the northern Great Plains landscape and its resources.[15] Snowfall in the mountains determined the level of water in creeks and rivers, and rainfall determined the abundance of resources on the plains. Binnema noted that "by late summer, especially in dry years, many water sources in the dry prairie had disappeared."[16] Developing and maintaining a relationship with the Thunder Maker was essential to Blackfeet existence.

According to the stories that the Blackfeet told the early recorders of Blackfeet life, there was an ancient time when the Blackfeet had no relationship with the Thunder. Instead they lived in fear of its deadly power and ability to withhold rain if it chose. However, the Blackfeet told Grinnell that they created a truce with the Thunder. This, they said, happened "long ago, almost in the beginning."[17] Several Blackfeet told the early recorders of Blackfeet life similar stories of the creation of a relationship between the Thunder and the Blackfeet.[18] However, a local schoolteacher on the reservation in the 1890s, Cora M. Ross, told Grinnell a version of the Thunder story that was widely accepted.[19]

The Blackfeet translator Joseph Tatsey described the Thunder to C. C. Uhlenbeck in 1910 as an otherworldly creature that "did not belong to this country."[20] Tatsey described a supernatural bird: "Its feathers were all of different colors, its bill was green-coloured, its legs were coloured the same." Its most important feature to the Blackfeet, he said, was that "when it opened its eyes, then it flashed lightning. When it flew, then the thunder roared."[21] The multicolored birdlike creature lived on the top of Chief Mountain in a stone lodge.[22] Clouds and rainbows were its tools for travel and for controlling the rainstorms.[23]

Thunder Maker's story began, according to Cora Ross, when the all-powerful Thunder kidnapped a Blackfeet man's wife. The man became distraught and went looking for her. As he traveled he asked each of the animals for assistance and guidance. However, the animals all feared the Thunder too, so they did not want to interfere in this dispute between the human and the Thunder. Finally the man stumbled upon the home of the Raven. The Raven was also a powerful supernatural entity. The Raven invited the human in and heard his sad story. The Raven empathized with him and then told him that it was impossible for a human to go up against a supernatural entity without supernatural power. Moved by the man's story the Raven decided to help.

The Raven gave the human two kinds of devices that contained supernatural power: the wing of a Raven and an arrow shaft made with an elk horn. The human then set out to find the home of the Thunder and retrieve his wife. Upon finding the Thunder's lodge he faced a test of supernatural power. After a time the Thunder conceded that the human, with the help of Raven, had "great medicine." The Thunder and the man made a truce. After returning the man's wife the Thunder gave the man and his wife a pipe to use in the springtime. The Thunder told the couple, "I bring the rain which makes all things grow, and for this you shall pray to me, you and all the people."[24]

Beginning with that first couple, the Blackfeet held a "Thunder Pipe" ceremony as instructed by the Thunder each spring.[25] According to the Blackfeet the Thunder Maker gave the humans one Thunder Pipe, which the Blackfeet had been passing down from owner to owner since the beginning.[26] Schultz was the first recorder of Blackfeet life to write about his experiences attending a Thunder Pipe ceremony. He wrote in 1884 that the Blackfeet still feared the power of the Thunder and its ability, through lightning, to kill humans. The couple who owned the Thunder pipe performed the ceremony as instructed by the Thunder in an effort to appease and remind the Thunder of their pact between the supernatural entity and humans.

For the Blackfeet a new year began with the sound of the first thunder.[27] At the sound of the first thunder the Blackfeet called the community together and then held their Thunder Pipe ceremony. At this ceremony the Blackfeet utilized nothing fresh and instead used foods and materials that they had saved from the previous year, such as dried tobacco, dried sage, dried berries, and dried meat. After Thunder Maker returned to its summer home in the north and after the Blackfeet performed their annual ceremony, Thunder Maker brought the rain to grow new plants. Part of the ceremony included praying to the Thunder for an abundant berry crop, and the participants each planted one dried berry for the coming year's crop. The Thunder Pipe ceremony was a celebration of both the new year and the renewal of life on the northern Great Plains.

The Blackfeet believed that the Thunder Maker was the most powerful of all weather phenomena because of its ability to kill humans with lightning, its ability to make humans suffer through drought, and its ability to generate new plant life with rain. Although it may seem to us in the twenty-first century that winter would have been the worst season to endure on the northern Great Plains, the Blackfeet viewed the summer as the most difficult. In the summer the Blackfeet had to deal with Thunder Maker. Since the "long ago" time individual Blackfeet had had relationships with multiple allies to do just that.

Bull Child

Clark Wissler met Bull Child in the summer of 1903 at the Blackfeet O'kan. Franz Boas, from the American Museum of Natural History, had sent Wissler on an expedition to Montana to study the "symbolism" of the tribes of the northern Great Plains. Wissler arrived near the end of June just as the community was preparing for the annual O'kan, which now coincided with the Fourth of July. Wissler learned at his first O'kan that Bull Child was one of the venerated religious leaders of the Blackfeet. From 1903 until Bull Child's death in 1908 Wissler and Duvall interviewed, corresponded with, and collected materials from him.[28] The ability that fascinated Wissler the most was Bull Child's power to change and control the weather.

Bull Child was born sometime in the 1830s and was probably in his seventies when Wissler first interviewed him.[29] By 1903 Bull Child was a well-known and well-respected ceremonial leader.[30] He lived in the mid-nineteenth century during a time that scholars such as John Ewers considered the high point of Blackfeet history. He was probably in his twenties when Lame Bull's treaty was signed in 1855. He was in his thirties and forties when the region grew into Montana Territory. He did not experience the near extinction of the bison until he was in his fifties. He had four wives, and only two of his children survived into adulthood.[31] Bull Child lived most of his life and adulthood on the prairies. This was exactly the type of person Wissler loved to interview (or have Duvall interview): a true "buffalo Indian."

The Blackfeet who lived through this time period were distinct from other Blackfeet. They experienced two important time periods in Blackfeet history. At midcentury they enjoyed the high point of significant political power, a large land base, diverse economic resources, and perhaps even wealth. By the end of the century they had endured the loss of their land base to the Americans, the loss of bison, numerous famines, and diseases. Those who survived into the twentieth century retained the knowledge of their former life on the northern Great Plains. Theirs was the knowledge that the early recorders of Blackfeet life competed to record.

Fig. 16. Bull Child and Mrs. Big Nose. Image #638.195, Joseph H. Sherburne Family Papers, Archives and Special Collections, Maureen and Mike Mansfield Library, University of Montana–Missoula.

O'kan, or the Sun Dance

Near the end of the summer the Blackfeet held one of their most important communal ceremonies—the O'kan. The O'kan celebrated the relationship between humans and their supernatural allies. The O'kan was a multiday ceremony made up of several individual rituals.[32] A significant part of each of these rituals was a reenactment of the O'kan's origin story. These told of the allies' introduction into the Blackfeet "visible" world from the "invisible" world. These reenactments were not merely to remember the original event as it *had been* in the past but to create a new relationship in the here and now.[33] To ensure that each O'kan was a success a "Weather Man" presided over the entire celebration. Bull Child was one of the most well known Weather Men at the turn of the twentieth century.

Walter McClintock had met Bull Child years before at an earlier O'kan. He photographed Bull Child and told the story of their meeting in his book *The Old North Trail*.[34] He described Bull Child as one of three "prominent medicine men" of the Blackfeet. As part of the O'kan the Blackfeet built a "booth" within the O'kan lodge for the Weather Men to stay in throughout the ceremony. Their role was to keep the Sun, as deity and natural element, physically present and visible throughout the O'kan during the daytime, as well as to keep the Thunder Maker and Wind Maker away. The Blackfeet built the booth out of cottonwood and juniper boughs for the Weather Men to live in throughout the O'kan. Both of these plants have supernatural origins with stories of their own. The Blackfeet used the earth taken from where the center pole was dug for the floor of the booth and spread white clay over it.

The Weather Men decided how many days to continue the O'kan based on how many days they wanted to keep the weather fair. Making "medicine" for several days in a row was hard work. The Weather Men also prayed for and blessed individual community members as part of their role at the O'kan. Women brought their children to Bull Child for "his blessing" that "they might be endowed with power and have an abundance to eat throughout their lives."[35] A lifetime of acquiring supernatural allies and control over the weather placed Bull Child in this prestigious position.

Receiving Power

Bull Child told Wissler and Duvall that he first received supernatural control over the weather when he was still a young man. He told them that he went up on Heart Butte, a small mountain on the southern part of what would become the reservation, where he "fasted and prayed for seven days."[36] He probably did this in the late 1840s or early 1850s.[37] Bull Child said that after seven days "the Sun appeared before me as a very old man, [he] gave me a drum and one song. He explained to me that this drum and the song were to be used in making clear weather."[38] With a supernatural ally such as the Sun, Bull Child could begin to change his own fortunes as a young man and use his new abilities to change the weather for going on raiding parties and for hunting. The Blackfeet believed that it was foolish to attempt to go on raids, travel, or hunt without some small ability to change the weather.

A story from Weasel Tail's youth provides a good comparison.[39] Weasel Tail told the ethnologist John Ewers that the first time he went on a raiding party he was only fifteen years old. Weasel Tail stated that he was anxious to make his mark and set out with a group of older men to raid the Crow. However, he soon learned that he could not keep up with them and they left him behind. Weasel Tail was then caught in a snowstorm, and after the snow settled he got snow blindness. He was blind and lost when a group of Cree or Métis peoples came upon him. They took pity on him and helped him find his way home. He was humiliated. From his first attempt at going to war Weasel Tail learned a lesson that many young Blackfeet understood: to never go without supernatural assistance and especially without some power over the weather.[40]

Bull Child was fortunate that he had access to a supernatural ally from a young age. As the years passed Bull Child's fortunes grew as he acquired more supernatural allies. The various major deities of the Blackfeet, such as the Sun, Moon, Morning Star, and Thunder, visited Bull Child and gave him various objects of power. The Sun returned to Bull Child and gave him a shell necklace that provided him the additional power to make the rain go away. Bull Child stated, "Since this time I have kept the shell and have exercised my power over the weather, and at the time of the sun dance I keep the rain away."[41] The Sun returned another time and gave Bull Child a headdress made out of a running-fisher (*Martes pennanti*) hide and other objects. This too was for directing the weather.[42] The Blackfeet believed that each alliance and corresponding object gave an individual some control over nature but not complete control. Over the years if a person was fortunate, like Bull Child, they acquired multiple alliances and multiple objects, which added up to a larger amount of control.

Sun Power

In their first published manuscript, *The Mythology of the Blackfoot Indians*, based on their interviews with Blackfeet men, Clark Wissler and David Duvall explained that the Blackfeet believed that certain objects held supernatural power.[43] James Willard Schultz explained this belief as "Na-to-ye. . . . The word means 'of the Sun' and is generally translated as 'medicine,' not physical but spiritual."[44] Wissler and Duvall explained that humans could acquire a supernatural ally, as well as its corresponding power, when the object with "Sun power" communicated with the person. This was usually done through speaking, in the visible world or in a dream. Wissler and Duvall observed that when the Sun endowed an object with supernatural power, it transformed into an entity with whom humans could communicate and a vessel for the Sun's supernatural power.[45] Wissler and Duvall further explained that after the object was endowed with power from the Sun, the human had access to that power once the object "transferred" the knowledge of its power to the human. Thus the process was in two parts: the Sun transferred supernatural power to an object, and the object transferred the knowledge of how to use the supernatural power to the human. Wissler and Duvall explained that this final step created a relationship with that one person.[46] Individuals such as Bull Child could accumulate dozens of objects endowed with supernatural power and with various uses, and only he could own and use them.

As previously mentioned, individuals could acquire objects with supernatural power in three ways.[47] The first was for a supernatural entity to seek out an individual and "speak" to that person through an object, as explained by Wissler and Duvall. The second way was for a human to go in search of supernatural assistance, usually by going to a place near the home of a supernatural and then suffering through physical deprivation until the supernatural entity took pity on the human. The third and easiest way was to "buy" supernatural power from another human who had already acquired it using any of the three methods. With the third way an individual could "buy" all or part of an object with supernatural power, and the "seller" would transfer their knowledge and ability to the purchaser.[48] The Blackfeet believed that the relationship between the supernatural and an individual remained intact, even with each new owner.

Once an individual "owned" an object, no matter how they acquired it they could "sell" the object to another and "buy" other objects. Individuals bought and sold dozens of these supernaturally endowed objects throughout their lives.[49]

Fig. 17. Holy woman at Little Badger, 1942. Photo courtesy Jessie Wilber Papers, MS 2252, Merrill G. Burlingame Special Collections, Montana State University, image #ORH 67.

Power Begets Power

Although the Blackfeet could use supernatural allies and power for a variety of purposes, one of the main reasons to have the allies was to change the natural environment in the Below world. Changing and controlling the weather played a key role in the Blackfeet belief system. The Blackfeet believed that humans existed in a universe where one supernatural power could trump other supernatural power, and to influence these weather systems the Blackfeet needed stronger supernatural power.

Individuals like Bull Child understood this system. As a young man Bull Child used his growing collection of supernatural objects to increase his status within the community and his own wealth. In addition to benefiting from using the objects himself, he also "rented" them out to younger men who had yet to acquire objects or to older men without sufficient supernatural allies. These men used his objects to change the natural world for hunting or for going to war. If the men were successful, Bull Child would get a share of their profits.[50]

As Bull Child got older his stature as a man connected to the supernatural grew and he acquired even more supernatural objects. From the Thunder he obtained the hide of a red-winged blackbird (*Agelaius phoeniceus*) that had "powers over the weather."[51] He also added a powerful robe design from the Thunder. Bull Child told Wissler and Duvall that the Thunder came to him in a dream and told him, "When wearing this robe, no matter how bad the weather may be, it will clear up. If the weather should be clear and you desire it to rain . . . it will rain."[52] Bull Child created the robe design as specified by Thunder Maker using first a bison robe and later a wool trade blanket. Bull Child eventually assembled a large array of objects until he was entirely covered from head to toe with a headdress, hair ornaments, bison robe, clothing, jewelry, accessories, and almost full body paint, all with connections to the supernatural world and all his allies.

Bull Child also purchased the powerful robe owned by Brings Down the Sun, a well-known North Peigan religious leader of the late nineteenth century. McClintock recorded the stories of Brings Down the Sun in his book *The Old North Trail.* Brings Down the Sun told McClintock that he went to the highest peak on the Porcupine Hills in what is now southern Alberta along the Rocky Mountain Front and spent ten days and ten nights fasting. While he was fasting the "Spirit of the Mountain" came to him and gave him the robe design, which was "endowed with wisdom and supernatural power."[53] The Mountain spirit gave Brings Down the Sun the "design and instructions" to use the robe.[54] McClintock claimed that by the time that Bull Child owned it, the robe was "famous among the Blackfeet."[55]

The Blackfeet recognized Bull Child both "for his power as a doctor" and as "a prominent medicine man."[56] Wissler claimed that it was unusual for a person to be both. He explained that the Blackfeet saw a difference between the two: a "doctor" was someone who healed physical illnesses, while a "medicine" man was someone knowledgeable about supernatural relationships. Wissler stated that two different types of people performed these duties in the community, and many doctors were women who used herbs to heal.[57] Wissler also made the distinction that a doctor's knowledge was not religious knowledge, whereas a medicine man could transfer his medicine to another person because it was connected to a supernatural ally.[58]

By the time that McClintock and Wissler visited, Bull Child's main role among the Blackfeet was as the primary Weather Man for the annual O'kan. Each year before the O'kan the family sponsoring it selected a person who possessed special powers over the weather to keep any storms, wind, and rain away and to guarantee sunlight throughout the ceremony. This person was known either as a Weather Priest, a Weather Dancer, or a Weather Man.[59]

Wissler witnessed for himself the power of Bull Child's role as a Weather Man. Wissler wrote, "In 1903 there was a contest between a number of rival medicinemen some of whom conjured for rain, others for fair weather: strange to say, clouds would threaten and then pass away during these days."[60] Wissler was impressed with Bull Child's ability to win the duel over the others. Bull Child recounted another story for Wissler of his ability to control the weather. Using his original drum and song from the Sun (which by then he had had for at least fifty years), he told Wissler that "on the fourth of July, 1902, while our people were in camp preparing for the sun dance, there came a great rain which threatened to flood the whole camp. I beat my drum and sang my song which kept the water away from my tipi." He added, however, that "I made up my mind to cause the water to drown out the tipi of my rival . . . and forced him to move."[61]

"I have great power"

By the time that Wissler met Bull Child, Bull Child was either in his late sixties or early seventies. Bull Child's role as a Weather Man at numerous O'kans solidified his place in Blackfeet society.[62] Similar to other Blackfeet at the turn of the twentieth century, Bull Child decided to sell his objects—but not their supernatural power. In the summer of 1904 Bull Child sold all the objects that he owned related to his abilities as a Weather Man, including his robe, headdress, necklace, whistle, drum, and other items, to the American Museum of Natural History.[63] Wissler and Duvall documented the stories and recorded the songs related to these objects. They regarded Bull Child as "absolutely sincere" in his efforts to document and explain his belief system.[64] We do not know why Bull Child decided to sell his objects to the American Museum of Natural History. We do know that he maintained an ongoing relationship, through visits and correspondence, with Wissler until Bull Child's death in the spring of 1908.[65]

The type of power that Bull Child possessed would have had many uses during his lifetime, and since he did not sell his power he would continue to maintain this power until his passing. However, after the Blackfeet settled onto the reservation its primary uses were at the annual O'kan and in asserting one's strength among rivals.

Wissler featured the items that he collected from Bull Child in his representation of Blackfeet religion at the American Museum of Natural History. They are still there today. Wissler commissioned a full-size mannequin of Bull Child and used it to display Bull Child's various objects. It was Wissler's final tribute to his close acquaintance. Wissler described him in this way:

The figure represents Bull Child, a prominent Blackfoot shaman, whose supernatural power gave him the ability to control the weather. Except for his robe, which was purchased from another shaman, all of his paraphernalia were made in accord with instructions received from supernatural beings in visions. His headdress of otter skin, his shell necklace, and his drum were given by the Sun and had the power to turn away rain or bring clear weather; his finger pendants symbolize control over the weather; and his robe had the power to cause rain or sunshine. The blue spots painted on his face represent stars; the crescents symbolize the moon; and the lines on his arms are rainbows. The eagle-wing wand in his left hand belongs to his medicine bundle; the right hand wand of the magpie, peacock, and dyed chicken feathers represent the moon. Bull Child also had supernatural protection against smallpox and bullets and the ability to prevent child bearing.[66]

When the early recorders of Blackfeet life first came to the reservation at the turn of the twentieth century to document and record the Blackfeet past, they were told stories of a different reality. It was a reality in which the Blackfeet had access to supernatural power through relationships with the forces of nature and supernatural entities. When the Sun told Bull Child, "This medicine lodge is ours [the Sun's and Moon's], the weather is ours, and when you wish the weather to be good . . . you must give me what I ask for," the Blackfeet obeyed.[67]

Not only did the Blackfeet believe that they could change and control the visible natural world, but they thought it was necessary for community well-being. The Blackfeet believed there existed three separate worlds, and from each of these worlds came specific elements that the Blackfeet could utilize to affect their earthly existence. Bull Child's power came from all three. The Blackfeet relationship with the supernatural and their understanding of nature gave them confidence and provided stability, despite their economic circumstances and political situation. As Wissler observed, "Once, it was told, that [Bull Child] became enraged at the power making the weather bad, shouting out, 'Now, you go ahead, if you want to. I have great power and can stop you when I will.'"[68]

And he did.

CHAPTER 6

Storytakers

Ethnographers Visit the Blackfeet

Grandma Gretchen was my grandfather's aunt. Her Blackfeet name was Holds Together Woman. Aimsback, my grandfather's father, married her two half-sisters, Calf Woman and Hollering in the Air Woman. It was common in those days to have more than one wife and to marry sisters. When Gretchen got older she helped take care of her sister's grandchildren. My uncle Gilbert was one of her favorites. She kept special treats for him in her old cupboard. When he went over to her house he would walk straight to her cupboard and ask for the candy or sweets that he knew she hid there for him. When she died he was too young to understand, and he was just told that Grandma went away, that she was not at home.

Grandma Gretchen was born in the 1870s and raised before the end of the buffalo days. She knew something of the old-time ways because she was in her early teens when those days came to an end. My family remembers her only as an old woman, because that is how they knew her. She did not wear contemporary store-bought clothing but wore homemade calico dresses. And instead of wearing homemade moccasins (like most women her age wore) she wore old men's dress shoes. No one is sure when she got into that habit. Similar to those of her generation she married several times. Unfortunately she never had biological children. Instead she took in children and raised them as her own.

Apparently one of the skills she learned as a child was how to do porcupine quillwork. Before the Blackfeet had access to trade beads they decorated their clothing, especially their clothing used for religious purposes, with dyed porcupine quills that the women flattened with their teeth and interwove into elaborate designs on tanned animal hides or robes. There was not much call for this type of work within the new reservation economy at the turn of the twentieth century. The ethnographer Clark Wissler commented in 1910 that Blackfeet quillwork had "almost become a thing of the past."[1]

Wissler knew that finding a quillworker would be difficult. He knew that doing quillwork was a long, laborious process. In the winter of 1905 he asked his Blackfeet collaborator David Duvall to find someone who could create a quilled blanket band for the American Museum of Natural History in New York. He wrote, "I should like to have in porcupine quill work, sewed with sinew one of those large blanket bands. . . . In choosing the colors I wish you would try to get the old ones used before the white people came among your people."[2]

Two years after he asked, Wissler finally received his request: "One quill worked blanket band for a man's blanket. Made in old style."[3] A blanket band was approximately four feet long. It took almost two years to complete because first the materials for the blanket band had to be collected and then the band made. His collaborator David Duvall explained that "quill work is much harder than beed [sic] work. She put in four months work on it and about five hours each day."[4] Upon seeing the band Wissler commented that it was "a fine piece of quill work."[5] In the winter of 1906 and 1907 Grandma Gretchen, then a woman in her thirties, created a masterpiece of Blackfeet woman's craftwork.

Holds Together Woman had an extraordinary talent. She learned the difficult tasks of taking the quills from a porcupine, dyeing them beautiful colors, and using them to create exquisite ornamentation on special and everyday objects. In the days before the Blackfeet had access to commercial glass beads and other manufactured embellishments Blackfeet women used elements from nature such as porcupine quills to decorate their robes, clothing, and household items. Quillwork was one of their ancient art forms.[6] In the pre-reservation days girls like Holds Together learned quillwork from older women. The Blackfeet believed that quillwork was a "sacred craft."[7] Although quillwork was an ancient craft, Holds Together Woman would be putting her skill to a new use. Holds Together Woman was not making this particular blanket band for herself or her family or to exchange or give as a gift. She knew that it would not be attached to any robe or blanket. It would never be worn by a person. She was making this object for a museum to sell for money. "She asked . . . $60.00 for it."[8]

Storytellers and Storytakers

By 1910 an unintended economy had emerged after the Blackfeet settled onto the reservation. The Blackfeet recognized that they could benefit from the plethora of outsiders visiting the reservation each summer. Dozens of individual Blackfeet, such as Holds Together Woman, began telling their stories, reciting their histories, singing their songs, posing for photographers, having their portraits painted, and making material objects for outsiders, all in exchange for cash—a rare commodity on the reservation. Some of the artisanry that had gone unused for many years was useful again. While the U.S. government had spent the previous twenty-five years punishing people for practicing their old ways, by 1910 the Great Northern Railroad was paying individual Blackfeet to wear their regalia to lure tourists to the newly created Glacier National Park, and the famous photographer Edward S. Curtis was paying Blackfeet to pose for him.

Today we might think of these interactions as exploitative. Perhaps they were. After all, these outsiders were entering a poverty-stricken community desperate for a cash economy. People needed money and not more debt or credit at the local mercantile. However, many records, such as the correspondence between David Duvall, Holds Together Woman, and Clark Wissler, show that negotiation regarding the price of their services on the part of Blackfeet individuals did occur. With each successive outside visitor Blackfeet individuals were learning the monetary value of their knowledge. In one instance an old widow contacted David Duvall, who in turn contacted Clark Wissler, to sell the objects her late husband had possessed. She let Wissler know that she knew her objects were valuable and that she could sell them to a museum. Wissler tried to negotiate her down, but after two years she got her price.[9]

Telling or selling stories therefore was not a one-sided transaction, with outsiders asking questions and the Blackfeet blindly answering. Whether it was a story or a song or an object, the Blackfeet learned they could and would get paid for it. A newspaper article about Edward Curtis's photography work among the Blackfeet at the turn of the century stated, "There isn't any mystery about the methods of Mr. Curtis. The average Indian will neither be cajoled nor bullied into posing. Mr. Curtis does very little urging. His rule is an old one—'money talks.'"[10] By 1910, even as the federal government increasingly restricted the Blackfeet reservation economic system, the Blackfeet had not lost control of their ability to tell or sell their own stories.

Between 1880 and 1910 a steady stream of outsiders made their way to the Blackfeet reservation. And as David Duvall explained to Clark Wissler, almost anyone could tell stories:

> So far as we know there are no restrictions against the telling of myths at certain times of the year. There is no detailed myths which can be narrated only to select audiences. . . . Neither are there myths peculiar to women or men, as the case may be, any one being at liberty to render any myth whatsoever. However, persons not versed in a ritual are often reluctant to narrate the myth accounting for its origin, because in a general way it is improper for one to speak in detail of medicines concerning which they have little knowledge.[11]

However, the storytakers were only interested in interacting with one type of person—what John C. Ewers called a "buffalo Indian," that is, those individuals who grew to adulthood on the open prairies. This focus limited the early recorders of Blackfeet life to interviewing or interacting with only a few residents of the reservation. The majority of these early recorders of Blackfeet life also did not speak Blackfeet, which meant they had to rely on interpreters. Between these two parameters the early recorders of Blackfeet life were left with few options for collaboration. For the most part we know the collaborators' names because these recorders of Blackfeet life name them within their documents. They also left behind unpublished documents hidden within archival records of their monetary transactions. These documents often named the people they interviewed and those from whom they collected songs or stories and from whom they purchased objects.

Ultimately the most used published works about the Blackfeet came from a few writers during this time who retold the stories of their Blackfeet collaborators. They include James Willard Schultz, George Bird Grinnell, Walter McClintock, Clark Wissler, Truman Michelson, and C. C. Uhlenbeck. After 1910 came a few others, such as John C. Ewers. They worked independently of each other to produce the majority of ethnographic materials that all scholars of Blackfoot history use today.[12] Contemporary scholars use the published and unpublished writings of these early recorders of Blackfeet history as their primary source for information on all things Blackfoot. I have done the same in this book. Contemporary scholars (often inaccurately) extrapolate from these stories to represent the history and culture of *all* Blackfoot peoples, in *all* places, at *all* times throughout history. I sometimes do this as well.

Numerous contemporary scholars have written about the lives of these outside storytakers.[13] I do not intend to repeat their efforts. However, I think it is important to know something of the men who came to the reservation to record the stories of the Blackfeet, what they wrote, and the extent to which there were or were not kinship connections to their Blackfeet collaborators. Based on family stories I knew that I was related to some of these collaborators.[14] So I attempted to figure out how people were related to each other or how they might have known each other. I assumed the interpreters and translators were interviewing their own relatives. Why? Because it is easier to interview a relative. I do the same thing today. And it is also proper protocol in Blackfeet society to speak initially to the elders of one's own family. In light of the difficult economic situation at the turn of the last century, it seemed obvious: why not hire your own relatives for various opportunities that included payments in cash?

The books and articles written about the Blackfeet from the turn of the last century used to be seen by scholars as objective histories. Contemporary scholars, including myself, now reevaluate these same works to find subjective histories representative of their place and time. However, after I looked at the genealogy of some of the Blackfeet storytellers and their connections to the storytakers, I came away with a new understanding. These histories reflect the knowledge of a small circle of mostly interconnected individuals willing to tell their stories.

James Willard Schultz, 1880s

One of the first outsiders to record Blackfeet knowledge could be considered more of an insider, as he had intimate knowledge of Blackfeet lifeways. James Willard Schultz came to Blackfeet territory in 1877 at the age of seventeen. He got a job in Fort Conrad on the Marias River working as a clerk for a trading company. At that time the primary language spoken in the region was Blackfeet, and he learned to speak the

Fig. 18. Sherburne Store, viewed from the west. Image #638.038, Joseph H. Sherburne Family Papers, Archives and Special Collections, Maureen and Mike Mansfield Library, University of Montana–Missoula.

language fluently. Within two years he had married Fine Shield Woman, a fifteen-year-old Blackfeet girl. They had a son, their only child, a few years later. They remained married for almost twenty-five years, until her death in the winter of 1903.[15] Schultz was not a trained ethnologist or even college educated, but he became one of the most prolific writers on the life of the Blackfeet.[16]

Schultz's articles, which began appearing in print in 1880, are the earliest published records of Blackfeet life. He published the first of these articles in *Forest and Stream,* a national weekly magazine that focused on outdoor activities. His articles were drawn from his own personal experiences on the prairies and in the mountains. His early articles in the magazine appeared under the column heading of "The Sportsman Tourist."[17] A few years after his wife died in 1903 he moved to California, and the majority of his writing shifted in genre, from nonfiction to fiction.[18] He published his best-known book, *My Life as an Indian* (fiction

Fig. 19. Butchering in shop, Badger Creek. Image #638.107, Joseph H. Sherburne Family Papers, Archives and Special Collections, Maureen and Mike Mansfield Library, University of Montana–Missoula.

based on fact) in 1907. He remained a professional writer throughout his life, producing dozens of articles and books.

Schultz was in a unique situation. He lived in Blackfeet territory for more than thirty years, he learned to speak the language, and he married into the tribe. George Bird Grinnell, the editor of *Forest and Stream* magazine, wrote of Schultz that "it is most unusual to find anyone . . . mingling in daily intercourse with Indians, who has the intelligence to study their traditions, history and customs, and the industry to reduce his observations into writing."[19] In his earliest articles Schultz wrote about his adventures with his friend Seen from Afar and others.[20] Within his writings he often identified the first-person voice of Seen from Afar and others by indenting or italicizing their words.[21] These were probably the first stories printed using the first-person voice of a "buffalo Indian." However, unlike later writers, Schultz did not appear to be specifically trying to tell the story of individual Blackfeet but instead was telling his own autobiographical story with the Blackfeet. When Schultz wrote his fourteen-part series "Life among the Blackfeet" for *Forest and Stream* he employed the objective, anonymous tone of the day and he no longer identified his friends or relatives by name.

Schultz's wife, Fine Shield Woman, was the daughter of Potato Woman and Pulling Down Lodge (also known as Bull Head). Schultz relied on these in-laws as well as Fine Shield's three brothers—Sam Yellow Wolf, Boy Chief, and Louis Champagne—for information.[22] Schultz probably also gleaned ethnographic information from his in-laws and from his son's in-laws on a daily basis without a structured interview process. The Schultzes lived with Fine Shield's extended family, spending most of their time with her uncle Yellow Wolf.[23] Schultz's son Lone Wolf, or Hart Schultz, married Margaret Eagle Head, the half-sister of David Duvall.[24] Margaret Eagle Head and David Duvall had the same mother, Yellow Bird.[25] Margaret's parents were Yellow Bird Woman and Eagle Head.

When he still lived on the reservation, Schultz and his family often stayed at the home of his wife's brother, Sam Yellow Wolf.[26] At that time Sam was married to Mary (Haggerty) Yellow Wolf. Mary was half African American and half Blackfeet. Mary Yellow Wolf's first marriage was to William Jackson, a longtime guide and interpreter for many reservation visitors.[27] Jackson had been an interpreter for both Walter McClintock and George Bird Grinnell. Mary and Sam Yellow Wolf raised the Jackson and Yellow Wolf children together. Schultz's main connection to the Blackfeet reservation after he moved to California was through his wife's relatives, the Yellow Wolf family.[28]

One of Mary and Sam Yellow Wolf's sons was Louis "Louie" Yellow Wolf. Louie Yellow Wolf eventually married my grandmother Annie's sister Ella Mad Plume.[29] Fine Shield Woman was my uncle Louie's aunt, Hart Schultz was his cousin, and James Willard Schultz was his uncle. However, Fine Shield woman died the same year that Louie Yellow Wolf was born, so he never knew her. He did know his uncle and cousin from their occasional visits to the Yellow Wolf home.

Unlike the writers who would follow, Schultz's experience was unparalleled, as Grinnell described. Schultz lived with the Blackfeet during the final years of the wild bison on the prairies and the early years of their transition to life on the reservation. <u>Unlike other non-Blackfeet who lived with the Blackfeet, such as the Catholic priests or government employees, Schultz did not have any intention of changing Blackfeet society.</u> And, like his in-laws, he too was adapting to the new economy, learning to make a living by selling his own stories.

George Bird Grinnell, 1890s

The man who purchased many of Schultz's stories was George Bird Grinnell. Grinnell first came to Montana and Blackfeet territory in 1885 while he was the editor of *Forest and Stream*. In 1892 Grinnell wrote several articles on Blackfeet life for *Science*, the *American Anthropologist*, and *Scribner's Magazine*. That same year he also published the first comprehensive work on the Blackfeet, *Blackfoot Lodge Tales: The Story of a Prairie People*. The book was based on his own research among the Blackfeet and the vignettes that James Willard Schultz had published in *Forest and Stream* from 1882 to 1884.[30] Schultz allowed Grinnell to incorporate his writings freely within *Blackfoot Lodge Tales*.[31] Although no one has ever done a word-for-word textual analysis, Grinnell did include a significant portion of Schultz's writing within his own. As a result the stories of Schultz's Blackfeet relatives became a central feature in Grinnell's work.

Grinnell had been visiting the reservation on a regular basis since 1885, and during that time he was able to interview a variety of individuals for the purpose of writing his book. During this time Grinnell also purchased items for Franz Boas and Clark Wissler at the American Museum of Natural History in New York City. Grinnell stated that in his work he "endeavored to show how Indians think and feel by letting some of them tell their own stories in their own fashion." He added, "I give the Blackfoot stories as they have been told to me by the Indians themselves."[32] Grinnell did not speak Blackfeet. Besides Schultz he used William Jackson (Mary Yellow Wolf's first husband) and William Russell, both educated mixed-blood Blackfeet, as his interpreters.[33] "Most of the stories," though, he credits to fourteen different men, some of whom had passed on by the time the book was published. They included Red

Eagle, Almost-a-Dog, Four Bears, Wolf Calf, Big Nose, Heavy Runner, Young Bear Chief, Wolf Tail, Mad Wolf (the adoptive father of Walter McClintock), Running Rabbit, White Calf, All Are His Children, Double Runner, and Lone Medicine Person.[34] One of Grinnell's main collaborators was the old Blackfeet leader White Calf. Grinnell's work with White Calf remains mostly unpublished.[35]

Grinnell divides his book into four sections. Grinnell begins *Blackfoot Lodge Tales* by telling his readers that the Blackfeet were "intensely religious."[36] The first three sections tell of the mythological origins stories and worldview of the Blackfeet. The fourth section tells of their daily life. Grinnell wrote that he wanted the Blackfeet to "explain in their own way how they look at the every-day occurrences of their life, what motives govern them, and how they reason."[37] *Blackfoot Lodge Tales* exemplifies what the Blackfeet believed to be the most important aspects about their lives and what motivated them, their relationship with the supernatural world, and their ability to develop alliances with the supernatural and change the world around them.

Blackfoot Lodge Tales continues to be the most widely read book written about the Blackfeet. It represents the first published work in which the author claims to be telling the stories of the Blackfeet as they wanted the stories told. We have every reason to believe Grinnell's Blackfeet collaborators.

Walter McClintock, 1890s to 1910s

After the publication of Grinnell's *Blackfoot Lodge Tales* and the numerous articles about the Blackfeet in popular magazines, many different outsiders began to arrive on the Blackfeet reservation. Walter McClintock came out to Montana from Philadelphia in 1896 because of a personal illness. His family believed that a trip out west would bring him back to health. From that time on he became a frequent visitor to the reservation. He interviewed individual Blackfeet, recorded their songs, and took hundreds of photographs. He never learned the Blackfeet language during his years of research and relied on various interpreters and translators, including David Duvall and William Jackson. McClintock published his first article, "Four Days in a Medicine Lodge," in *Harper's New Monthly*

Magazine in 1900. Ten years later he published his seminal work, *The Old North Trail: Life, Legends and Religion of the Blackfeet Indians*. He based this book on his relationship with the elder Siyeh, or Mad Wolf, and his wife, Gives to the Sun. They adopted him as their own. *The Old North Trail* is also about the North Peigan elder Brings Down the Sun and other Blackfeet ceremonial leaders. McClintock relied on his adoptive Blackfeet family to provide the majority of the information for his work. Unlike many recorders of Blackfeet lives of that time McClintock identified in his publications almost every person with whom he interacted. Much later in life McClintock published a new series of articles in the Southwest Museum's magazine, but they essentially rehashed his original experiences with Siyeh and his family.

In addition to writing about Mad Wolf and his adoptive Blackfeet family McClintock took hundreds of photos of late nineteenth-century and early twentieth-century Blackfeet life. McClintock's Blackfeet photographs continue to captivate people. Fortunately most of McClintock's research survives, including his photographs, recorded songs, correspondence, typed notes, and manuscripts.[38] Like many recorders of Blackfeet life of that time McClintock came to the reservation only during the summertime and often only during the annual O'kan, or Medicine Lodge.

David Duvall told Truman Michelson that he did not like working for McClintock because he was not treated well and was not paid well.[39] Mad Wolf corresponded (through a translator) with McClintock, often asking him for assistance or when he would be returning to the reservation.[40] McClintock's replies to Mad Wolf seem terse. Unfortunately these interactions reveal the complicated and perhaps difficult relationships he had with his adoptive Blackfeet family and his Blackfeet translator.

McClintock's *The Old North Trail* remains one of the most comprehensive books on the ceremonial life of the Blackfeet. By focusing on one Blackfeet family and viewing events through the eyes of the author, the book allows the reader to sit in on each ritual throughout the summer ceremonial season. McClintock also shares with the reader the various gender roles of his family members. The Blackfeet women Menake and Nitana shared their knowledge of the botany of the Blackfeet. They helped McClintock collect plant specimens, and he sent them to the

Carnegie Institute in Pittsburgh. He published "Materia Medica of the Blackfeet" in 1909 and included it in the appendixes to *The Old North Trail*. As was the case for *Blackfoot Lodge Tales*, in *The Old North Trail* Mad Wolf and Gives to the Sun shared what was important to them, their unique worldview, their relationships with the supernatural, and their knowledge of the natural world.

Clark Wissler and David Duvall, 1900s to 1910s

Franz Boas, probably the most influential figure in modern anthropology, sent his student Clark Wissler, a recent graduate of Indiana University and Columbia University, to study the Blackfeet in the summer of 1903. He was the first trained academic to systematically document Blackfeet lifeways. At that time Wissler worked for the American Museum of Natural History. He never learned how to speak the Blackfeet language, which was unusual for Boas's students. Instead he worked closely with the Blackfeet collaborator David C. Duvall.

Not much is known about David Duvall. We do know that he attended Carlisle Indian Industrial Institute and learned to be a blacksmith. He had a small blacksmith shop in Browning. David Duvall had worked as a collaborator or translator for Grinnell, McClintock, Wissler, Michelson, and perhaps others. Duvall relied primarily on his own relatives, his in-laws, and several others for his interviews for Wissler. His methodology in recording and translating stories was thorough. As Wissler noted, "Mr. Duvall read the descriptive parts of the manuscript to well-informed Indians, recording their corrections and comments, the substance of which was incorporated in the final version."[41] Wissler had to rely on Duvall because he suffered from a debilitating disease that made it difficult for him to travel.

David Duvall's mother was Yellow Bird Woman, whose parents were Big Plume and Kills at Night. Both his mother and the family of his wife, Holds Together Woman (or Gretchen), were members of the Fat Melters band, who lived on the south side of the reservation. It was through the Fat Melters band that Duvall found many of his consultants. David Duvall's wife Gretchen's parents were Good Gun (or Running Wolf) and Spear Woman. Gretchen was a half-sister to my great-grandfather

Aimsback's two wives, Hollering in the Air and Calf Woman.[42] David and Gretchen Duvall were my great-grandfather's sister and brother-in-law and the aunt and uncle of my grandfather Iòkimau (or Francis). However, David Duvall died the same year that my grandfather was born, so my grandfather only knew his aunt Gretchen.

David Duvall and Clark Wissler spent significant time interviewing Gretchen's paternal uncle, Bull Child. In addition, the stories of Bull Child are featured in several of Wissler's publications, and Bull Child has his own museum exhibit at the American Museum of Natural History. Bull Child corresponded with Wissler on a regular basis, via a translator at the local mercantile, from 1903 when they first met until Bull Child's death in 1908.[43]

Wissler also contracted Duvall to make material objects for the American Museum of Natural History. Duvall's wife, Gretchen, made some objects, especially those decorated with porcupine quills. And Duvall's other relatives made other objects, such as all the Blackfeet "Indian games" and toys at the natural history museum, and others.[44] Duvall interviewed his maternal uncle Eagle Child, who was one of Yellow Bird Woman's brothers.[45] (Eagle Child and his wife, Charging Both Sides, were also the maternal aunt and uncle of my great-grandfather Aimsback.)[46] Duvall also interviewed his mother's maternal uncle, Strangling Wolf, and his aunt Old Lady Strangling Wolf (her name is not in the records, however). Duvall also conducted a significant number of interviews with his mother's fourth husband, Japy Takes Gun on Top.[47]

David Duvall and Clark Wissler's collaboration ended abruptly in 1911, when, because of a domestic dispute, Duvall committed suicide. Oddly enough George Bird Grinnell just happened to be in Browning the day that Duvall killed himself. Grinnell wrote a letter to Wissler giving him the unfortunate news.[48] After the death of Duvall, Clark Wissler enlisted the assistance of Duvall's cousin James Eagle Child to provide translation and family connections. But this relationship did not work out.[49] Wissler did not return to the Blackfeet reservation.

Wissler published *Mythology of the Blackfoot Indians* in 1908. It was the one and only time that he listed Duvall as a coauthor. Wissler published five other major works on the Blackfeet that relied heavily on Duvall's field notes, including *Material Culture of the Blackfoot Indians* in 1910, *The Social Life of the Blackfoot Indians* in 1911, *Ceremonial Bundles of the Blackfoot Indians* in 1912, *Societies and Dance Associations of the Blackfoot Indians* in 1913, and *The Sun Dance of the Blackfoot Indians* in 1918. The work done by Wissler and Duvall is by far the most extensive collection of ethnographic materials ever produced on the Blackfeet.

Truman Michelson, 1910s

Truman Michelson was a linguist and an ethnologist. He received his doctorate from Harvard University in 1904. He also studied privately with Franz Boas from 1909 to 1910 before beginning his career at the Bureau of American Ethnology (BAE) at the Smithsonian Institution.[50] Beginning in his first year with the BAE in 1910 he conducted a survey of Algonquian languages. The Blackfeet language was classified as Algonquian, and so he went to the Blackfeet reservation in northwest Montana for the summer. He spent only one month on the reservation, and there is no evidence that he ever returned. However, he published five articles on his visit—three on Blackfeet folklore and two scientific discussions of Blackfeet as an Algonquian language. And he left hundreds of pages of unpublished field notes in both Blackfeet and English at the National Anthropological Archives.

Michelson strove to document the language so that scientists who had no working knowledge of it could read the words he wrote out and pronounce them correctly. He was critical of other linguists who produced texts that other scholars could not reproduce later without intimate knowledge of the language.[51] He worked primarily with David Duvall as his translator. And Michelson and Duvall have some of the best unpublished Blackfeet language materials available. Unlike other outside visitors Michelson recorded almost all the Blackfeet storytellers and songs on a Dictaphone. Michelson stated that "Duvall repeated the separate words of the informant. I wrote them down and repeated it to the satisfaction of Duvall and the informant. Subsequently I repeated them again to the satisfaction of Duvall, making corrections where needed: these were found to be extremely few."[52] After the stories were written in Blackfeet, the two men then translated them into English.

Michelson also utilized the services of Julia White Swan and her daughter Norah Thomas as translators. He apparently connected with them at the Holy Family Mission. Michelson and Duvall ultimately interviewed Eagle Child, Mountain Chief, Little Young Man, Julia Wades-in-the-Water, George Pablo, Henry No Bear, Black Bear, Big Moon, Bear Medicine, and Reuben Black Boy (who eventually worked as John C. Ewers's main translator). He also recorded the songs of Yellow Calf, Eagle Child, White Elk, Horn, Big Moon, Little Young Man, and other unidentified singers. Many of these men were members of the Crazy Dog Society.[53]

Of all the stories that Truman Michelson collected he published only about a half dozen. In his article "Piegan Tales" he wrote that collecting the stories "was merely incidental to obtaining first-hand knowledge of the [Blackfeet] language."[54] Michelson was aware of the collection of stories on Blackfeet mythology already published by Clark Wissler and David Duvall in 1908 and saw no need to duplicate it. His goal was to study the Algonquian language. Michelson left behind hundreds of pages of handwritten and recorded stories from his interviews with the Blackfeet in 1910, which the Blackfeet today consider to be important.

Cornelius C. Uhlenbeck, 1910s

The linguistics professor C. C. Uhlenbeck came from the Netherlands to conduct in-depth research on the Blackfeet language during the summer of 1910 and 1911.[55] He brought his graduate students and his family. They stayed at the Holy Family Mission on Two Medicine River and relied on a few individuals for their study. Uhlenbeck was the most prolific scholar of the Blackfeet language. He published *Original Blackfoot Texts from the Southern Piegans* in 1911 and *A New Series of Blackfoot Texts from the Southern Piegans* in 1912. His student J. P. B. de Josselin de Jong published *Blackfoot Texts from the Southern Peigans* [sic] *Reservation* in 1914. Uhlenbeck's most comprehensive linguistic study was his dictionary series, *An English-Blackfoot Vocabulary: Based on Material from the Southern Peigans* [sic], and its corresponding volume, *A Blackfoot-English Vocabulary: Based on Material from the Southern Peigans* [sic], both published in the early 1930s. The linguistic work conducted by Uhlenbeck is invaluable.

Uhlenbeck worked primarily with Joseph Tatsey. Tatsey worked both

Fig. 20. Sewing department, Cut Bank Boarding School. Image #638.128, Joseph H. Sherburne Family Papers, Archives and Special Collections, Maureen and Mike Mansfield Library, University of Montana–Missoula.

as a translator and as a collaborator, providing a wide variety of his own stories of Blackfeet history and lifeways. Uhlenbeck also utilized the help of Margaret Champagne and "Mission boys" John Tatsey, James Vielle, and Peter Bear Leggings as translators. Uhlenbeck's main collaborator was Bear Chief, a member of the Never Laughs band, the same band as my grandmother's family. Uhlenbeck also interviewed Mountain Chief, Jim Blood, White Quiver, Green Grass Bull, Eli Guardipee, Old Child, Walter Mountain Chief, Chief All Over, Four Horns, Many Guns, and many others. The summer before, in 1910, Uhlenbeck's graduate student Josselin de Jong had worked primarily with Walter Mountain Chief (Síkimiáχkitopi or Black Horse Rider), and others.

According to the diary of Willy Uhlenbeck, her husband also either interviewed or visited with my grandmother Annie Mad Plume's father Elmer Mad Plume, her uncles Richard and David Mad Plume, and her grandfather Mad Plume during the summer of 1911.[56] However, nowhere

Fig. 21. Dining hall, Cut Bank Boarding School. Image #638.132, Joseph H. Sherburne Family Papers, Archives and Special Collections, Maureen and Mike Mansfield Library, University of Montana–Missoula.

in the published record are they identified as being collaborators. It is possible that their contributions to his research were never incorporated into the final work. Uhlenbeck stated, "It is a pity, that some well-informed and experienced men among the tribe were not disposed to impart their valuable knowledge, and that some others, who were willing to help me along, could not spend so many hours with me, as I should have liked and needed."[57] His wife's diaries reflect both old men like my great-grandfather Mad Plume, who just stopped by to see the visitors from another place, and those whom Uhlenbeck tried to interview but could never persuade to be recorded.[58]

John C. Ewers, 1940s to 1950s

With each passing year more and more people died from disease and old age, and likewise with each passing year recorders of Blackfeet life knew that there would be fewer "buffalo Indians" for them to record.[59]

By the 1940s few remained. In the early 1940s the ethnologist John C. Ewers arrived at the Blackfeet reservation to work for the Indian Arts and Crafts Board, which built the Museum of the Plains Indian in Browning. Ewers set out to interview as many pre-reservation Indians as he could find. By this time most Blackfeet were bilingual; a few, usually the old, continued to be monolingual Blackfeet speakers. Although Ewers used interpreters with his older collaborators, he did not need to rely on his interpreters to access collaborators to the same extent as the earlier ethnographers. He systematically created a list based on the census and the local government agent's knowledge of the "buffalo Indians." He then tried to interview each person on the list. His collaborators did not have the same kinship relationships as those of earlier ethnographic efforts, because Ewers, not his interpreters, selected who he was going to interview. He relied primarily on Reuben and Cecile Black Boy for translation. His favorite collaborator, however, was Weasel Tail, a Kainai elder who lived on the Blackfeet reservation. But Ewers interviewed many others. His work produced two seminal studies on Blackfeet life—*The Horse in Blackfeet Culture* (1955) and *The Blackfeet: Raiders on the Northwestern Plains* (1958)—as well as dozens of articles and monographs. His massive collection of field notes from his interviews with the last "buffalo Indians" and the material objects he collected are in the National Museum of Natural History, Smithsonian Institution, in Washington DC and at its facilities in Suitland, Maryland.

"From very ancient times"

The storytakers came to the Blackfeet reservation with the intention of recording the stories and history of the Blackfeet. They were interested in Blackfeet life on the northern Great Plains when the bison were abundant and the Blackfeet were free from colonial restrictions. However, the storytellers had their own intentions as well. The interactions between the recorders and the recorded, the storytakers and the storytellers, was more than just for money or for the benefit of contemporary scholars. The Blackfeet did not create objects or tell stories that were devoid of meaning. They infused their objects, stories, and songs with the religious significance that they viewed as important and necessary to tell. The

Blackfeet told Grinnell, as recorded in *Blackfeet Indian Stories*, that "the stories here told come down to us from very ancient times," and they imparted the stories' importance to him.[60] When Holds Together Woman created a blanket band it was not just a pretty object for a museum. It was also a visible mnemonic device that told the story of a history of relationships with the invisible realm. Similar to a Christian person wearing a crucifix to declare their worldview, a blanket band was a visible reminder of the Blackfeet cosmology.

Elk Horn told Clark Wissler a few years before Holds Together Woman made her blanket band that creating a blanket band was a more complex process than just sewing it together. Elk Horn said that the women who created these bands had to follow proper religious protocol every day while working on their creation. Elk Horn stated that, "in conferring the power to put the band on—[the designer was required to] paint face red all over—[with a] black dot on each cheek."[61] The face paint design had reflected the meaning of the Blackfeet cosmology inscribed on the band. Elk Horn explained that the "black spots" on the maker's face represented the major deities of the Blackfeet. She painted the Sun on her forehead, the Mistaken Morning Star on her chin, the Moon on her left cheek, and the Morning Star on her right cheek. A smaller dot on her nose represented the "stationary star," or North Star.[62]

Elk Horn further explained that even though a blanket band had to look a specific way (because they all look the same), "the color and design [of the band] may be any way" depending on the designer's preference.[63] A Blackfeet woman created a blanket band as a singular object that then could be sewn across the middle of a bison robe or blanket that a person wore to public occasions. In this way, if a robe became old or worn out, the band could be removed and attached to a new robe. A typical blanket band was approximately four feet long, four inches wide, with four six-inch disks or circles placed evenly across the band. The result looked something like this: ●■●■●■●. The disks on a blanket band represented from left to right the four major deities in the Blackfeet worldview: the Sun, the Moon, the Mistaken Morning Star, and the Morning Star.[64] Blanket bands were yet another place for the Blackfeet to tell a story of how a young man, a human, went to the Sky world, befriended a star, was pitied by the Moon, killed some monsters, impressed the wrathful Sun, won over the beautiful maiden, and returned to the earth to share the power of his supernatural allies with his relatives.

The starry night sky was a real place that the Blackfeet could see every night; it was not imagined. The Blackfeet believed they were part of a living universe with which they could interact and with whom they had a relationship. Their own religious iconography gave them hope and reminded them that if that young man could do it, so could they.

CHAPTER 7

All That Remain

From the Prairies to the Atomic Age

My mother was born in 1940. She was the third child and third daughter of my grandparents Annie Mad Plume and Francis Aimsback.[1] They lived with my grandfather's parents, Páyotayàkχkumei, or Aimsback, and Kayetså'χkumi, or Hollering in the Air, on the south side of the reservation on Blacktail Creek. Within the next year my uncle Francis would also be born; he was the first son and grandson. Aimsback and Hollering in the Air never called my grandfather "Francis." They called him Iòkimau, and he went by this name his entire life. Iòkimau is a shortened form of the word ixtáiòkimau, which means "to make pemmican."[2] Since his parents adopted my grandfather when they were in their late forties, they raised him more like a grandchild than as a son. And by the time my mother was born her grandparents were considered ancient.

My mother remembers living with her grandparents, even though they would pass on while she was still young. Aimsback and Hollering in the Air did not learn to speak English and did not convert to Christianity. My grandfather Iòkimau learned to speak English at Holy Family Mission, the Catholic on-reservation boarding school. He did not attend Holy Family until he was a young teenager, and he attended only a few years.[3] Like all the male students at Holy Family he spent about two-thirds of his day out working on the mission farm in order for the mission to sustain itself. He also learned to play in the brass band at Holy Family, which was common for all male students. The brass band even played in front of John Philip Sousa once, or so the family story goes.

In the old days it was common for the youngest child in the family to live with the parents as their parents aged. My grandfather played that role in his family, apparently much to the chagrin of my grandmother. (She had many stories of living with her in-laws, but don't we all.) Aimsback and Hollering in the Air were both religious leaders on the south side of the reservation. My grandfather and grandmother assisted in their activities. My grandmother assisted Hollering in the Air with her role as a holy woman, especially at the annual O'kan. My grandfather learned all the songs of the various religious ceremonies and sang for his father. My mother and her siblings attended these events along with their parents. They grew up being purified every day and having their faces painted. Aimsback and Hollering in the Air owned O'maχkskimikokàup, or the "Big Rock" tipi, which they put up at various religious events, and they owned medicine bundles and several other religious objects.

My mother remembers that her parents always kept a part of their main living room empty of any furniture. The old-time Blackfeet did not like to sit on chairs. They preferred the ground or floor. Her grandmother Hollering in the Air used to always carry with her a piece of rolled-up canvas. My mother remembers her grandmother brushing off where she sat, carefully unrolling her canvas, and placing it on the ground to sit on. Sitting on chairs was another change to which the "buffalo Indians" did not readily adapt.

Aimsback named all of his grandchildren with Blackfeet names, and he called them by those names. Each one of the names that Aimsback selected for his grandchildren was taken from events in his own life. To older Blackfeet like Aimsback and his wife, English names held no meaning; they were just words. Blackfeet names, however, were rich with meaning and significance.[4] Names expressed the intertwined and interwoven histories and stories of relationships between humans and the supernatural world. Told collectively, Blackfeet names constituted a continuous narrative of the people, places, events, and history of the Blackfeet.

Aimsback named my mother Sépistaki, or Owl Woman. It seems like a simple name. However, the Blackfeet did not view owls as part of the natural world. Owls were not birds. The Blackfeet believed that owls were the reincarnation of powerful religious leaders (humans) who had passed on. In the afterlife these religious leaders became owls, simultaneously natural and supernatural, who could communicate with humans when they chose. The Blackfeet viewed communicating with an owl as a fortunate event. In the old days the Blackfeet thought that owls could give humans the power to heal, to be lucky in war, to acquire wealth, and to change nature itself.[5]

Aimsback had a relationship with an owl that lived on Blacktail Creek. Whenever Aimsback rode his horse along Blacktail Creek the owl talked to him and gave him advice. Aimsback believed that owls were the "spirits of people long dead." He believed, as did other Blackfeet, that if an owl hooted, a person should "request the owl for help," asking, "Father, help me! Give me good luck in the future."[6] In 1940, at the dawn of the atomic age, Aimsback gave my mother a simple name: Sépistaki, or Owl Woman. It was to remind everyone that he had a complex relationship with the larger universe. The owl spoke to Aimsback to tell him that he was not alone and to emphasize their longtime relationship, reminding him, "We are the ones that take care of you."[7]

Aim While Moving through the Air

Aimsback was what the scholar John C. Ewers called a "buffalo Indian." Aimsback was born sometime in the 1860s. He grew up on the prairies, in what is now central Montana, where his family hunted bison, gathered roots, berries, and medicine, and worshiped near the Sweet Pine Hills. He lived with and belonged to the A'pekaïks, or Skunks band, like its leader, who was his father, Unistássamme, or Calf Looking.[8] Aimsback was probably in his early twenties when the "starvation winter" occurred on the newly created Blackfeet reservation in 1883–84. Aimsback suffered through the transition from the loss of bison on the prairies, to relocating farther west to the mountains, through starvation and disease, to living a sedentary life on the reservation. In 1905 Clark Wissler described this transition to Franz Boas: "[The Blackfoot] industrial life was destroyed about thirty years ago, when the United States and Canadian Governments confined them to reservations. . . . Art and religion are all that remain."[9]

Aimsback married two sisters, Calf Woman and Hollering in the Air, which was common in his time. Calf Woman and Hollering in the Air were the daughters of Little Plume and Spear Woman. They were members of Iχ'púχsimaiks, or the Fat Melters band.[10] Aimsback's wives were also half-sisters with Gretchen Duvall, the wife of David Duvall.[11] However, after Calf Woman died, he did not marry another. He remained married only to Hollering in the Air for the rest of his life.[12] Aimsback could not have children. Instead he adopted. He was probably in his forties when he adopted my grandfather in the 1910s.[13] Aimsback and the Skunks band eventually settled on the south side of the reservation, initially at Birch Creek and then at Blacktail Creek.[14] My grandfather grew up on

Blacktail Creek. His mother, Hollering in the Air, arranged his marriage with my grandmother's family. This was common at the time. After he married my grandmother they lived with his parents and raised their young children, including my mother, at Blacktail.

There are brief glimpses of Aimsback's life that can be found within the historical record, beginning with the 1907 tribal census used to determine allotments. Despite the fact that the Dawes General Allotment Act was passed in 1887 and that numerous other reservations had already been allotted, the Blackfeet had not been allotted at the time. The U.S. government conducted an extensive (although in no way perfect) census in 1907 and 1908 before determining families to be allotted land. The government apparently made an effort to allot land to individual families where they had settled on the reservation. The U.S. government allotted Aimsback land at Blacktail Creek, where the Skunks band had settled. The allotment process continued from 1907 to 1912 on the Blackfeet reservation, at which point the surplus lands of the reservation were supposed to open up to white settlers. However, the Blackfeet fought the opening up of their reservation, and in 1919 Congress passed a resolution allowing the Blackfeet to allot their surplus lands to tribal members.[15] It was not until after the government settled the surplus land situation on the Blackfeet reservation that they began a new agricultural program.

The U.S. government had initially divided the reservation into four agricultural districts in the late nineteenth century. However, when Fred Campbell became the new agency superintendent in 1921 he expanded the number of districts to twenty-nine "chapters."[16] He then started the Piegan Farming and Livestock Association and a "Five Year Industrial Program" in an effort to focus on small-market and subsistence-level farming and not large-scale farming and ranching.[17] The Haskell Indian School's national newspaper, the *Indian Leader*, reported that Blackfeet "chapter-membership averaged about 15 families, and these families were associated together through relationship or marriages prior to the time of allotments and were allotted in communities accordingly, so that a chapter membership, in many instances, comprises a large family group."[18] Unbeknown to the Blackfeet agent, Campbell had essentially reauthorized the Blackfeet band system overnight. This move to

Fig. 22. Aimsback and Hollering in the Air. Photo courtesy National Archives and Records Administration (Record Group 75), Denver.

a certain extent allowed band relationships to remain intact for a while at the beginning of the twentieth century. Even though many Blackfeet families, especially those living on the south side of the reservation, had continued to live in communities centered on their old band affiliations, now they could do it with government sanction.[19]

At some point in the early twentieth century my great-grandfather's name Páyotayàkχkumei (Payottaayawaahkomi), or Aim While Moving through the Air, was translated into English as Aims-Back.[20] It was probably translated by a government worker for a government census in the nineteenth century and then used thereafter. My grandfather said that the name described the ability of a person to turn backward while riding on a horse and then accurately shoot a bow and arrow. Aim While Moving through the Air was an elegant name. It described a skill that was necessary for his former life on the northern Great Plains and unfortunately a skill that was no longer required in his new sedentary life as a farmer. It also described a relationship between Aimsback and his supernatural allies, who provided him with the gift and ability to aim while moving through the air.

Capitalism and Competition

In one of those odd flukes of historical research my husband and nephew discovered a file on Aimsback in the President's Subject Files for the Great Northern Railway Company at the Minnesota Historical Society in Saint Paul, Minnesota. It was serendipitous to say the least, because nowhere in the archival finding aid was there a mention of his name. My husband took our (then) young nephew, Martin Beck, with him to the Minnesota Historical Society one day to show him what historians do and to help us conduct research on a book project we were working on.[21] And on that day they found a file on Aimsback, my great-grandfather. Eureka!

Apparently Fred Campbell and the Blackfeet agency acquired funds from the Great Northern Railway to sponsor the winning prize for an agricultural contest on the Blackfeet reservation. The prize was an award-winning steer, which apparently the Great Northern would transport by railcar from Minnesota to Montana. This contest occurred in the early 1920s after the U.S. government had divided the Blackfeet reservation into twenty-nine agricultural chapters or districts, which formed the Piegan Farming and Livestock Association (PFLA).[22] It is difficult to know if the competition was among all twenty-nine chapters or if it was only the final competition between the two chapters listed in the file. The thin file held a fascinating array of drawings, letters, and documents of that year's final competition between the Bull Shoe and Aimsback Chapters of the PFLA on the south side of the reservation.[23]

The purpose of the PFLA was to encourage small-market and subsistence farming on the reservation and to engender social change within Blackfeet families. Within the file was held a five-page list used to tally the competition points with merits and demerits: building a "chicken house," plus ten points; owning a chicken, plus five points; owning "more than two dogs," minus ten points. The points reflected the new American assimilationist efforts the U.S. government hoped to encourage: work horses and farm animals, yes; dogs, no. The file contained detailed information regarding the contest, which took place over the summer and fall growing seasons between the Bull Shoe and Aimsback Chapters of the PFLA.[24]

Finding a list of the relative merits and demerits of my own family's home life was shocking, to say the least. There were even points assessed for the "general appearance of home including children"—plus fifteen points! However, the file also included cartoonlike drawings that I assume were meant for entertainment and were reminiscent of the "winter counts" of old. These cartoons depicted Bull Shoe and Aimsback in a tug-of-war. In one they are both holding on to the end of the prize steer, with Bull Shoe pulling its tail and Aimsback pulling its horns. The steer looks comically toward its readers in mock alarm. Bull Shoe is depicted in short hair, wearing modern clothing and cowboy boots, whereas Aimsback is shown with long braids, moccasins, and work clothes. The drawing depicted the two sides of the Blackfeet narrative at that time: those who appear to have Americanized and those who were still in the process of transitioning. The drawings were made by Richard Sanderville, a well-known Blackfeet official from the south side of the reservation.[25]

The file also included a written report to the president of Great Northern explaining the contest, the point system, and the ultimate winner at the end of the season. The purpose of having a contest was to create a friendly competition between chapters and to introduce American values such as capitalism, individualism, and thrift. Campbell stated, "At the meeting of the Bull Shoe chapter last week, Judge No Coat in his remark stated that he felt that their chapter would be entirely disgraced if they would allow the Aimsback chapter to lead the bull over the hill." The Bullshoe Chapter won, with 738 points; the Aimsback Chapter acquired only 460 points.[26] It had been more than seventy years since the first efforts to introduce the Blackfeet to farming—the 1855 Lame Bull's treaty (back before Aimsback was probably even born). In the 1920s the U.S. government was still trying to figure out ways to transform the Blackfeet into farmers.

On the one hand it was historically fascinating to view a file with such rich history and documentation of governmental public policy and process. Historians have long written about allotment, agriculture, forced assimilation, and the acculturation process in tribal communities. I have read (with historical objectivity) many of those works. However, it is another experience altogether to view the story of your own family being judged in such a public way in a competition that literally graded the contents of one's own family, dirty laundry and all.

These efforts of encouraging capitalism did not garner what the U.S. government hoped for; none of Aimsback's descendants ever became farmers. However, similar to other Blackfeet, I do own a dog. Minus ten points.

Industrial Survey

In the spring of 1921 the U.S. government conducted an "industrial survey" of farming cooperatives on several reservations, including the Blackfeet reservation. The U.S. government took photographs of each Native American family within the survey area, usually sitting or standing in front of their home. The survey then reported on the condition of the family, home, and farm. Data taken included information on food and food storage systems, such as the existence of a root cellar, the types and number of canned or preserved goods on hand, and other stored vegetables. It listed farming equipment and the numbers of farm animals, such as cattle, sheep, goats, and chickens. It listed the types of grains under cultivation to sell to the market and what was in the home garden. These reports often used value-laden language that compared the lifestyles of Native American families to standard, middle-class American ideals for home and family.[27]

"Aimsback and wife" garnered a two-page report in the 1921 Blackfeet Industrial Survey. It included a black-and-white photo of Aimsback and Hollering in the Air. A caption stated that they had an eighteen-year-old son and a nine-year-old son (my grandfather). But it did not include a photo with the boys. The photo showed them both wearing moccasins; Hollering in the Air's are plain, while Aimsback's were vividly beaded. They both have long braids and plain clothing. He is wearing work pants and a work coat, with a scarf around his neck. She is wearing a long plaid dress and a plain neck scarf, and she is covered in a large plaid shawl. Compared to other photographs of Blackfeet in the Industrial Survey, Aimsback and Hollering in the Air's clothing would have been considered to be the common dress that the old-timers would wear on the reservation.[28]

The Industrial Survey also reported if the Blackfeet families were either in "ward" or "trust" status. The tribe began issuing "trust patents" to allotments in February 1918.[29] However, in 1921 Aimsback was listed under "ward" status. Aimsback and Hollering in the Air's home fared well by comparison to others. The reported stated theirs "was a quite well improved two room house, very clean and well kept." The survey reported that Aimsback had broken and seeded ten acres of wheat and was planning a one-acre home garden that year. He had four horses but no cattle or chickens. The report noted that "this is a very attractive allotment and Aimsback seems to have the proper spirit."[30] *Yikes*

The "Five Year Industrial Program" and the Piegan Farming and Live-stock Association encouraged the efforts of Blackfeet farmers. On the south side of the reservation they held "farmers' institutes" in the nearby village of Heart Butte to teach details about farming. The PFLA and these gatherings also engendered a political voice for the group's new leadership.[31] When Agent Campbell tried at one of the farmers' institutes to encourage some Blackfeet to move to different allotments, Aimsback "stated that after considering all the different features that he thought it was better to remain on his own allotment rather than to leave home and allow his home to deteriorate."[32]

Throughout the "Five Year Industrial Program" Aimsback apparently served as one of the leaders in the PFLA. Like his father, who had been the leader of the Skunks band, Aimsback grew to be the leader of a chapter of the PFLA. In 1923 Aimsback and Hollering in the Air traveled to Washington DC with a contingent of Blackfeet leaders. They were all photographed standing in front of the U.S. Capitol. The Bureau of American Ethnology also took photographs of both Aimsback and Hollering in the Air while they were in Washington DC.[33] In addition to the transcontinental travel opportunity that PFLA leadership entailed, Aimsback and Hollering in the Air also entered the competitions and harvest fairs created to encourage and reward participation.[34]

Despite all this effort on the part of the U.S. government, states the historian Paul Rosier, "the allotment policy failed miserably on the Blackfeet reservation, as it did elsewhere in the nation."[35] Participants such as Henry Magee stated that the small subsistence farms were "hardly enough to be economically profitable," that they "lack[ed] sufficient farm machinery" to make their allotments successful. Magee added that "in his own case he found there was so much time spent in meetings, discussions, etc. [h]e did not have time to tend to his farming and attend them all."[36]

The purpose of the agricultural program in the 1920s was to develop self-sufficient and self-sustaining farms and gardens growing domesticated American crops. However, a decade after the startup of the Blackfeet Industrial Program, a significant amount of the food preserved by Blackfeet women continued to come from native plant sources and not from their new American home gardens. The federal government's Extension Service reported in 1933 that "among native fruits and berries canned by Indian women on the Reservation in the 12th Annual Mid-Winter Fair were: canned—chokecherry syrup, huckleberries, strawberries, gooseberries, sarvis berries, bullberries, chokecherry jelly; dried fruits—choke cherries, sarvis berries, dried meats, pemmican etc."[37] These are all Native species, and none came from the introduced species of the American gardens.

My grandmother's stories of Aimsback and Hollering in the Air never told of their farming history or his leadership in an agricultural chapter on the reservation. Besides farming they also got seasonal work at the newly created Glacier National Park as part of its emerging tourism economy. Glacier Park even sold their images in full Native regalia on postcards, even though in reality, as the 1921 Industrial Survey photographs show, Aimsback wore old trousers and a tattered jacket with his moccasins and Hollering in the Air wore a homemade plaid dress in their everyday life. Why didn't my family share this history that is documented in the archives? Probably because, similar to other "buffalo Indians," Aimsback and Hollering in the Air were concerned with a different kind of relationship to the natural and supernatural world.

Big Rock Tipi

Aimsback believed that the Blackfeet lived in a universe with three interconnected worlds. He believed that on earth lived both supernatural and natural beings. He taught my grandfather these same beliefs. He believed that humans could find supernatural allies that would help them live a prosperous life. He thought it was foolish to do otherwise. Aimsback held a belief similar to Mad Wolf's observation that "the Blackfeet are firm believers in the Supernatural and in the control of human affairs by both Good and Evil Powers in the invisible world."[38]

The most important belief that Aimsback taught my grandfather was that the Blackfeet believed that with supernatural allies they could have some semblance of "control over human affairs," over the natural world, and ultimately over their own destiny. It made them positive and hopeful. My grandfather always told us to "pray for the unfortunate people," because he truly believed he was a fortunate person. But that belief was based on his and his parents' relationship with the supernatural.

In the 1930s the Federal Writers' Project hired Cecile Black Boy, the daughter of Going After Water, a well-known Blackfeet "skilled craftswoman," to interview the Blackfeet about their stories and "legends."[39] Cecile Black Boy ultimately recorded 245 Blackfeet stories for the Montana Federal Writers' Project.[40] One unique project that Cecile worked on was that she attempted to record the stories of the many different painted tipis of the Blackfeet. George Bird Grinnell and S. A. Barrett wrote about the painted tipis as well.[41] However, neither Grinnell nor Barrett tried to collect all the stories of the various painted tipis among the Blackfeet.

One of the stories that Cecile Black Boy collected was the story of the "Big Rock" tipi. It was the tipi owned by Aimsback and Hollering in the Air. Grinnell stated that "the paintings on the lodges represent sacred animals or objects which possess protective powers and the painting was adopted and is continued to insure good luck."[42] The story of the Big Rock tipi to a certain extent was well known among the Blackfeet, even though owning the tipi was unique to Aimsback's experiences with the supernatural.

Cecile Black Boy described it as the "Legend of the Big Rock Teepee which was given to the abandoned child who later grew up over night and became a great kind of warrior."[43] The story is long and includes many characters, twists, and turns, and it details an epic journey or quest for justice. And unlike most Western legends the story of the Big Rock tipi does not have a "moral." It is instead a story of the origin of the tipi. Like several other Blackfeet stories this one begins with the abandonment of children, their being taken captive by a supernatural evil woman, their escape, their being found by an elderly grandmother and her supernatural dog, the transformation of a young boy into a man, his revenge on their abductors, and his ultimate ascent to leadership, all with the help of his new supernatural ally. As Cecile Big Boy recounted, "This boy [now man] remembered the lodge where all the children had been killed by the old woman. It was a teepee of big rocks and in later years he painted his teepee the same way the Big Rock teepee is painted now."[44]

In 1944 two professors from Montana State University, Olga Ross Hannon and Jessie Wilber of the Art Department, photographed Aimsback and Hollering in the Air's tipi at the annual Heart Butte O'kan. Jessie Wilber later created a color silk screen of their tipi.[45] John C. Ewers also attended the same O'kan as the two professors.[46] He wrote that "these tipis were of religious significance, being a part of a complex of sacred objects and rituals and taboos surrounding the Indian owners as long as they possessed the tipis."[47] He recounted, though, how in 1944 "it was a small encampment of but 13 lodges and a larger number of tents. Only four of

Fig. 23. Minnie Aimsback and the Big Rock tipi, Heart Butte, 1944. Photo courtesy Jessie Wilber Papers, MS 2252, Merrill G. Burlingame Special Collections, Montana State University, image #ORH 108.

Fig. 24. Heart Butte, general tipis, 1942. Photo courtesy Jessie Wilber Papers, MS 2252, Merrill G. Burlingame Special Collections, Montana State University, image #ORH 6.

the 13 were painted (Albert Mad Plume's, Aimsback's, Swims Under's and Running Crane's)."[48] Part of the Big Rock tipi Aimsback and Hollering in the Air owned was a fossil with supernatural connection that they carried with them their entire lives. And then my grandfather and grandmother owned it. In the old days the Blackfeet utilized supernatural fossils such as "worm rocks," which controlled insects that might be harming their edible plants, as well as "oyster rocks" to cross over rivers, "copper rocks" that made humans stronger and resilient, and "buffalo rocks" to entice buffalo to their deaths.[49] Some of these fossils or rocks were owned as separate religious objects. The Aimsbacks' fossil or rock provided them "protective powers," and it was part of their tipi's religious bundle.

A New Kind of Indian

I thought it would be challenging to look for "real stories," as my grandmother called them, about the Blackfeet relationship with their supernatural allies, but I found instead that these stories were ubiquitous. They seemed to be everywhere. All of the early recorders of Blackfeet life recorded them. Clark Wissler even commented in 1912 that "a considerable collection of these tales could be made without difficulty."[50] If the stories left behind by the old-time Blackfeet were not stories of the hardships of daily life or the transition to being farmers but of their belief in the supernatural and their relationship with nature, I decided that should be my focus. I began this book by looking at life on the reservation in 1910, the year before my grandfather was born, in an effort to begin to understand the stories that the old-time Blackfeet did not share. And I wanted to end by reflecting on the lives of my grandfather's parents, who, as Wissler told Boas, lived in a world of "art and religion."[51]

The Blackfeet at the turn of the twentieth century were not afraid to share information about Blackfeet religious belief. As Mad Wolf told McClintock, "I will reveal many things in order that you may know there is nothing harmful in our worship. You can then explain our religion to the white people, for we know you are straight and will speak the truth."[52] Almost fifty years after Mad Wolf spoke to McClintock, John C. Ewers recorded that the "earlier generations" or the "buffalo Indians" that he interviewed in the 1940s were "not secretive." They invited him to attend the "most secret medicine ceremony," and they wanted their stories "recorded for the record."[53]

In the summer of 1910 David Duvall interviewed Mountain Chief about the history of the Blackfeet. Mountain Chief told Duvall a story that his father had told him about an old man predicting the future of the Blackfeet. Mountain Chief stated, "When his father was a young man he saw a very old man with a cane walking in a circle about a lodge, foretelling the future. [The old man] said that the Piegans [Blackfeet] would soon die out." Mountain Chief's father said that the old man predicted that a transformation would take place in the future and out of this transformation would emerge "a different people, a new kind of Indian, they would sit in the branches of trees."[54]

By the beginning of the twentieth century Mountain Chief's father's stories were coming to fruition. "A new kind of Indian" was emerging. The historian Paul Rosier has recounted how the Blackfeet from 1885 to 1915 "had become poor, hungry, and neglected, living in the margins." He describes how the tribe created a "syncretic Blackfeet political culture," one that blended Blackfeet methods of decision making with newly introduced, U.S.-created political structures.[55] In the same time period a similar process was taking place in terms of individual economy. At the turn of the twentieth century the "old system" was gone, and the Blackfeet were learning how to navigate the new economy. However, even with this new American system the Blackfeet did not prosper; they continued to suffer through periods of disease, malnutrition, and starvation well into the twentieth century. A visiting U.S. senator stated during the time of my grandparents' births that "starvation is the primary though indirect cause of many deaths among [the full-blood community]."[56] The statement was especially true for those on the south side of the reservation, where Aimsback and Hollering in the Air lived.

By the turn of the twentieth century the Blackfeet were learning to blend the new methods of farming and ranching with the old methods of hunting and gathering, albeit while confined to a much smaller landscape. They continued to struggle to make a living from numerous U.S. government economic development ventures of the early twentieth century, such as the tribal cattle operation, subsistence agricultural programs, or wage-labor digging irrigation ditches.[57] The Blackfeet also added new methods of gaining a living, such as selling their stories, songs, pictures, and objects to interested outsiders.

Aimsback was a "buffalo Indian." He had been born in a tipi, traveled with the seasons on a horse and with a travois, and experienced a world without roads or fences. However, the early twentieth century was a time of transition for the Blackfeet and for the northern Great Plains. The buffalo were gone, and the "buffalo Indians" were forced to do something alien to them. They had to stay in one place. Bear Chief, the leader of the Never Laughs band, my grandmother's band, stated what all knew at the time regarding the changing times: "'When the buffalo went away,' he said, 'I saw that we must change.'"[58] They moved into enclaves along the rivers and creeks within the boundaries of the modern-day reservation. They built log cabins and began to eat beef. Their children began to learn to speak a new language.

However, some like Aimsback continued to believe in the power of their supernatural allies. He believed he could talk to nature and that it would talk back. His understanding of and relationship with the supernatural provided him confidence and stability in an unstable changing world. These are the stories that my family shared. Once while Aimsback, Hollering in the Air, and my grandfather Iòkimau were out in the pasture cutting hay they stopped for a meal in their old canvas tent. Hollering in the Air was putting dry meat into the woodstove when they suddenly heard a very loud crackling sound. This sound hit them so violently that they all fell to the ground. Aimsback heard a voice calling out to him, and it said, "My name is Natoas Kistakumaki—Holy Thunder Woman." She told him that she did not kill them, although she had the power to do so. Instead she wanted to communicate with Aimsback, become one of his supernatural allies, and bring him good fortune. She told him, "I wanted to strike you folks, so you folks can live a good life."

Epilogue

And the Dogs Have Separated

Several years ago, after about twenty years of learning about plants and the natural world with my grandmother and after she had told me many different family stories, she ended that day by announcing, "Now, you are an old woman."[1] What she meant by this was that I had finally learned what she wanted to share and that I would be able to share her knowledge with others. The stories she shared were stories she had begun learning in the 1910s from old-timers or "buffalo Indians" about Blackfeet life before the reservation.

This book seeks to explore many different interconnected subjects: life on the reservation at the turn of the century, the role of outside scholars who recorded information about Blackfeet knowledge, the Blackfeet who told stories to outsiders, the Blackfeet belief system and how it informed their understanding of nature, and their resilience despite hardship. The 1880s to the 1910s was a complex time for the Blackfeet. The older generation, the ones who reached adulthood before the reservation, were struggling with disorientation. They learned that their vast environmental knowledge was of little use within the confines of the reservation and the reservation economy.

Both of my maternal grandparents were born in the 1910s on the Blackfeet reservation in northwest Montana. They were both raised by older extended family members. Their own parents could not raise them due to a variety of factors, primarily the changing economy and its impact on family structure. They were both raised by people much older than their own parents. In my grandmother's case she was raised by two old women: her maternal grandmother and her great-grandmother. My grandfather was adopted by two older family members who were the age of his grandparents. This older generation was in the process of experiencing a dramatic transition. Most lived into their adult years according to the Blackfeet nomadic lifestyle of hunting, gathering wild roots and berries, and living out on the prairies before the demise of the bison. At the turn of the twentieth century the U.S. government expected them to be farmers, plant small home gardens, herd cattle, and, most dramatically, live in one place.

The older generation's life experiences were different from those of their children or their grandchildren who were born on the reservation. At the beginning of the twentieth century the Blackfeet were undergoing a rapid social and economic shift. Although the bison had disappeared almost twenty-five years before my grandparents were born, the effects of that collapse on the Blackfeet social and economic lifestyle were still being felt in the newly created reservation community. For the older generation life was difficult. They were accustomed to a close and intimate relationship with a large area the size of Montana, not one where they had limited connection to much smaller ecosystems. Their understanding and views of nature were shaped by their experiences of life on the prairies and their distinctive worldview.

While this dramatic shift was occurring on the reservation, modern America discovered these old-time Indians. They believed that Indians, like the bison, would soon be gone. Dozens of museum curators, academics, government officials, and amateurs flocked to the Blackfeet reservation to gather information and collect material culture. With them a new economy emerged on the reservation. Old-timers learned they could make money selling old stories, old songs, and even their old clothing and moccasins. Instead of going bison hunting for a living, now old men told stories about bison hunting. Instead of sewing bison-hide tipis, now old women told stories about how to design a bison-hide tipi. Selling the nostalgia of the past became a part of their present-day lives.

The stories they told and sold were not always the types of stories that these early recorders of Blackfeet life were expecting. The stories they told spoke of resilience, strength, and relationships with the supernatural. Blackfeet religion provided this older generation with continuity and stability in their chaotic lives. George Bird Grinnell pointed this out in "Indians and Their Stories," his preface to *Blackfoot Lodge Tales*, in 1892. He observed how non-Natives wrote about Native Americans as if they were non-Natives without taking into account how Native Americans might think and represent themselves differently. He added that "the feelings which lead an Indian to perform a particular action are not those which would induce a white man to do the same thing."[2] By this he meant that the Blackfeet were motivated by their religious belief system. He pointed out that "the Indian is intensely religious. No people pray more earnestly nor more frequently. This is especially true of all Indians on the Plains."[3] At the foundation of the Blackfeet belief system was a different perception of everyday reality.

I began this book by recounting my own "Aha" moment when I realized that the old-time Indians did not believe that they live "in harmony and balance" with nature the way we portray them today. Instead they believed that they could "change and control" nature. What a powerful worldview! This book is an effort to tell a part of this story of the Blackfeet religious belief system and their understanding of the natural world. Now, at its closing, I am sure that readers will be wondering to what extent (if any) and in what ways the religious beliefs and relationship with the natural world persist into the twenty-first century. How has generational turnover affected those beliefs? What are the legacies of the turn-of-the-twentieth-century history written about in this book? Are the Blackfeet still shaped by that history? If so, how?

I am not sure that I can (or want to) answer all of those questions. I will say that the Blackfeet are still affected by the colonial policies and politics of the past and we did not become farmers. Others have written of this history.[4] We continue to persist into the twenty-first century. I am fortunate to have two grown daughters, who often learned about plants and family stories from my grandmother. I was fortunate to have spent as much time as I did with my grandmother. She was fortunate to have learned from her two old "buffalo Indian" grandmothers, women who had both hunted bison and gathered roots and berries on the northern Great Plains. The North Peigan religious leader Brings Down the Sun recognized the changing times at the turn of the last century when he observed, "At one time animals and men were able to understand each other. We still talk to the animals just as we do to people, but they now seldom reply, except in dreams."[5]

I wrote the majority of this book on the Blackfeet reservation. One night as I was finishing this book I had a dream.[6] In the dream a grizzly bear came to my camp. (I live up in the mountains during the summers.) I was in my sleeping bag in my tent, but I was not alarmed. I just thought I would wait. However, after looking around, the bear poked its head under the tent covering. It greeted me forehead to forehead, nose to nose. I could feel its large head next to mine, as well as the heat and moisture from its breathing. It took a deep breath and slowly breathed in my breath. And then it left.

The next morning I felt as if I had done strenuous exercise—I felt out of breath. I decided to make strong coffee and sit for a moment. After this (being a modern Blackfeet), I contacted my family and friends and told them of the dream. My friend Leslie immediately contacted me back, saying "Wow! That's powerful!" She added that for the Ojibwe, "Bears are our warrior clan, our front-line protectors in battle. They also govern the medicine found in the woods." My immediate family also responded with "Wow!"

As I sat there drinking my coffee, my breathing did not completely return to normal. I thought, WWOTD, or what would the old-timers do? My grandmother had told me that in the old days the way that women purified themselves was to bathe in a river or lake, then smudge with the incense of certain plants, and then paint their faces with earth minerals. I thought I should do as the old people would have done.

I set up kindling for a fire and put my incense next to it. I then went down to the lake, which was completely still in the cool early morning. I walked into the water. As I turned around to look back at the shore, I saw a grizzly bear about twenty yards up the shore walking toward me. I waited as it continued to walk closer. I thought it was going to walk by me. But then in a moment it was gone. I listened and looked to see if it was climbing the hill or walking the other direction, but somehow it had completely disappeared.

Brings Down the Sun's observation may have been true. Maybe our ability as humans to talk to animals has changed. But clearly *their* efforts to continue to communicate with us have not changed even into the twenty-first century. Once after my grandmother told a story of Spotted Bear and his relationship with the natural and supernatural world, she said to me something that I will repeat again: "That was really true . . . a real story. You can write it down."

At the end of a story the Blackfeet say *ki ánetòyi imitáiks*, which translates to "and the dogs have separated."

NOTES

PREFACE

1. Works that have addressed various issues related to scholarship about Native peoples include, among others, Deloria, *Red Earth, White Lies*; Mihesuah, ed., *Natives and Academics*; L. Smith, *Decolonizing Methodologies*; and Said, *Culture and Imperialism*.

2. DeMarce, *Blackfeet Heritage*; Josselin de Jong, "Social Organization"; Uhlenbeck, *New Series of Blackfoot Texts*; and Uhlenbeck, *Original Blackfoot Texts*.

3. Powwow culture on the Blackfeet reservation was a new activity during my childhood. And it was not until my adulthood that many Blackfeet began to view powwows as part of "authentic" Blackfeet cultural activity. Since the new powwow culture was foreign to her understanding of the Blackfeet experience, my grandmother referred to powwows as something "those hippie Indians" did.

4. Uhlenbeck and Van Gulik, *English-Blackfoot Vocabulary*, 157.

5. It is possible that he was named after the Irish nationalist who became the acting governor of Montana Territory, Thomas Francis Meagher.

6. "Constitution and By-Laws for the Blackfeet Tribe."

7. I wrote three brief articles about the Blackfeet side of my family: one on my grandmother, LaPier, "Blackfoot Botanist"; one on my great-grandfather Aimsback, LaPier, "From the Natural to the Supernatural"; and one on names, LaPier, "What's in a Name?"

8. Peterson and Brown, *New People*.

9. Throughout my life I have identified myself as Métis, Chippewa, and Ojibwe—but never "breed."

10. I wrote two book chapters about the Métis in Montana, some of which is a history of my family: LaPier, "Métis Life along Montana's Front Range"; and LaPier, "Between Hay and Grass." I also wrote a magazine article: LaPier, "Métis Miskihkiya."

11. My uncle Francis and aunt Shirley Wall went in search of our Irish family records in the 1990s. They found records that our ancestors were from the Wall and Conklin families and came to Montana via Boston and Ireland. I have a great-great-grandfather Patrick Conklin. They are also listed in DeMarce, *Blackfeet Heritage.*

12. L. P. Hartley was a British novelist who wrote that phrase in his novel *The Go-Between*, 17.

13. Farr, "Troubled Bundles, Troubled Blackfeet."

14. The Piegan Institute is a private nonprofit on the Blackfeet reservation with a mission to revitalize the Blackfeet language. I began working with the Piegan Institute in 1991, while I was employed at NAES College, a private, Native-controlled college. However, it was not until 1999 that I began an ongoing working relationship with the Piegan Institute, directing research projects and raising funds. I raised around $4 million during that time. My relationship with Piegan Institute ended after the deaths of two of its founders, Thomas Little Plume in 2008 and Darrell Robes Kipp in 2013. In 2008 I founded, with Darrell Robes Kipp and a group of Blackfeet women, a new community-based organization called Saokio Heritage.

15. See LaPier and Crow Shoe, "Blackfeet Vocabulary Terms for Items of Material Culture."

16. Tribal Council Minutes, December 2, 1943, in possession of John C. Ewers, Series xiv, Box 2, John C. Ewers Papers (hereafter, Ewers Papers), National Anthropological Archives, National Museum of Natural History, Smithsonian Institution, Washington DC (hereafter, NAA-SI).

17. Deloria, *God Is Red.*

18. Nabokov, *Forest of Time*, 53.

19. Wissler and Duvall, *Mythology of the Blackfoot*, 17. Wissler was an ethnographer from the American Museum of Natural History who along with his Blackfeet collaborator, David Duvall, recorded more stories than any other early recorder.

20. Wissler and Duvall, *Mythology of the Blackfoot*, 17 (emphasis added).

21. Grinnell, *Blackfoot Lodge Tales.*

22. See Prothero, *God Is not One*; and Martin, *Jesuit's Guide to (Almost) Everything.*

23. Hallowell, "Ojibway Ontology."

24. Father Emile Legal, O.M.I., "1885 Field Notes on Customs, Legends and Other Stories among the Blackfoot People," translated by Maurice Goutier, O.M.I., Oblates of Mary Immaculate Papers, Provincial Archives of Alberta, Edmonton AB.

25. "Reckoning Time," in Wissler, *Social Life of the Blackfoot Indians*, 44–50.

26. Harrod, *Animals Came Dancing*, xix–xx.

27. Ewers, *The Blackfeet*, 89.

28. Dempsey, *Blackfoot War Art*, 25–63.

29. Harrod, *Renewing the World*, 20.

30. Harrod, *Animals Came Dancing*, xx.

31. L. Smith, *Decolonizing Methodologies*, 28.

32. Ewers, personal note to self, Series XIV, Box 3, Ewers Papers.

33. Ewers, *The Blackfeet*, ix.

INTRODUCTION

1. See the preface for a discussion of Blackfeet versus Blackfoot Confederacy and the original name, Amskapi Pikuni.

2. McClintock, *Old North Trail*.

3. Agnes (No Runner) Wells (born 1905) and her husband, Albert Wells (born 1902), were respected cultural leaders of their day. They were interviewed by scholars, including Howard Harrod, who was researching Blackfeet religious beliefs for his dissertation and his book, *Mission among the Blackfeet*.

4. Farr, "Troubled Bundles, Troubled Blackfeet," 8.

5. H. Dempsey and Moir, *Bibliography of the Blackfoot*.

6. Ewers, *The Blackfeet*, 18.

7. H. Dempsey and Moir, *Bibliography of the Blackfoot*. Of course scholars have written a lot more in the last quarter century.

8. Ewers used the phrase "buffalo Indian" to describe Blackfeet who were born, raised, and lived to adulthood before the demise of the bison herds. Ewers and other ethnographers preferred interviewing only "buffalo Indians" because of their distinct knowledge of "nomadic" life on the northern Great Plains.

1. NO NOTHING

1. "An act to ratify and confirm an agreement with the Gros Ventre, Piegan Blood, Blackfeet, and River Crow Indians in Montana, and for other purposes," May 1, 1888, in Kappler, *Indian Affairs, Laws and Treaties*, 1:261–66; and also in Ewers, *The Blackfeet*, 304. More than two hundred Blackfeet men signed the executive agreement in February 1888 to sell the Sweet Grass Hills, an area of strategic political value and religious significance.

2. Her name is often translated as Red Shell Woman, but a more literal translation is Salmon-Colored Supernatural Fossilized Shell Woman. See my article on names: LaPier, "What's in a Name?"

3. DeMarce, *Blackfeet Heritage*, 162.

4. Adam White Man, interview by John Ewers, interpreted by Louis Bear Child, September 7, 1951, "Blackfeet Political Organization #1, Piegan Bands," Series xiv, Box 4, Ewers Papers.

5. Father J. B. Carroll married my great-grandparents at Holy Family Mission.

6. Carroll, "Fourth of July Dishonored," 28. In this article Father Carroll correctly called the Blackfeet the "South Piëgan Indians."

7. O'kan is often translated as "Sun Dance" or "Medicine Lodge." However, neither phrase is a literal translation.

8. The most complete study of the O'kan is found in Wissler, *Sun Dance of the Blackfoot Indians*. He conducted his research on the O'kan beginning in the summer of 1903.

9. Wissler, *Sun Dance of the Blackfoot Indians*, 231.

10. Carroll, "Fourth of July Dishonored," 29.

11. Carroll, "Fourth of July Dishonored," 32.

12. United States, Office of Indian Affairs, *Annual Report of the Commissioner of Indian Affairs, for the Year 1882*, 98–100.

13. United States, Office of Indian Affairs, *Annual Report of the Commissioner of Indian Affairs, for the Year 1880*, 105–7.

14. Carroll, "Fourth of July Dishonored," 29.

15. Browning Mercantile Company Records, 1907–27, Box 1, Manuscript Collection 230, Montana Historical Society, Helena MT.

16. MS 2823, 2826, and 2827, Truman Michelson Papers, NAA-SI (hereafter, Michelson Papers).

17. Carroll, "Fourth of July Dishonored," 30.

18. They published more than a dozen articles and manuscripts on the Blackfeet language (see bibliography) from their 1910 and 1911 summer fieldwork, including Blackfeet stories based on interviews with the Blackfeet. See, e.g., Uhlenbeck, *Original Blackfoot Texts*; Uhlenbeck, *New Series of Blackfoot Texts*; and Josselin de Jong, *Blackfoot Texts*.

19. Bottomly-O'Looney, "Sitting Proud," 68.

20. Gidley, *Edward S. Curtis*, 71–72.

21. Carroll, "Fourth of July Dishonored," 30.

22. Wissler, *Sun Dance of the Blackfoot Indians*, 259.

23. Wissler, *Sun Dance of the Blackfoot Indians*, 260.

24. Wissler, *Sun Dance of the Blackfoot Indians*, 232 (emphasis added).

25. Morrisroe, "Blessing."

26. The Blackfoot Confederacy is the term used when referring to the four tribal groups: the Siksika, Kainai, Pikuni, and Inaksiks.

27. "Treaty with the Blackfeet, 1855," in Kappler, *Indian Affairs, Laws and Treaties*, 2:736–40.

28. During the summer of 1832 in his "Letter No. 8" the artist George Catlin identified four distinct groups: the "Pe-a-gans, Blackfoot, Blood and Small Robes." Catlin, *North American Indians*, 51.

29. Brink, *Imagining Head-Smashed-In*.

30. Binnema, *Common and Contested Ground*; Binnema, "Allegiances and Interests."

31. Ewers, *The Blackfeet*, 188.

32. "Treaty with the Blackfeet, 1855," in Kappler, *Indian Affairs, Laws and Treaties*, 2:736–40; Ewers, *The Blackfeet*, 212. Lame Bull's treaty was the last in a series of treaties negotiated by Washington governor Isaac Stevens in 1855. As a group they are often referred to as the Stevens treaties.

33. "Treaty with the Blackfeet, 1855," in Kappler, *Indian Affairs, Laws and Treaties*, 2:736–40.

34. Ewers, *The Blackfeet*, 241, 245.

35. The United States stopped making treaties with tribes in 1871. After this date most land cessions were one-sided deals.

36. United States, Office of Indian Affairs, *Annual Report of the Commissioner of Indian Affairs, for the year 1878*.

37. United States, Office of Indian Affairs, *Annual Report of the Commissioner of Indian Affairs, for the Year 1884*.

38. United States, Office of Indian Affairs, *Annual Report of the Commissioner of Indian Affairs, for the Year 1886*, 171.

39. Ewers, *The Blackfeet*, 273, 306, 313, 318.

40. Ewers, *The Blackfeet*, 227.

41. Three Calf, interview by John Ewers, translated by Reuben Black Boy, November 10, 1943, in "Rations," Series xiv, Box 17, Ewers Papers.

42. Schultz, "Life among the Blackfeet [first paper]." (For more on bands see chap. 5.)

43. Ewers, *The Blackfeet*, 230.

44. Unknown author, "Fort Benton Journal" (kept primarily by Andrew Dawson and Alexander Rose), 1855–56, Pierre Chouteau Jr. and Company Records, Manuscript Collection 4, Box 1, Montana Historical Society Archives, Helena MT.

45. Three Calf, interview by John Ewers, translated by Reuben Black Boy, November 10, 1943, in "Rations."

46. Copy of *Annual Report of the Commissioner of Indian Affairs*, 1875, Series xiv, Box 1, Ewers Papers.

47. John Old Person, interview by John Ewers, May 11, 1942, Series xiv, Box 1, Ewers Papers.

48. Foley, *Historical Analysis*, 75.

49. Richard Sanderville, interview by John Ewers, n.d., Series xiv, Box 1, Ewers Papers.

50. Richard Sanderville, interview by John Ewers, n.d., Series xiv, Box 4, Ewers Papers.

51. Richard Sanderville, interview by John Ewers, n.d., Series xiv, Box 2, Ewers Papers.

52. Quoted in United States Senate, *Subcommittee Report*, 233.

53. Ewers, *The Blackfeet*, 292; copy of C. H. Howard, Special Report on the Condition of the Blackfeet Indians, November 16, 1883, Series XIV, Box 2, Ewers Papers.

54. Ewers, *The Blackfeet*, 292–93; United States, Office of Indian Affairs, *Annual Report of the Commissioner of Indian Affairs, for the Year 1883*.

55. Reuben Allen to Commissioner of Indian Affairs, April 9, 1884, copy in Series XIV, Box 2, Ewers Papers.

56. DeMarce, *Blackfeet Heritage*, 162.

57. Harrod, *Mission among the Blackfeet*, 47.

58. Ewers, *The Blackfeet*, 294.

59. Rosier, *Rebirth of the Blackfeet Nation*, 14.

60. Adam White Man, interview by John Ewers, translated by Louis Bear Child, "Blackfeet Political Organization #1, Piegan Bands," September 7, 1951, Series xiv, Box 4, Ewers Papers.

61. Reuben Black Boy, interview by John Ewers, July 31, 1947, Series xiv, Box 6, Ewers Papers.

62. Foley, *Historical Analysis*, 74, 76, 79–81.

63. Foley, *Historical Analysis*, 93.

64. Quoted from a letter of George Bird Grinnell, September 25, 1888, in Foley, *Historical Analysis*, 104.

65. Quoted from a letter of George Bird Grinnell, November 30, 1888, in Foley, *Historical Analysis*, 107.

66. Quoted in Foley, *Historical Analysis*, 131.

67. Quoted in Foley, *Historical Analysis*, 132.

68. Copy of George Steele report to Commissioner of Indian Affairs, April 15, 1895, in possession of John Ewers, Series xiv, Box 2, Ewers Papers.

69. Inspector Province McCormick's August 1895 report quoted in Foley, *Historical Analysis*, 205.

70. Copy of Annual Report, Commissioner of Indian Affairs, 1888, xxi, in Series xiv, Box 2, Ewers Papers.

71. Ewers, *The Blackfeet*, 311.

72. Quote from the 1895 negotiations as printed in Foley, *Historical Analysis*, 190.

73. Quote from the 1895 negotiations as printed in Foley, *Historical Analysis*, 188.

74. Copy of Annual Report, Commissioner of Indian Affairs, 1875, in Series xiv, Box 1, Ewers Papers.

75. Quote from the 1895 negotiations as printed in Foley, *Historical Analysis*, 193.

76. Foley, *Historical Analysis*, 307.

77. Copy of Annual Report, Commissioner of Indian Affairs, 1898, in Series xiv, Box 2, Ewers Papers.

78. Foley, *Historical Analysis*, 273.

79. Quoted in Foley, *Historical Analysis*, 274.

80. Quoted in Foley, *Historical Analysis*, 294.

81. John Ewers, "White Calf," Series xiv, Box 11, Ewers Papers.

82. Harrod, *Mission among the Blackfeet*, 58–60.

83. Ewers, "White Calf."

84. Ewers, *The Blackfeet*, 317.

85. Quoted in Uhlenbeck, *New Series of Blackfoot Texts*, 224.

86. Soer, "Piëgans," 18, 19.

87. Soer, "Piëgans," 22.

2. INVISIBLE REALITY

1. Of the four tribes within the Blackfoot Confederacy, the South Piegan and the North Peigan are the most closely related, because they were probably one group before the nineteenth century. In this case I will use observations made by an early recorder of Piegan life, not of the South Piegan but the North Peigan.

2. Father Emile Legal, O.M.I., "1885 Field Notes on Customs, Legends and Other Stories among the Blackfoot People," translated by Maurice Goutier, O.M.I., 4, Oblates of Mary Immaculate Papers, Provincial Archives of Alberta, Edmonton AB.

3. Wissler and Duvall, *Mythology of the Blackfoot*, 7.

4. The Blackfeet told George Bird Grinnell that their "religious system includes a number of minor deities or rather natural qualities and forces, which are personified and given shape. These are included in the general terms Above Persons, Ground Persons, and Under Water Persons." Grinnell, *Blackfoot Lodge Tales*, 259.

5. Grinnell, *Blackfoot Lodge Tales*, 258–60.

6. Wissler, *Ceremonial Bundles of the Blackfoot Indians*, 103.

7. Wissler and Duvall, *Mythology of the Blackfoot*, 94.

8. Grinnell, *Blackfoot Lodge Tales*, 263.

9. McClintock, *Tragedy of the Blackfoot*, 4.

10. Clark Wissler to Franz Boas, July 9, 1903, Accession Records, Donor Clark Wissler, 1903, Department of Anthropology Archives, American Museum of Natural History, New York NY (hereafter, AMNH).

11. Wissler, *Ceremonial Bundles of the Blackfoot Indians*, 69–279.

12. The contemporary historian William Farr also explained this process of "buying" and "selling" supernatural power in an article, "Troubled Bundles, Troubled Blackfeet."

13. The Blackfeet had bison robes with pictographs of warriors' activities or winter counts with pictographs of annual events and other types of recordings.

14. Frantz and Russell, *Blackfoot Dictionary*. The word for tipi is *niitóyis* (singular form) or *niitóyiistsi* (plural form), which combines two word stems: *niit* + *moyís*, or real + dwelling.

15. Grinnell, "Lodges of the Blackfeet"; "Painted-Tipis," in Wissler, *Ceremonial Bundles of the Blackfoot Indians*, 220–41; Uhlenbeck, "Origin of the Otter-Lodge";

Barrett, "Painted Lodge or Ceremonial Tipi"; McClintock, "Blackfoot Tipi," in *Masterkey*; McClintock, *Blackfoot Tipi* (leaflet); and McClintock, *Painted Tipis and Picture Writing of the Blackfoot Indians* (leaflet).

16. "Painted-Tipis," in Wissler, *Ceremonial Bundles of the Blackfoot Indians*, 220–41.

17. The basic design only included elements of the Sky world and Below world. A representation of the Water world was not painted onto the tipi unless it was related to the individual tipi owner's personal design.

18. The archives of Montana State University have photos and a lithograph of this tipi recorded at the 1943 O'kan (Sun Dance) at Heart Butte. MSU also holds the records of the Federal Writers' Project (WPA), in which Cecile Black Boy recorded the stories of "Painted Lodges," including the "Big Rock teepee" story.

19. Grinnell, "Lodges of the Blackfeet."

20. Wissler and Duvall, *Mythology of the Blackfoot*, 17.

21. Wissler and Duvall, *Mythology of the Blackfoot*, 17.

22. Wissler and Duvall, *Mythology of the Blackfoot*, 5.

23. Paie is often translated as Scar Face, but the literal translation is Ridge. The scar on Paie's face looked like a ridge on the landscape; see Uhlenbeck, *Original Blackfoot Texts*, 50–57. Other versions of Paie are found in Curtis, *North American Indian*, 6:59–69; Schultz and Donaldson, *Sun God's Children*, 71–76; Wissler and Duvall, *Mythology of the Blackfoot*, 61–65; Grinnell, *Blackfoot Lodge Tales*, 93–103; Josselin de Jong, *Blackfoot Texts*, 80–82; McClintock, *Old North Trail*, 491–505; and Wissler, *Sun Dance of the Blackfoot Indians*, 269–70.

24. LaPier, "Smudging."

25. Wissler, *Sun Dance of the Blackfoot Indians*, 270.

26. The story of Soatsaki, or Feather Woman, is sometimes called "The Girl Who Married the Star" or the story of "The Fixed Star," and it can be found in Josselin de Jong, *Blackfoot Texts*, 95–97; and Wissler and Duvall, *Mythology of the Blackfoot*, 58–61.

27. Wissler and Duvall, *Mythology of the Blackfoot*, 60.

28. "Reckoning Time," in Wissler, *Social Life of the Blackfoot Indians*, 44–50.

29. Joseph Tatsey, "The Bunched Stars," in Uhlenbeck, *New Series of Blackfoot Texts*, 112–13; also in Wissler and Duvall, *Mythology of the Blackfoot*, 71–72; and McClintock, *Old North Trail*, 490.

30. Buffalo jumps were steep cliffs that the Blackfeet used to kill bison. The Blackfeet pursued the bison toward the cliff and then the bison "jumped" (technically, fell) to their deaths. See Brink, *Imagining Head-Smashed-In*.

31. The Blackfeet believe that the weasel is a transformative supernatural animal. The Blackfeet believe it can help humans change form. See Ewers, "Notes on the Weasel in Historic Plains Indian Culture."

32. Julia White Swan told her version of "The Woman Who Turned into a Bear"

to David Duvall, who translated it for Truman Michelson. It was rare that the recorders of Blackfeet life ever interviewed women, and fortunately White Swan's version was published in Michelson, "Piegan Tales," 244–46.

33. Wissler and Duvall, *Mythology of the Blackfoot*, 17.

34. Legal, "1885 Field Notes," 4, Oblates of Mary Immaculate Papers.

3. VISIBLE REALITY

1. Although Grinnell used the word "Blackfoot" in his title, his book is about the Amskapi Pikuni, or the South Piegan in Montana, and not about the entire Blackfoot Confederacy.

2. Schultz, "Life among the Blackfeet—Third Paper."

3. Fagan, *Little Ice Age*; Sherow, *Grasslands of the United States*, 307.

4. The early recorders of Blackfeet life collected stories of life on the prairies that were marked by longer and colder winters and wetter summers with occasional hot, dry, or droughty periods. However, some recorders did not understand that they were documenting through the lens of this era of global climate shift. As we are entering a new era of climate change on the northern Great Plains and globally, we do not know how the Blackfeet would live on the prairies today. And we cannot take their knowledge of the past and use it in today's new world.

5. Recent scholarship by the environmental historian Theodore Binnema and archaeologist Jack Brink describes the complex understandings that the Blackfeet had of both plant and animal ecology, which informed their strategic use of these resources. See Binnema, *Common and Contested Ground*; and Brink, *Imagining Head-Smashed-In*.

6. Uhlenbeck, *New Series of Blackfoot Texts*.

7. The translation of Kainaikoan should be Many Leaders Man, for: Kainai, or Many Leaders + koan, Man. The Kainai are one of the groups of the Blackfoot Confederacy, now located in Alberta, Canada. However, in the nineteenth century the Canadian government did not translate Kainai as Many Leaders; they translated it as Blood, which stemmed from the fact that the Kainai people painted their faces with red ocher. The Americans then translated the Kainaikoan name (now his surname) to Blood. His American name became Jim Blood.

8. "How the Ancient Peigans Lived," in Uhlenbeck, *New Series of Blackfoot Texts*, 1–38.

9. Josselin de Jong, *Blackfoot Texts*, 120–21.

10. "Bands," in Wissler, *Social Life of the Blackfoot Indians*, 18–22.

11. Schultz, "Life among the Blackfeet [first paper]."

12. Grinnell, *Blackfoot Lodge Tales*, 208–10.

13. Scholars often use sources and evidence primarily collected during the reservation period to tell us about Blackfeet life in prehistoric times. And scholars

also often use only Blackfeet sources to extrapolate about the whole of the Blackfoot Confederacy.

14. There are of course many references to the Blackfeet and other Blackfoot Confederacy tribes in first contact records. These are minimal, however, and are from the fur traders' or priests' perspectives. The information gathered in the late nineteenth and early twentieth century was the result of a systematic effort to collect Blackfeet perspectives.

15. Brink, *Imagining Head-Smashed-In.*

16. Schultz and Donaldson, "Sacred Tobacco Rites," in *Sun God's Children*, 122–58.

17. Ewers, *The Blackfeet*, 9.

18. "A family of 6, say a man and wife with four children would need: 2 horses to carry lodge poles; 1 to carry the lodge; 1 horse for the travois; 2 horses for packing parfleches—it would take a good ten head for [the] purposes for such a family. NOTE—The ten would include 4 riding horses for hunting and general use of the family." Chewing Black Bones and Rides at the Door, interview by John Ewers, translated by Reuben Black Boy, March 1, 1943, "Family Use of Horses," Series xiv, Box 7, Ewers Papers.

19. Ewers, *Horse in Blackfeet Culture*, 20–21.

20. Each year a different woman sponsored the O'kan. To participate in the O'kan each year Blackfeet bands traveled to within the designated site selected by the woman. The woman announced her intention to sponsor the O'kan in the early spring when the *okonok*, or serviceberry (*Amelanchier alnifolia*), was in bloom. The woman's band sent runners to each band to announce her intentions and invite the bands to the designated place. When the okonok was fully ripe in the late summer the Blackfeet held the O'kan. See Wissler, *Sun Dance of the Blackfoot Indians.*

21. Schultz, "Life among the Blackfeet—Fourth Paper"; Wissler, *Social Life of the Blackfoot Indians*, 44. Wissler wrote that the concept of four seasons, including spring and autumn, were introduced to the Blackfeet by the "whites."

22. Uhlenbeck, *New Series of Blackfoot Texts*, 1–38. The spellings of all Blackfeet words within this story remain the same as those in Uhlenbeck's version.

23. The Kainai, Siksika, and Inaksiks wintered along different rivers in the northern Great Plains.

24. Blackfeet agency detective Andre Dusold letter, copy from the National Archives, in "Blackfoot Habitat—Winter 1875," Series xiv, Box 1, Ewers Papers.

25. Ewers, *Horse in Blackfeet Culture*, 125.

26. Uhlenbeck, *New Series of Blackfoot Texts*, 1–38.

27. Weasel Head, interview by John Ewers, translated by Reuben Black Boy, March 6, 1943, "Piegan on March," Series xiv, Box 7, Ewers Papers.

28. Cecile Black Boy, interview by John Ewers, August 25, 1951, "Medicine Bundles," Series xiv, Box 4, Ewers Papers.

29. Tobacco seeds are very small, smaller than poppy seeds. The Blackfeet probably created this mixture because the seeds were so small and difficult to plant by themselves, and this mixture also served as a natural fertilizer.

30. White Calf, interview by George Bird Grinnell, October 25, 1897, Grinnell Diary, 1897, #327, George Bird Grinnell Papers, Southwest Museum, Los Angeles CA (hereafter, Grinnell Papers).

31. Commercial tobacco (*Nicotiana tabacum*) cultivated in the nineteenth century was originally from South America and had a high nicotine content. The tobacco the Blackfeet grew (*Nicotiana quadrivalvis*) had a low nicotine content. Winter, "Food of the Gods."

32. Jack Brink explores in *Imagining Head-Smashed-In* how the prehistoric peoples of the northern Great Plains hunted buffalo.

33. Wissler, *Material Culture of the Blackfoot Indians*, 41.

34. Stirrups, of course, were developed only after the Blackfeet started using horses. Wissler, *Material Culture of the Blackfoot Indians*, 93.

35. Wissler, *Material Culture of the Blackfoot Indians*, 163.

36. Weasel Head, interview by John Ewers, translated by Reuben Black Boy, March 9, 1943, "Hunting Buffalo," Series xiv, Box 16, Ewers Papers.

37. "How the Ancient Peigans Lived," in Uhlenbeck, *New Series of Blackfoot Texts*, 1–38.

38. "Parfleche," in Wissler, *Material Culture of the Blackfoot Indians*, 79–82.

39. Wissler, *Material Culture of the Blackfoot Indians*, 22.

40. Three Calf, interview by John Ewers, translated by Reuben Black Boy, November 8, 1943, "Making Pemmican," Series xiv, Box 16, Ewers Papers.

41. Wissler, *Material Culture of the Blackfoot Indians*, 100–101.

42. Wissler, *Material Culture of the Blackfoot Indians*, 21.

43. Green Grass Bull, interview by John Ewers, translated by Reuben Black Boy, July 21, 1947, "Pipes," Series xiv, Box 16, Ewers Papers.

44. "How the Ancient Peigans Lived," in Uhlenbeck, *New Series of Blackfoot Texts*, 1–38.

45. Wissler, *Material Culture of the Blackfoot Indians*, 21.

46. Wissler, *Material Culture of the Blackfoot Indians*, 104.

47. Grinnell, *Blackfoot Lodge Tales*, 201–2.

48. Wissler, *Material Culture of the Blackfoot Indians*, 125.

49. Wissler, *Material Culture of the Blackfoot Indians*, 123.

50. Wissler, *Material Culture of the Blackfoot Indians*, 125.

51. Wissler, *Material Culture of the Blackfoot Indians*, 92, 96.

52. Wissler, *Material Culture of the Blackfoot Indians*, 158.

53. Wissler, *Material Culture of the Blackfoot Indians*, 23.

54. Wissler, *Material Culture of the Blackfoot Indians*, 63.

55. "How the Ancient Peigans Lived," in Uhlenbeck, *New Series of Blackfoot Texts*, 1–38.

56. Wissler, *Material Culture of the Blackfoot Indians*, 99.

57. "How the Ancient Peigans Lived," in Uhlenbeck, *New Series of Blackfoot Texts*, 1–38.

58. Weasel Head, interview by John Ewers, translated by Reuben Black Boy, March 8, 1943, "Daily Care of Horse Herds," Series xiv, Box 6, Ewers Papers.

59. Short Face, interview by John Ewers, n.d., Series xiv, Box 6, Ewers Papers.

60. "How the Ancient Peigans Lived," in Uhlenbeck, *New Series of Blackfoot Texts*, 1–38.

61. Weasel Head interview by Ewers, translated by Reuben Black Boy, "Daily Care of Horse Herds," March 8, 1943.

62. Although not in the written record, it was well known that the Blackfeet used tanned antelope hides for underwear.

63. Wissler, *Material Culture of the Blackfoot Indians*, 120; Grinnell, *Blackfoot Lodge Tales*, 196.

64. Wissler, *Material Culture of the Blackfoot Indians*, 72, 74.

65. "How the Ancient Peigans Lived," in Uhlenbeck, *New Series of Blackfoot Texts*, 1–38.

66. Lazy Boy, interview by John Ewers, translated by Reuben Black Boy, December 6, 1943, "Pipes," Series xiv, Box 16, Ewers Papers.

67. "How the Ancient Peigans Lived," in Uhlenbeck, *New Series of Blackfoot Texts*, 1–38.

68. Tom Spotted Eagle, interview by John Ewers, translated by Louis Bear Child, n.d., "Blackfeet Political Organization #2—Winter Camps 1870's," Series xiv, Box 4, Ewers Papers.

69. Weasel Tail, interview by John Ewers, translated Reuben Black Boy, August 7, 1947, "On Grass Use for Horses," Series xiv, Box 6, Ewers Papers.

70. Three Calf, interview by John Ewers, translated by Reuben Black Boy, August 13, 1947, "Horses Feed," Series xiv, Box 6, Ewers Papers.

71. "How the Ancient Peigans Lived," in Uhlenbeck, *New Series of Blackfoot Texts*, 1–38.

72. Blackfeet agency detective Andre Dusold letter, copy from the National Archives, 1895, "Blackfoot Habitat—Winter 1875."

73. Jim Walters, interview by John Ewers, January 20, 1943, "Shelter—nineteenth century tipi," Series xiv, Box 4, Ewers Papers.

74. "How the Ancient Peigans Lived," in Uhlenbeck, *New Series of Blackfoot Texts*, 1–38.

75. David Duvall Papers, Department of Anthropology Archives, AMNH (hereafter, Duvall Papers).

76. Wissler, *Social Life of the Blackfoot Indians*, 54.

77. We were both working on a project for the National Museum of Natural History, Smithsonian Institution, which eventually became a lexicon, "Blackfeet Vocabulary Terms for Items of Material Culture."

78. LaPier, "Relationship with the Land."

79. Uhlenbeck, "How the Ancient Peigans Lived," in *New Series of Blackfoot Texts*, 1–38. Although a South Piegan man told this story in 1911, museums and scholars use this information to tell the story of all Blackfoot Confederacy people in prehistoric times. The Glenbow Museum in Calgary created a map within their permanent exhibit, *Nitsitapiisinni: The Story of the Blackfoot People*, based on this story. They also publish the map in the Blackfoot Gallery Committee's *Nitsitapiisinni*. Most recently Jack Brink's *Imagining Head-Smashed-In* used this story to help "reimagine" prehistoric life at Head-Smashed-In Buffalo Jump in Alberta.

80. LaPier, "Silent, Sacred and Wild."

81. Adam White Man, interview by John Ewers, translated by Louis Bear Child, September 7, 1951, "Blackfeet Political Organization #2 — Winter Camps 1870's," Series xiv, Box 4, Ewers Papers.

82. John Ewers, "Blood Band," Series xiv, Box 4, Ewers Papers.

4. CLOSED SEASON

1. Wissler, *Ceremonial Bundles of the Blackfoot Indians*, 276.

2. Western Christians celebrate Easter the first Sunday after the first full moon after the vernal equinox, which can happen anytime from March 22 to April 25. Thurnston, "Easter Controversy."

3. Schultz, "Life among the Blackfeet — Fourth Paper."

4. Wissler, *Ceremonial Bundles of the Blackfoot Indians*, 246.

5. Wissler, *Ceremonial Bundles of the Blackfoot Indians*, 169.

6. Crooked Meat Strings, interview by Jane Richardson Hanks, translated by Mary White Elk, Manuscript 8458, File 6, Box 1, Jane Richardson Hanks Papers, Glenbow Museum, Calgary AB. Crooked Meat Strings added, "This is not done by the rich. The rich purchase holy objects."

7. Binnema, *Common and Contested Ground*, 65–68, 74. Binnema states that "the historic Blackfoot people developed from the Old Woman's phase." Old Woman's phase (in archaeological terms) emerged 1,200 BP and expanded from 1,200 BP to 800 BP.

8. Brink, *Imagining Head-Smashed-In*, xii. Brink argues that humans have lived on the northern Great Plains for twelve thousand years.

9. Brink, *Imagining Head-Smashed-In*.

10. Morgan, "Beaver Ecology/Beaver Mythology."

11. In the case of Wissler, Duvall sent Wissler his handwritten English translations.

Wissler's editorial assistant, Bella Weitzner, typed up the notes and did the first edit into standard English. Wissler then read them, added questions in the margins, and mailed the material back to Duvall to read to the people he had interviewed. Duvall retranslated the text back into Blackfeet and asked the clarifying questions. They were returned to New York City for a final edit by Weitzner and Wissler. See Wissler, *Ceremonial Bundles of the Blackfoot Indians*, 70; and correspondence between Duvall and Wissler, Department of Anthropology Archives, AMNH; and MS 2823, 1–3, Michelson Papers.

12. Wissler, *Ceremonial Bundles of the Blackfoot Indians*, 69.

13. Wissler and Duvall, *Mythology of the Blackfoot*, 14.

14. The versions of the story of Beaver medicine can be found in Grinnell, *Blackfoot Lodge Tales*, 117–24; McClintock, *Old North Trail*, 103–12; Wissler and Duvall, *Mythology of the Blackfoot*, 81–83; Josselin de Jong, *Blackfoot Texts*, 86–91; Uhlenbeck, *New Series of Blackfoot Texts*, 72–92; and David Duvall, "Blackfeet Notes," unpublished, in Duvall Papers. I was also told a version by my grandmother Annie Mad Plume Wall and my aunt Theresa Still Smoking.

15. Duvall, "Blackfeet Notes," Duvall Papers; Wissler, *Ceremonial Bundles of the Blackfoot Indians*, 190–91.

16. In most stories the human was a young man, but in some it was a young woman and in one an old woman.

17. Wissler, *Ceremonial Bundles of the Blackfoot Indians*, 103.

18. Wissler, *Ceremonial Bundles of the Blackfoot Indians*, 103.

19. Wissler, *Ceremonial Bundles of the Blackfoot Indians*, 169.

20. As stated earlier some stories have a female lead. In all of the stories the human who lived with the beavers "transferred" his or her knowledge to the next human man. Thereafter the term "Beaver man" was used to refer to the owner of a Beaver bundle even though it was owned by a married couple.

21. Schultz, "Life among the Blackfeet—Fourth Paper." Schultz wrote that the Blackfeet believed that all the animals and birds had their own languages, songs, and dances.

22. Cecile Black Boy, interview by John Ewers, August 25, 1951, "Remaking of Ceremonial Objects," Series xiv, Box 4, Ewers Papers. Cecile Black Boy preferred using the word "title" to explain the exchange of ownership of a bundle. The title of the person is not what is being exchanged but the title of ownership of the object, the Beaver bundle.

23. Wissler, *Ceremonial Bundles of the Blackfoot Indians*, 103.

24. Wissler, *Ceremonial Bundles of the Blackfoot Indians*, 146.

25. Wissler, *Ceremonial Bundles of the Blackfoot Indians*, 101.

26. Cecile Black Boy interview by Ewers, August 25, 1951, "Remaking of Ceremonial Objects." John Ewers was asked to step in and explain to the Denver Art

Museum the Blackfeet concepts of "ownership" because of a misunderstanding. The Denver Art Museum thought they had purchased the "one and only" version of a painted tipi. In the mind of the Blackfeet owner, however, the museum had purchased the physical object devoid of religious meaning. After the purchase the owner painted another identical tipi for himself, which retained its supernatural power.

27. Cecile Black Boy interview by Ewers, August 25, 1951; and Ewers commentary, both in "Remaking of Ceremonial Objects," Series xiv, Box 4, Ewers Papers.

28. Japy Takes Gun on Top, interview by David Duvall, "Blackfoot Notes," 206–300, Duvall Papers. Japy Takes Gun on Top told Duvall that sometimes the new owners sought out others to invest in the bundle. These individuals paid for individual hides or skins and their corresponding songs. This practice lessened the overall burden of the large purchase price.

29. Japy Takes Gun on Top interview by Duvall, "Blackfoot Notes," 206–300.

30. Grinnell Diary, 1897, #327, October 25, 1897, Grinnell Papers.

31. Winter, "Food of the Gods."

32. I also heard the stories of tobacco from my grandmother Annie Mad Plume Wall and my aunt Theresa Still Smoking.

33. The story of tobacco can be found in Ewers, The Blackfeet, 169–70; Grinnell, Blackfoot Lodge Tales, 268–71; Johnston, Plants and the Blackfoot, 52–53; Schultz, Blackfeet and Buffalo, 344–46; and Wissler, Ceremonial Bundles of the Blackfoot Indians, 200–204.

34. After the Blackfeet stopped growing tobacco, they placed commercial tobacco in the Beaver bundle, which then became consecrated during the winter.

35. Wissler noted that historically the only two rituals "carried out by the whole tribal organization" were the O'kan and planting tobacco. Wissler, Sun Dance of the Blackfoot Indians, 229.

36. Grinnell Diary, 1897, #327, October 25, 1897.

37. Three Bears, interview by David Duvall, "Blackfoot Notes," 302–6, Duvall Papers.

38. Alexander Johnston wrote, "Amos Leather, also called 'Berry-eater,' died in 1969. Much Blackfoot Indian culture was lost with his death. The 72-year-old elder was the sole custodian of many songs, rituals and dances of the Blackfoot nation of Alberta and Montana. . . . He knew all 230 songs of the Tobacco Planting ritual, a spring festival from the time when the Blackfoot raised tobacco as a crop. This collection of songs died with Mr. Leather." Johnston, Plants and the Blackfoot, 2.

39. Three Bears interview by Duvall, "Blackfoot Notes," 302–6. Three Bears told Duvall that tobacco plants were little people, which Ewers referenced as well.

40. My grandfather used to regale us with the adventures of the little people. I spent many hours of my childhood looking for them.

41. John Ewers collected replicas of little people objects and clothing that are

now held in the material object collections of the National Museum of Natural History, Smithsonian Institution, Washington DC.

42. Grinnell Diary, 1897, #327, October 25, 1897.
43. Three Bears interview by Duvall, "Blackfoot Notes," 302–6.
44. Grinnell Diary, 1897, #327, October 25, 1897.
45. McClintock, *Old North Trail*, 528.
46. See LaPier, "Smudging," 16–17. The Blackfeet used more than two dozen different dried plants or other natural elements for incense.
47. Wissler, *Ceremonial Bundles of the Blackfoot Indians*, 114, 127.
48. Ewers, *The Blackfeet*, 30. Similar to the practice of using shared smoking to maintain personal behavior in their own group, the Blackfeet smoked with outside groups to encourage honest relationships.
49. Ewers, *The Blackfeet*, 230. The U.S government purchased 2,660 pounds of tobacco for 460 lodges. This quantity would amount to 5.78 pounds of tobacco per lodge per year. If it was used only for ceremonial purposes, for six months out of the year, it totaled a little less than 1 pound per month.
50. Uhlenbeck, *New Series of Blackfoot Texts*, 14.
51. Winter, "Food of the Gods."
52. Wissler, *Social Life of the Blackfoot Indians*, 51.
53. Wissler, *Social Life of the Blackfoot Indians*, 51.
54. As mentioned earlier, Green Grass Bull told John Ewers that "men sometimes swore to tell the truth by saying they would talk straight as a willow pipe stem." Green Grass Bull, interview by John Ewers, translated by Reuben Black Boy, July 21, 1947, "Pipes," Series xiv, Box 16, Ewers Papers.
55. Schultz, "Life among the Blackfeet—Fourth Paper."
56. According to Blackfeet stories, the bison originated in the Water world as a supernatural underwater being and came to the Below world as an animal. Uhlenbeck, *Original Blackfoot Texts*, 6–12.
57. Japy Takes Gun on Top interview by Duvall, "Blackfoot Notes," 206.
58. Japy Takes Gun on Top interview by Duvall, "Blackfoot Notes," 211.
59. Japy Takes Gun on Top interview by Duvall, "Blackfoot Notes," 211–12.
60. Japy Takes Gun on Top interview by Duvall, "Blackfoot Notes," 212–13. Japy added, "If this is done in the summer time rain and hail storms may be expected."
61. Japy Takes Gun on Top interview by Duvall, "Blackfoot Notes," 215.
62. Wissler, *Ceremonial Bundles of the Blackfoot Indians*, 128.
63. Wissler, *Social Life of the Blackfoot Indians*, 45. However, it is possible that this practice began during the Little Ice Age, when winters could have lasted seven months.
64. Wissler, *Social Life of the Blackfoot Indians*, 44.
65. Wissler, *Ceremonial Bundles of the Blackfoot Indians*, 171.

66. Three Bears interview by Duvall, "Blackfoot Notes," 300–301.

67. Wissler, *Ceremonial Bundles of the Blackfoot Indians*, 277.

68. Wissler, *Ceremonial Bundles of the Blackfoot Indians*, 272.

69. Japy Takes Gun on Top interview by Duvall, "Blackfoot Notes," 294.

70. Japy Takes Gun on Top interview by Duvall, "Blackfoot Notes," 290.

5. OPENED SEASON

1. Gilbert was interviewed about his experiences at Khe Sanh in two books: Hammel, *Khe Sanh*; and Prados and Stubbe, *Valley of Decision*.

2. Many Guns, *Pinto Horse Rider*.

3. Many Guns was a member of the Never Laughs band, which was my grandmother's father's band. One of Many Guns's brothers was Under Mink (Tim No Runner), and one of his sisters was Singing This Way. Tim No Runner was my grandmother's maternal grandfather; Singing This Way was her paternal aunt. Uhlenbeck, *Original Blackfoot Texts*, 124–25.

4. Binnema, *Common and Contested Ground*, 17.

5. Binnema, *Common and Contested Ground*, 18.

6. Grinnell, *Blackfoot Lodge Tales*, 259.

7. "The Home of the Wind Maker," in McClintock, *Old North Trail*, 60–62.

8. Schultz, "Life among the Blackfeet—Fourth Paper."

9. Grinnell, *Blackfoot Lodge Tales*, 260.

10. "The Legend of the Snow Tipi," in McClintock, *Old North Trail*, 133–38. McClintock used both the name "Cold Maker" and "Maker of Storms and Blizzards" for the overarching supernatural entity. The Blackfeet recognized that within winter there were multiple weather patterns.

11. "The Legend of the Snow Tipi," in McClintock, *Old North Trail*, 136.

12. McClintock, *Old North Trail*, 139.

13. Grinnell, *Blackfoot Lodge Tales*, 259.

14. Grinnell, *Blackfoot Lodge Tales*, 277.

15. Binnema, *Common and Contested Ground*, 21.

16. Binnema, *Common and Contested Ground*, 42.

17. Grinnell, *Blackfoot Lodge Tales*, 113.

18. Early scholars of Blackfeet life recorded different versions of Thunder or the origin of the Thunder Pipe story. In 1884 Schultz wrote about his firsthand experience attending a Thunder Pipe ceremony in "Life among the Blackfeet—Eighth Paper." Grinnell wrote the "Origin of Medicine Pipe" in 1892 in *Blackfoot Lodge Tales*, 113–16, and rewrote the same story in 1913 as "How the Thunder Pipe Came," in Grinnell, *Blackfeet Indian Stories*, 53–59. See also McClintock, *Old North Trail*, 425; and Uhlenbeck, *New Series of Blackfoot Texts*, 65–66. I also heard similar stories of Thunder from my grandmother Annie Mad Plume Wall.

19. Grinnell, *Blackfoot Lodge Tales*, xxx. Cora Ross was not Blackfeet.

20. Uhlenbeck, *New Series of Blackfoot Texts*, 65–66. Tatsey was half Blackfeet, and he worked as a Blackfeet-English translator for Uhlenbeck and others on the reservation.

21. Uhlenbeck, *New Series of Blackfoot Texts*, 65–66.

22. McClintock, *Old North Trail*, 519–20. The Blackfeet gave McClintock the same description of a rainbow-colored bird with green claws in the 1890s as Uhlenbeck got in the 1910s.

23. McClintock, *Old North Trail*, 487. McClintock wrote that the Blackfeet called rainbows "rain lariats" or "rain-ropers."

24. "Origin of the Medicine Pipe," in Grinnell, *Blackfoot Lodge Tales*. 113–16. He rewrote the same story as "How the Thunder Pipe Came" in *Blackfeet Indian Stories*, 53–59.

25. Schultz, "Life among the Blackfeet—Eighth Paper."

26. Wissler and Duvall, *Mythology of the Blackfoot*, 89.

27. Grinnell, *Blackfoot Lodge Tales*, 115–16.

28. David Duvall interviewed many people from his own family or from his wife's family. Bull Child was Duvall's wife's paternal uncle (her father's brother), which makes him my great-grandmother's uncle.

29. DeMarce, *Blackfeet Heritage*, 50–51.

30. McClintock, *Old North Trail*, 310.

31. DeMarce, *Blackfeet Heritage*, 50–52. When the U.S. government conducted a census for the 1907–12 allotment, all four of Bull Child's wives had died. It is unclear from the records if he had multiple wives at one time or was married four times in a row. He probably was polygamous, as that was common in his time.

32. The most complete discussions of the O'kan are found in Wissler, *Ceremonial Bundles of the Blackfoot Indians*; and Wissler, *Sun Dance of the Blackfoot Indians*.

33. To the Blackfeet these were not reenactments or retellings; the purpose of the rituals was for the participants to experience the original experience for the first time.

34. The majority of McClintock's photographs are now available online at the website of the Beinecke Rare Book and Manuscript Library, Yale University. There are seventeen photos that show Bull Child.

35. McClintock, *Old North Trail*, 316.

36. Wissler, *Ceremonial Bundles of the Blackfoot Indians*, 72.

37. In the 1840s and 1850s the Blackfeet lived primarily in central Montana and not up near the Rocky Mountains. It was not until the 1870s and 1880s that the Blackfeet lived near the mountains.

38. Wissler, *Ceremonial Bundles of the Blackfoot Indians*, 72.

39. Weasel Tail was a "buffalo Indian" interviewed by John Ewers in the early 1940s. Weasel Tail eventually became a very well known warrior, and like Bull Child

he survived into the twentieth century. The ethnologist John Ewers recorded his life story. "Weasel Tail" file, Ewers Papers.

40. "Weasel Tail" file, Ewers Papers.
41. Wissler, *Ceremonial Bundles of the Blackfoot Indians*, 73.
42. Wissler, *Ceremonial Bundles of the Blackfoot Indians*, 74.
43. Wissler, *Ceremonial Bundles of the Blackfoot Indians*, 103.
44. Schultz, "Origin of the Medicine Lodge," 82.
45. This process was similar to "transubstantiation" and the "totality of the presence" found within Catholic theology, in which God both transforms and is present within an earthly object. The material object remains, but its essence becomes supernatural. Pohle, "Real Presence of Christ in the Eucharist."
46. Wissler, *Ceremonial Bundles of the Blackfoot Indians*, 103.
47. I divide this process of acquisition into three categories; two involve intercession with a supernatural and one involves purchase. Crooked Meat Strings, of the Siksika, told Jane Richardson Hanks of a similar method: "There are two kinds of owners of power: a) Those who buy lots of medicines and never dreams, b) Those who dream lots of medicines[;] (a) can never lend medicines, but (b) can lend. So (a) is called atsim.apitapi—owner by buying. (b) is nato'si—holy man." Crooked Meat Strings, interview by Jane Richardson Hanks, interpreted by Mary White Elk, September 12, 1938, File 6, Box 1, Jane Richardson Hanks Papers, Glenbow Museum, Calgary AB.
48. Wissler, *Ceremonial Bundles of the Blackfoot Indians*, 72.
49. Farr, "Troubled Bundles, Troubled Blackfeet."
50. Wissler, *Ceremonial Bundles of the Blackfoot Indians*, 100.
51. Wissler, *Ceremonial Bundles of the Blackfoot Indians*, 100.
52. Wissler, *Ceremonial Bundles of the Blackfoot Indians*, 74.
53. McClintock, *Old North Trail*, 429.
54. McClintock, *Old North Trail*, 519.
55. McClintock, *Old North Trail*, 310.
56. Wissler, *Ceremonial Bundles of the Blackfoot Indians*, 98; McClintock, *Old North Trail*, 312–14.
57. Wissler, *Ceremonial Bundles of the Blackfoot Indians*, 270.
58. Wissler, *Ceremonial Bundles of the Blackfoot Indians*, 270–73.
59. Wissler, *Sun Dance of the Blackfoot Indians*, 259; McClintock, *Old North Trail*, 314.
60. Wissler, *Sun Dance of the Blackfoot Indians*, 259.
61. Wissler, *Ceremonial Bundles of the Blackfoot Indians*, 72.
62. Wissler, *Sun Dance of the Blackfoot Indians*, 258–60.
63. David Duvall and Clark Wissler Correspondence, 1904, Series xvi, File 1, Box 2, Department of Anthropology Archives, AMNH.
64. Wissler, *Ceremonial Bundles of the Blackfoot Indians*, 71.

65. Clark Wissler Papers, Department of Anthropology Archives, AMNH.

66. Text from museum display at the American Museum of Natural History. Recorded by the author.

67. Wissler, *Ceremonial Bundles of the Blackfoot Indians*, 73.

68. Wissler, *Sun Dance of the Blackfoot Indians*, 259.

6. STORYTAKERS

1. Wissler, *Material Culture of the Blackfoot Indians*, 55.

2. Clark Wissler to David Duvall, December 9, 1905, Accession Records, Donor D. C. Duvall, 1905, Department of Anthropology Archives, AMNH.

3. Accession Records, Donor D. C. Duvall, 1907, Department of Anthropology Archives, AMNH.

4. David Duvall to Clark Wissler, May 9, 1907, Accession Records, Donor D. C. Duvall, 1907, Department of Anthropology Archives, AMNH.

5. Clark Wissler to H. C. Bumpus, June 3, 1907, Accession Records, Donor D. C. Duvall, 1907, Department of Anthropology Archives, AMNH.

6. Archaeologists have uncovered quillwork objects on the northern Great Plains from the sixth century. See Bebbington, *Quillwork of the Plains*, 6.

7. Ewers, *Blackfeet Crafts*, 29.

8. Duvall to Wissler, May 9, 1907, Accession Records, Donor D. C. Duvall, 1907, Department of Anthropology Archives, AMNH.

9. David Duvall to Clark Wissler, December 15, 1905, Accession Records, Donor D. C. Duvall, 1906, Correspondence, Department of Anthropology Archives, AMNH.

10. Quote from an October 1900 article in the *San Francisco Sunday Call*, reprinted in Gidley, *Edward S. Curtis*, 58.

11. Wissler and Duvall, *Mythology of the Blackfoot*, 17–18.

12. Although all these men were studying the South Piegan in Montana, their work is used by scholars who study one or all of the four tribal groups that are part of the Blackfoot Confederacy.

13. Numerous biographies of the early recorders of Blackfeet life have been written, including Egan, *Short Nights of the Shadow Catcher*; Freed and Freed, *Clark Wissler*; Freed and Freed, "Clark Wissler and the Development of Anthropology in the United States"; Hagan, *Theodore Roosevelt and Six Friends of the Indian*; Hanna, *Stars over Montana*; Punke, *Last Stand*; S. Smith, *Reimagining Indians*.

14. I used the Blackfeet census records, allotment records, and Josselin de Jong and Uhlenbeck's lists of family names. I did not use online genealogy sites such as Ancestry.com.

15. Hanna, foreword to *Recently Discovered Tales of Life among the Indians*, by Schultz, xi–xviii.

16. H. Dempsey and Moir, *Bibliography of the Blackfoot*. Dempsey and Moir list seventy-eight separate articles or books written by Schultz.

17. Schultz, "Life among the Blackfeet [first paper]."

18. Schultz and Kennedy, "Return to the Beloved Mountains," 27.

19. Grinnell, *Blackfoot Lodge Tales*, xxx.

20. Schultz, "White Buffalo Cow."

21. For examples, see Schultz, "White Buffalo Cow"; and Schultz, "'Piskan' of the Blackfeet."

22. DeMarce, *Blackfeet Heritage*, 62, 286. Fine Shield's maternal grandparents were Diving Round Woman and Buffalo Painted Lodge, and her paternal grandparents were Bird Tail Woman and Double Coming Up the Hill.

23. Dyck, "Lone Wolf Returns." Hart Schultz recounted his childhood memories of growing up on the Blackfeet reservation.

24. DeMarce, *Blackfeet Heritage*, 231.

25. DeMarce, *Blackfeet Heritage*. 231.

26. Dyck, "Lone Wolf Returns."

27. DeMarce, *Blackfeet Heritage*, 286.

28. Dyck, "Lone Wolf Returns."

29. Louie and Ella never had children and spent significant time with my aunt Theresa Still Smoking and her family. The Montana Historical Society holds the photographs taken by Louie and Ella Yellow Wolf.

30. Between 1882 and 1884 Schultz wrote a series of fourteen articles about the Blackfeet for *Forest and Stream*. Some of these articles were reproduced in Schultz, *Recently Discovered Tales of Life among the Indians*. They are all listed in this book's bibliography.

31. Grinnell, *Blackfoot Lodge Tales*, xxix–xxx.

32. Grinnell, *Blackfoot Lodge Tales*, xxvii.

33. Grinnell, *Blackfoot Lodge Tales*, xxx.

34. Grinnell, *Blackfoot Lodge Tales*, xxx–xxxi.

35. Grinnell Diary, 1897, #327, October 25, 1897, Grinnell Papers.

36. Grinnell, *Blackfoot Lodge Tales*, xxviii.

37. Grinnell, *Blackfoot Lodge Tales*, xxvii.

38. McClintock's archives are split between the Beinecke Library at Yale University and the Southwest Museum in Pasadena, California.

39. Michelson Papers.

40. Walter McClintock Papers, Beinecke Rare Book and Manuscript Library, Yale University, New Haven CT.

41. Wissler, *Social Life of the Blackfoot Indians*, 3.

42. DeMarce, *Blackfeet Heritage*, 93; Department of Anthropology Archives, AMNH.

43. DeMarce, *Blackfeet Heritage,* 50–51, 93; Department of Anthropology Archives, AMNH.

44. Wissler Correspondence, Department of Anthropology Archives, AMNH.

45. DeMarce, *Blackfeet Heritage,* 284; Department of Anthropology Archives, AMNH.

46. DeMarce, *Blackfeet Heritage,* 18.

47. DeMarce, *Blackfeet Heritage,* 284; Department of Anthropology Archives, AMNH.

48. Grinnell to Wissler, July 10, 1911, Grinnell correspondence, Department of Anthropology Archives, AMNH.

49. Wissler Correspondence, Summer 1912, Department of Anthropology Archives, AMNH.

50. Cooper, "Truman Michelson," 281.

51. Michelson, Review of *Original Blackfoot Texts.*

52. MS 2823, Michelson Papers.

53. MS 2827, Michelson Papers. It is possible that Michelson names other individuals within his numerous handwritten manuscripts.

54. Michelson, "Piegan Tales," 238.

55. Eggermont-Molenaar, *Montana, 1911.* Uhlenbeck also brought his wife along. Eggermont-Molenaar translated her diaries, which share information about life at the Holy Family Mission and in the Two Medicine valley.

56. Willy Uhlenbeck's diaries mention various visits by Mad Plume and his sons Richard, David, and Elmer at different times throughout the summer of 1911. Eggermont-Molenaar, *Montana, 1911,* 103, 104, 106, 141, 161.

57. Uhlenbeck, *New Series of Blackfoot Texts,* viii.

58. Eggermont-Molenaar, *Montana, 1911.*

59. From about the 1910s to 1940s several other recorders of Blackfeet life came to the Blackfeet reservation, including Edward S. Curtis, who wrote a chapter on the Blackfeet for his multivolume series, *The North American Indian.* S. A. Barrett came in 1921 from the Milwaukee Public Museum; he wrote several articles, all of which are listed in the bibliography. William Wildschut came in 1924 from the Museum of the American Indian, Heye Foundation, in New York. He also wrote articles; see the bibliography. The Federal Writers' Project of the Works Progress Administration came in the 1930s; it hired Cecile Black Boy to collect stories on lodges or tipis. Claude Schaeffer worked from 1947 to 1954 reinterviewing many of the same people John Ewers had interviewed; see H. Dempsey, "Claude Everett Schaeffer."

60. Grinnell, *Blackfeet Indian Stories,* v.

61. Elk Horn, interview by Clark Wissler, translator unknown, "Blackfoot Field Notes, 1903–1905," Clark Wissler, 1870–1947, Misc. Box, Department of Anthropology Archives, AMNH.

62. Clark Wissler drawings, "Blackfoot Face & Body Designs," Clark Wissler, 1870–1947, Misc. Box, Department of Anthropology Archives, AMNH.

63. Elk Horn interview by Wissler, translator unknown.

64. Elk Horn interview by Wissler, translator unknown.

7. ALL THAT REMAIN

1. After his parents died my grandfather started using his "Irish" legal name, Thomas Francis Wall. As noted earlier, he was probably named by his birth family after the famous Irish nationalist and Montana Territory governor Thomas Francis Meagher. He did go by his Blackfeet name Iòkimau all his life.

2. Uhlenbeck and Van Gulik, *English-Blackfoot Vocabulary*, 157.

3. Holy Family Mission attendance records, Bureau of Catholic Indian Missions Records, Marquette University Archives, Milwaukee WI.

4. I wrote an article on how Blackfeet names are a reflection of the supernatural alliances with humans; see LaPier, "What's in a Name?"

5. Clark Wissler collected objects with either owl feathers, owl skins, or owl heads, now at the American Museum of Natural History, described in "Personal Charms and Medicines," in Wissler, *Ceremonial Bundles of the Blackfoot Indians*, 91–100.

6. Blackfoot Bird Lore–Misc. Notes [ca. 1934–54], M-1100-144, Claude Schaeffer Papers, Glenbow Museum, Calgary AB.

7. Annie Mad Plume Wall, personal communication.

8. Josselin de Jong, *Blackfoot Texts from the Southern Peigans Reservation*, 123.

9. Clark Wissler to Franz Boas, May 12, 1905, Wissler Correspondence, Accession Records, Donor Clark Wissler, 1903, Department of Anthropology Archives, AMNH.

10. Josselin de Jong, *Blackfoot Texts from the Southern Peigans Reservation*, 123. The Fat Melters first settled at Big Badger Creek and then at Two Medicine, according to Adam White Man: "On September 7, with Dr. Schaeffer, Adam White Man and Louis Bear Child, I went over the Big Badger by car and Adam pointed out the sites of the various bands in early Old Agency Period, moving from west to east." Adam White Man, interview by John Ewers, interpreted by Louis Bear Child, September 7, 1951, Series xiv, Box 4, Ewers Papers.

11. DeMarce, *Blackfeet Heritage*, 93. They all had the same mother, Spear Woman.

12. DeMarce, *Blackfeet Heritage*, 18.

13. Our family does not know precisely when Aimsback adopted our grandfather. Aimsback also adopted an older son, George.

14. Adam White man interview by Ewers, interpreted by Louis Bear Child, September 7, 1951.

15. Rosier, *Rebirth of the Blackfeet*.

16. MC 67, Box 1, Campbell Family Papers, Montana Historical Society, Helena MT.

17. Ewers, *The Blackfeet*, 320; Rosier, *Rebirth of the Blackfeet Nation*, 34–35.

18. "The Five Year Program on the Blackfoot Indian Reservation," *Indian Leader* (Lawrence KS), March 16, 1923, 2–3.

19. "Blackfeet Political Organization," Series xiv, Box 4, Ewers Papers.

20. Donald Frantz and Mizuki Miyashita, personal communication. They both translated the name and rewrote it in modern Blackfeet based on the Uhlenbeck spelling.

21. We were researching the 1912 Chicago Land Show, sponsored by the Great Northern Railway, for our book, LaPier and Beck, *City Indian*.

22. Articles and books on economic change and agriculture on the Blackfeet reservation include Rosier, *Rebirth of the Blackfeet Nation*; Samek, *Blackfoot Confederacy*; and Wessel, "Agent of Acculturation."

23. Folder 12252, Browning (MT), Bull donated to Indians, 1925–28, President's Subject Files, Great Northern Railway Company (hereafter, President's Subject Files, GNR), Minnesota Historical Society, Saint Paul MN.

24. Folder 12252, Browning (MT), Bull donated to Indians, 1925–28, President's Subject Files, GNR.

25. Folder 12252, Browning (MT), Bull donated to Indians, 1925–28, President's Subject Files, GNR.

26. Folder 12252, Browning (MT), Bull donated to Indians, 1925–28, President's Subject Files, GNR.

27. Blackfeet Industrial Survey, compiled 1921–21, Record Group 75: Records of the Bureau of Indian Affairs, 1793–1999, National Archives and Records Administration, Denver (hereafter, RG 75, NARA-Denver).

28. Blackfeet Industrial Survey, compiled 1921–21, RG 75, NARA-Denver.

29. John C. Ewers asked the Blackfeet land office clerk in 1942 about when the "first trust patents [were] issued the Indians on the Blackfeet reservation Feb. 18, 1918." Series xiv, Box 2, Ewers Papers.

30. Blackfeet Industrial Survey, compiled 1921–21, RG 75, NARA-Denver.

31. Paul Rosier recounts the rise of the PFLA as a political organization on the Blackfeet reservation. He argues that it represented a significant number of full-bloods from the south side of the reservation who challenged the leadership of the newly formed Blackfeet Tribal Business Council. See Rosier, *Rebirth of the Blackfeet Nation*.

32. Blackfeet Industrial Survey, compiled 1921–1921, RG 75, NARA-Denver.

33. Portraits of Aimsback and Mrs. Minnie Aimsback, Photographs, NAA-SI.

34. President's Subject Files, GNR.

35. Rosier, *Rebirth of the Blackfeet Nation*, 59.

36. Henry Magee, interview by John C. Ewers, June 21, 1942, Series xiv, Box 2, Ewers Papers.

37. Agricultural Extension Report, 1933, 29, Series xiv, Box 2, Ewers Papers.

38. McClintock, *Old North Trail*, 167.

39. "Going After Water (ca. 1869–1963), Fullblood. Mother of Cecile Black Boy.

Formerly wife of Short Robe, later of Bird Rattler. Skilled craftswoman." Ewers's list of "buffalo Indians," Series xiv, Box 3, Ewers Papers.

40. "Cecile Black Boy—WPA Legends Study," Cecile Black Boy Papers, Federal Writers' Project, Merrill G. Burlingame Special Collections (hereafter, Cecile Black Boy Papers), Montana State University Library, Bozeman MT.

41. Grinnell, "Lodges of the Blackfeet"; Barrett, "Painted Lodge or Ceremonial Tipi."

42. Grinnell, "Lodges of Blackfeet."

43. There is no evidence that Cecile Black Boy interviewed Aimsback or Hollering in the Air about the "Big Rock" tipi because it was a commonly known story, but it is possible.

44. "Big Rock Teepee," story in "Cecile Black Boy—WPA Legends Study," Cecile Black Boy Papers.

45. Aimsback tipi, Object Identifier X76.35.05, Merrill G. Burlingame Special Collections, Montana State University Library, Bozeman MT.

46. "I [JCE] visited the encampment on July 5, 1944, in company with Mrs. Hannon and Miss Wilbur [sic] of Montana State College." Sun Dance Encampment at Heart Butte, Series xiv, Box 7, Ewers Papers.

47. Ewers, *Blackfeet Indian Tipis*, foreword.

48. Sun Dance Encampment at Heart Butte, Series xiv, Box 7, Ewers Papers. Albert Mad Plume was my grandmother Annie's paternal uncle.

49. Examples of sacred rocks can be found at the Denver Art Museum's collection of Blackfeet *iniskim*, which includes a variety of these objects.

50. Wissler, *Ceremonial Bundles of the Blackfoot Indians*, 270.

51. Clark Wissler to Franz Boas, May 12, 1905, Wissler Correspondence, Department of Anthropology Archives, AMNH.

52. Quoted in McClintock, *Old North Trail*, 174.

53. Series xiv, Box 3, Ewers Papers.

54. Mountain Chief, interview by Truman Michelson, translated by David Duvall, June 21, 1910, MS 2827, Michelson Papers.

55. Rosier, *Rebirth of the Blackfeet Nation*, 2, 6.

56. Senator Harry Lane reported on his visit to the Blackfeet reservation in United States, Congress, *Blackfeet Indian Reservation*.

57. Rosier, *Rebirth of the Blackfeet Nation*.

58. "Reading of the Robe," 271.

EPILOGUE

1. I began apprenticing with my grandmother and my aunt Theresa while I still lived in Chicago and continued when I returned home to Montana. This apprenticeship took place over a twenty-year period.

2. Grinnell, *Blackfoot Lodge Tales*, x.

3. Grinnell, *Blackfoot Lodge Tales*, xii.

4. See, e.g., Rosier, *Rebirth of the Blackfeet Nation*; Samek, *Blackfoot Confederacy*; and Wessel, "Agent of Acculturation."

5. Quoted in McClintock, *Old North Trail*, 476.

6. This is a much shorter version of the entire episode that occurred that morning. I have had other dreams in that same camping location, and I have consulted with religious leaders and family.

BIBLIOGRAPHY

MANUSCRIPT AND ARCHIVAL MATERIALS

American Museum of Natural History, New York NY (AMNH)
 Accession Records, Department of Anthropology Archives
 Department of Anthropology Records, Department of Anthropology Archives
 David Duvall Papers, Department of Anthropology Archives
 Clark Wissler Papers, Department of Anthropology Archives
Beinecke Rare Book and Manuscript Library, Yale University, New Haven CT
 Walter McClintock Papers
Glenbow Museum, Calgary AB
 Jane Richardson Hanks Papers
 Claude Schaeffer Papers
Marquette University Archives, Milwaukee WI
 Bureau of Catholic Indian Missions Records
Merrill G. Burlingame Special Collections, Montana State University Library, Bozeman MT
 Cecile Black Boy Papers, Federal Writers' Project
 James Willard Schultz Papers
Minnesota Historical Society, Saint Paul MN
 President's Subject Files, Great Northern Railway Company (GNR)
Montana Historical Society, Helena MT
 Browning Mercantile Company Records
 Campbell Family Papers
 Pierre Chouteau Jr. and Company Papers
National Anthropological Archives, National Museum of Natural History, Smithsonian Institution, Washington DC (NAA-SI)

John C. Ewers Papers

Photographs

Truman Michelson Papers

National Archives and Records Administration, Denver CO

Record Group 75, Records of the Bureau of Indian Affairs

Provincial Archives of Alberta, Edmonton AB

Oblates of Mary Immaculate Papers

Southwest Museum, Pasadena CA

George Bird Grinnell Papers

PUBLISHED WORKS

Barrett, S. A. "The Blackfoot Iniskim or Buffalo Bundle: Its Origin and Use." *Milwaukee Public Museum Yearbook* 1 (1921): 80–84.

———. "The Blackfoot Sweat Lodge." *Milwaukee Public Museum Yearbook* 1 (1921): 73–80.

———. "Collecting among the Blackfoot Indians." *Milwaukee Public Museum Yearbook for 1921* (1922): 22–28.

———. "A New Ethnology Group—The Plains Indians—Blackfoot." *Milwaukee Public Museum Yearbook* 2 (1922): 173–76.

———. "The Painted Lodge or Ceremonial Tipi." *Milwaukee Public Museum Yearbook for 1921* (1922): 85–88.

Bebbington, Julia M. *Quillwork of the Plains.* Calgary AB: Glenbow Museum, 1982.

Binnema, Theodore. "Allegiances and Interests: Niitsitapi (Blackfoot) Trade, Diplomacy, and Warfare, 1806–1831." *Western Historical Quarterly* 37, no. 3 (Autumn 2006): 327–49.

———. *Common and Contested Ground: A Human and Environmental History of the Northwestern Plains.* Norman: University of Oklahoma, 2001.

Blackfoot Gallery Committee. *Nitsitapiisinni: The Story of the Blackfoot People.* Toronto: Key Porter Books, 2001.

Bottomly-O'Looney, Jennifer. "Sitting Proud: The Indian Portraits of Joseph Scheuerle." *Montana: The Magazine of Western History* 58, no. 3 (Autumn 2008): 64–72.

Brink, Jack. *Imagining Head-Smashed-In: Aboriginal Buffalo Hunting on the Northern Plains.* Edmonton AB: Athabaska Press, 2008.

Carroll, J. B., S.J. "The Fourth of July Dishonored." *The Indian Sentinel* (1910): 28–33.

Catlin, George. *North American Indians.* 1844. New York: Penguin Books, 2004.

"Constitution and By-Laws for the Blackfeet Tribe of the Blackfeet Indian Reservation of Montana." 1998. www.narf.org/nill/constitutions/blackfeet/.

Cooper, John M. "Truman Michelson." *American Anthropologist,* n.s., 42, no. 2 (April–June 1939): 281–85.

Curtis, Edward S. *The North American Indian: Being a Series of Volumes Picturing and Describing the Indians of the United States and Alaska.* Vol. 6. Seattle, 1911.

Deloria, Vine, Jr. *God Is Red: A Native View of Religion.* Updated ed. Golden CO: Fulcrum, 1994.

———. *Red Earth, White Lies: Native Americans and the Myth of Scientific Fact.* Boulder CO: Fulcrum, 1997.

DeMarce, Roxanne, ed. *Blackfeet Heritage, 1907–1908.* Browning MT: Blackfeet Heritage Program, 1980.

Dempsey, Hugh A. "Claude Everett Schaeffer, 1901–1969." *American Anthropologist* 72, no. 6 (1970): 1409–10.

Dempsey, Hugh A., and Lindsay Moir. *Bibliography of the Blackfoot.* Lanham MD: Scarecrow Press, 1989.

Dempsey, L. James. *Blackfoot War Art: Pictographs of the Reservation Period, 1880–2000.* Norman: University of Oklahoma Press, 2007.

Dyck, Paul. "Lone Wolf Returns to That Long Ago Time." *Montana: The Magazine of Western History* 22, no. 1 (Winter 1972): 18–41.

Egan, Timothy. *Short Nights of the Shadow Catcher: The Epic Life and Immortal Photographs of Edward Curtis.* Boston: Houghton Mifflin Harcourt, 2012.

Eggermont-Molenaar, Mary. *Montana 1911: A Professor and His Wife among the Blackfeet.* Lincoln: University of Nebraska Press, 2005.

Ewers, John C. *Blackfeet Crafts.* Washington DC: U.S. Department of the Interior, 1945.

———. *The Blackfeet: Raiders on the Northwestern Plains.* Norman: University of Oklahoma Press, 1958.

———. *The Horse in Blackfeet Culture.* Smithsonian Institution, Bureau of American Ethnology Bulletin 159. Washington DC: U.S. Government Printing Office, 1955.

———. "Notes on the Weasel in Historic Plains Indian Culture." *Plains Anthropologist* 22, no. 78 (1977): 253–62.

———. *Blackfeet Indian Tipis: Design and Legend.* Bozeman MT: Museum of the Rockies, Montana State University, 1976–2016. http://arc.lib.montana.edu/indian-great-plains/ewers-forward.php.

Fagan, Brian. *The Little Ice Age: How Climate Made History, 1300–1850.* New York: Basic Books, 2002.

Farr, William E. "Troubled Bundles, Troubled Blackfeet: The Travail of Cultural and Religious Renewal." *Montana: The Magazine of Western History* 43, no. 4 (Autumn 1993): 3–18.

Foley, Michael F. *An Historical Analysis of the Administration of the Blackfeet Indian Reservation by the United States, 1855–1950's.* Report for the U.S. Indian Claims Commission, Docket Number 279-D, 1974.

Frantz, Donald G., and Norma Jean Russell. *Blackfoot Dictionary of Stems, Roots, and Affixes.* 2nd ed. Toronto: University of Toronto Press, 1995.

Freed, Stanley A., and Ruth S. Freed. "Clark Wissler and the Development of Anthropology in the United States." *American Anthropologist*, n.s., 85, no. 4 (December, 1983): 800–825.

———. *Clark Wissler: September 18, 1870–August 25, 1947*. National Academy of Sciences of the United States of America Biographical Memoirs. Washington DC: National Academy Press, 1992.

Gidley, Mick, ed. *Edward S. Curtis and the North American Indian Project in the Field*. Lincoln: University of Nebraska Press, 2003.

Grinnell, George Bird. *Blackfeet Indian Stories*. 1913. Helena MT: Riverbend Publishing, 2005.

———. *Blackfoot Lodge Tales: The Story of a Prairie People*. 1892. Lincoln: University of Nebraska Press, 2003.

———. "The Lodges of the Blackfeet." *American Anthropologist*, n.s., 3, no. 4 (October–December 1901): 650–68.

Hagan, William T. *Theodore Roosevelt and Six Friends of the Indian*. Norman: University of Oklahoma Press, 1997.

Hallowell, A. Irving. "Ojibway Ontology, Behavior and World View." In *Contributions to Ojibwe Studies: Essays, 1934–1972*, edited and with introductions by Jennifer S. H. Brown and Susan Elaine Gray, 535–68. Lincoln: University of Nebraska Press, 2010.

Hammel, Eric. *Khe Sanh: Siege in the Clouds*. New York: Crown, 1989.

Hanna, Warren L. Foreword to *Recently Discovered Tales of Life among the Indians*, by James Willard Schultz. Compiled and edited by Warren L. Hanna. Missoula MT: Mountain Press Publishing, 1988.

———. *Stars over Montana: A Centennial Celebration of the Men Who Shaped Glacier National Park*. Guilford CT: Twodot Press, 1989.

Harrod, Howard L. *The Animals Came Dancing: Native American Sacred Ecology and Animal Kinship*. Tucson: University of Arizona Press, 2000.

———. *Mission among the Blackfeet*. Norman: University of Oklahoma Press, 1971.

———. *Renewing the World: Plains Indian Religion and Morality*. Tucson: University of Arizona Press, 1987.

Hartley, L. P. *The Go-Between*. 1953. New York: New York Review Books, 2002.

Holterman, Jack, et al. *A Blackfoot Language Study*. [Browning MT]: Piegan Institute, 1996.

Johnston, Alex. *Plants and the Blackfoot*. Occasional Paper No. 15. Lethbridge AB: Lethbridge Historical Society, 1987.

Josselin de Jong, J. P. de. *Blackfoot Texts from the Southern Peigans Reservation, Teton County, Montana, with the Help of Black-Horse-Rider, Collected and Published with an English Translation*. Amsterdam: Johannes Müller, 1914.

———. "Social Organization of the Southern Peigans." *Internationales Archiv für Ethnographie* 20, no. 5 (1912): 191–96.

Kappler, Charles J., comp. and ed. *Indian Affairs, Laws and Treaties*. 2 vols. 2nd ed. Washington DC: Government Printing Office, 1904.

LaPier, Rosalyn. "Between Hay and Grass: A Brief History of Two Métis Communities in Central Montana." In *Proceedings of the International Conference of Metis History and Culture*, edited by William Furdell, 105–20. Great Falls MT: University of Great Falls, 1997.

———. "Blackfeet Botanist: Annie Mad Plume Wall." *Montana Naturalist* (Fall 2005): 4–5.

———. "From the Natural to the Supernatural: Discovering the Piegan People's World View." *Montana Naturalist* (Winter 2009–10): 6–7.

———. "Métis Life along Montana's Front Range." In *Beyond . . . The Shadows of the Rockies: History of the Augusta Area*, 33–41. Augusta MT: Augusta Historical Society, 2007.

———. "Métis Miskihkiya: Métis Life in Montana." *Montana Naturalist* (Winter 2013–14): 4–5.

———. "Relationship with the Land—Seasonal Round." *Niitsitapiisinni: Our Way of Life*, Glenbow Museum, Calgary AB, Spring 2006. www.glenbow.org/blackfoot /teacher_toolkit/pdf/Land_SeasonalRound.pdf.

———. "Silent, Sacred and Wild." *Crown of the Continent and the Greater Yellowstone Magazine*, no. 1 (2015): 58–61.

———. "Smudging: Plants, Purification and Prayer." *Montana Naturalist* (Spring–Summer 2016): 16–17.

———. "What's in a Name?" *Montana Naturalist* (Spring–Summer 2015): 6–8.

LaPier, Rosalyn R., and David R. M. Beck. *City Indian: Native American Activism in Chicago, 1893–1934*. Lincoln: University of Nebraska Press, 2015.

LaPier, Rosalyn R., and Shirlee Crow Shoe. "Blackfeet Vocabulary Terms for Items of Material Culture." Report for the National Museum of Natural History, Washington DC, 2004.

Many Guns, Tom. *Pinto Horse Rider*. Browning MT: Blackfeet Heritage Program, 1979.

Martin, James, S.J. *The Jesuit's Guide to (Almost) Everything: A Spirituality for Real Life*. New York: HarperOne, 2012.

McClintock, Walter. "The Blackfoot Tipi." *The Masterkey*. Los Angeles: Southwest Museum, 10, no. 3 (May 1936): 85–96.

———. *The Blackfoot Tipi*. Southwest Museum Leaflets, no. 5. Los Angeles: Southwest Museum, 1936.

———. *The Old North Trail: Life, Legends and Religion of the Blackfeet Indians*. 1910. Lincoln: University of Nebraska, 1999.

———. *Painted Tipis and Picture Writing of the Blackfoot Indians*. Southwest Museum Leaflets, no. 6. Los Angeles: Southwest Museum, 1936.

———. *The Tragedy of the Blackfoot*. Southwest Museum Papers, no. 3. Los Angeles: Southwest Museum, 1930.

Michelson, Truman. "Piegan Tales." *Journal of American Folklore* 24, no. 92 (April–June 1911): 238–48.

———. Review of *Original Blackfoot Texts*, by C. C. Uhlenbeck. *American Anthropologist*, n.s., 13, no. 2 (April–June 1911): 326–30.

Mihesuah, Devon A., ed. *Natives and Academics: Researching and Writing about American Indians*. Lincoln: University of Nebraska Press, 1998.

Morgan, Rosalind Grace. "Beaver Ecology/Beaver Mythology." PhD diss., University of Alberta, 1991.

Morrisroe, Patrick. "Blessing." *The Catholic Encyclopedia*. Vol. 2. New York: Appleton, 1907. http://www.newadvent.org/.

Nabokov, Peter. *A Forest of Time: American Indian Ways of History*. Cambridge: Cambridge University Press, 2002.

Peterson, Jacqueline, and Jennifer S. H. Brown, eds. *The New People: Being and Becoming Métis*. Winnipeg: University of Manitoba Press, 1985.

Pohle, Joseph. "The Real Presence of Christ in the Eucharist." *The Catholic Encyclopedia*. Vol. 5. New York: Appleton, 1909. http://www.newadvent.org/cathen/05573a.htm.

Prados, John, and Ray W. Stubbe. *Valley of Decision: The Siege of Khe Sanh*. Boston: Houghton Mifflin, 1991.

Prothero, Stephen R. *God Is not One: The Eight Religions That Run the World—and Why Their Differences Matter*. New York: HarperOne, 2011.

Punke, Michael. *Last Stand: George Bird Grinnell, the Battle to Save the Buffalo, and the Birth of the New West*. Washington DC: Smithsonian Books, 2007.

"The Reading of the Robe." *Forest and Stream* 46, no. 14 (April 4, 1896): 271.

Rosier, Paul. *Rebirth of the Blackfeet Nation, 1912–1954*. Lincoln: University of Nebraska University, 2001.

Said, Edward. *Culture and Imperialism*. New York: Vintage, 1994.

Samek, Hana. *The Blackfoot Confederacy, 1880–1920: A Comparative Study of Canadian and U.S. Indian Policy*. Albuquerque: University of New Mexico Press, 2011.

Schultz, James Willard. *Blackfeet and Buffalo: Memories of Life among the Indians*. Norman: University of Oklahoma Press, 1962.

———. "Life among the Blackfeet [first paper]." *Forest and Stream* 21, no. 18 (November 29, 1883): 343–44.

———. "Life among the Blackfeet—Second Paper." *Forest and Stream* 21, no. 19 (December 6, 1883): 362.

———. "Life among the Blackfeet—Third Paper." *Forest and Stream* 21, no. 20 (December 13, 1883): 383.

———. "Life among the Blackfeet—Fourth Paper." *Forest and Stream* 21, no. 21 (December 20, 1883): 405.

———. "Life among the Blackfeet—Fifth Paper." *Forest and Stream* 21, no. 22 (December 27, 1883): 433–34.

———. "Life among the Blackfeet—Sixth Paper." *Forest and Stream* 21, no. 23 (January 3, 1884): 450.

———. "Life among the Blackfeet—Seventh Paper." *Forest and Stream* 21, no. 24 (January 10, 1884): 470–71.

———. "Life among the Blackfeet—Eighth Paper." *Forest and Stream* 21, no. 25 (January 17, 1884): 492.

———. "Life among the Blackfeet—Ninth Paper." *Forest and Stream* 21, no. 26 (January 24, 1884): 512.

———. "Life among the Blackfeet—Tenth Paper—Folk-Lore." *Forest and Stream* 22, no. 1 (January 31, 1884): 5.

———. "Life among the Blackfeet—Eleventh Paper—Folk-Lore." *Forest and Stream* 22, no. 2 (February 7, 1884): 24–25.

———. "Life among the Blackfeet—Twelfth Paper—Folk-Lore." *Forest and Stream* 22, no. 4 (February 21, 1884): 64.

———. "Life among the Blackfeet—Thirteenth Paper—Folk-Lore." *Forest and Stream* 22, no. 7 (March 13, 1884): 122.

———. "Life among the Blackfeet—Fourteenth Paper—Folk-Lore." *Forest and Stream* 22, no. 8 (March 20, 1884): 143.

———. *My Life as an Indian: The Story of a Red Woman and a White Man in the Lodges of the Blackfeet.* New York: Doubleday, Page, 1907.

———. "The Origin of the Medicine Lodge." *Forest and Stream* 29, no. 5 (August 25, 1887): 82.

———. "The 'Piskan' of the Blackfeet." *Forest and Stream* 18, no. 18 (June 1, 1882): 344.

———. *Recently Discovered Tales of Life among the Indians.* Compiled and edited by Warren L. Hanna. Missoula MT: Mountain Press Publishing, 1988.

———. "The White Buffalo Cow." *Forest and Stream* 16, no. 12 (April 21, 1881): 224.

Schultz, James Willard, and Jessie Louise Donaldson. *The Sun God's Children.* Boston: Houghton Mifflin, 1930.

Schultz, James Willard, and Michael Kennedy. "Return to the Beloved Mountains." *Montana: The Magazine of Western History* 7, no. 3 (Summer 1957): 26–33.

Sherow, James Earl. *The Grasslands of the United States: An Environmental History.* Santa Barbara CA: ABC-CLIO, 2007.

Smith, Linda Tuhiwai. *Decolonizing Methodologies: Research and Indigenous Peoples.* 2nd ed. London: Zed Books, 2012.

Smith, Sherry L. *Reimagining Indians: Native Americans through Anglo Eyes, 1880–1940.* New York: Oxford University Press, 2002.

Soer, A., S.J. "The Piëgans." *The Indian Sentinel* (1910): 17–23.

Thurnston, Herbert. "Easter Controversy." *The Catholic Encyclopedia*. Vol. 5. New York: Appleton, 1909.

Uhlenbeck, C. C. *A New Series of Blackfoot Texts from the Southern Piegans Blackfoot Reservation, Teton County, Montana*. Amsterdam: Johannes Müller, 1912.

———. *Original Blackfoot Texts from the Southern Piegans Blackfoot Reservation, Teton County, Montana*. Amsterdam: Johannes Müller, 1911.

———. "The Origin of the Otter-Lodge." In *Festschrift: Vilhelm Thomsen zur Vollendung des siebzigsten Lebensjahres am 25 Januar 1912*. Leipzig: Otto Harrassowitz, 1912.

Uhlenbeck, C. C., and R. H. Van Gulik. *A Blackfoot-English Vocabulary Based on Material from the Southern Peigans*. Amsterdam: Noord-Hollandsche Uitgevers-Maatschappij, 1934.

———. *An English-Blackfoot Vocabulary: Based on Material from the Southern Peigans*. Amsterdam: Koninklijke Akademie van Wetenschappen, 1930.

United States. Congress. *Blackfeet Indian Reservation: Serial One, Hearings before the Joint Commission of the Congress of the United States to Investigate Indian Affairs*. 63rd Cong., 2nd sess., part 6, February 21, 1914. Washington DC: GPO, 1914.

United States. Office of Indian Affairs. *Annual Report of the Commissioner of Indian Affairs, for the Year 1878*. Washington DC: Government Printing Office, 1878.

———. *Annual Report of the Commissioner of Indian Affairs, for the Year 1880*. Washington DC: Government Printing Office, 1880.

———. *Annual Report of the Commissioner of Indian Affairs, for the Year 1882*. Washington DC: Government Printing Office, 1882.

———. *Annual Report of the Commissioner of Indian Affairs, for the Year 1883*. Washington DC: Government Printing Office, 1883.

———. *Annual Report of the Commissioner of Indian Affairs, for the Year 1884*. Washington DC: Government Printing Office, 1884.

———.*Annual Report of the Commissioner of Indian Affairs, for the Year 1886*. Washington DC: Government Printing Office, 1886.

United States. Senate. *Subcommittee Report*. 48th Cong., 1st sess., *Senate Report 238, 1883–1885*.

Wessel, Thomas. "Agent of Acculturation: Farming on the Northern Plains Reservations, 1880–1910." *Agricultural History* 60, no. 2 (Spring 1986): 233–45.

Wildschut, William. "Blackfoot Beaver Bundles." *Indian Notes* (Museum of the American Indian, Heye Foundation), 1 (1924): 138–41.

———. "Blackfoot Pipe Bundles." *Indian Notes* (Museum of the American Indian, Heye Foundation), 5, no. 4 (1928): 419–33.

Winter, Joseph C. "Food of the Gods: Biochemistry, Addiction, and the Development of Native American Tobacco Use." In *Tobacco Use by Native North Americans: Sacred Smoke and Silent Killer*, edited by Joseph C. Winter, 305–29. Norman: University of Oklahoma Press, 2000.

Wissler, Clark. *Ceremonial Bundles of the Blackfoot Indians.* Anthropological Papers of the American Museum of Natural History. Vol. 7, part 2. New York: American Museum of Natural History, 1912.

———. *Material Culture of the Blackfoot Indians.* Anthropological Papers of the American Museum of Natural History. Vol. 5, part 1. New York: American Museum of Natural History, 1910.

———. *The Social Life of the Blackfoot Indians.* Anthropological Papers of the American Museum of Natural History. Vol. 7, part 1. New York: American Museum of Natural History, 1911.

———. *The Sun Dance of the Blackfoot Indians.* Anthropological Papers of the American Museum of Natural History. Vol. 16, part 3. New York: American Museum of Natural History, 1918.

Wissler, Clark, and D. C. Duvall. *Mythology of the Blackfoot Indians.* Anthropological Papers of the American Museum of Natural History. Vol. 2, part 1. New York: American Museum of Natural History, 1908.

INDEX

Page numbers in italic indicate illustrations.

Amelanchier alnifolia, 3, 52, 54–55, 128, 150n20; wood, 55

American Anthropologist, 107

American Museum of Natural History, 60, 89, 100, 107, 110, 111

American settlers, 45

Amskapi Pikuni tribe. See Blackfeet

animals, 77, 87. See also Kse-ōhts-uh-pēks-sēks (under animals); Raven (supernatural entity); Sō-ōhts'uh-pēks-sēks (beyond animals); Spŭhts'-ah-pēk-sēks (above animals); and individual animals

annuities. See under Blackfeet: annuity payments and rations to

antelope, 57–58; clothing, 58; uses of, 57–58

Apatohsi Pikuni tribe, xvii, 6–7, 25, 48, 63

A'pekaiĭks. See Skunks band (Blackfeet)

apprenticeship of author, xvi, xxxi–xxxii, 135, 137–38. See also under Blackfeet: traditional, education

Arctostaphylos uva-ursi, 75

arranged marriage, xviii

ashes. See tobacco ashes

assimilation efforts, federal government, 19, 101, 136–38. See also civilization policy

authenticity of Indian scholars, xi–xv

autumn, 50, 58, 59. See also closed season

awl, 40

axes, 12

Å'χkomonoàsiu (Green Lake), 57

Azure, Roselyn, xlii

bacon, 21

Badger Creek, xxxiii, 58; agency headquarters at, 12, 13, 17

Badger-Two Medicine area, xxxiii, 23, 45

bags. See under antelope: uses of

band system. See Aápaitapì band; Blackfeet: bands; Blackfeet: band system; Blackfoot Confederacy: bands; Fat Melters band; Lone Eater's band; Never Laughs band (Blackfeet); Skunks band (Blackfeet)

Bannock MT, 10

Barrett, Samuel A., 31, 130, 162n59

barter, 12–13

Battle Coulee (Itsipútsimaup), 50–51

beads, 99

beadwork, 17, 100

Bear Chief, 16, 67, 114, 134

Bear Gulch, 60

Bear Leggings, Peter, 114

Bear Medicine, 113

Bear Paw Mountains, 10; mining in, 15

Bear River. See Marias River

bears, 57

bears, supernatural, 26, 39–40, 138–39

Beaver, supernatural. See Kitaiksísskstaki (Not Real Beaver [supernatural entity])

Beaver bundles, xxiii, 65, 66, 68–75, 76, 77, 79

Beaver medicine, 68–75, 77–78

Beaver men, 69, 73–74, 78–80

beavers, 23, 27, 65, 77; fur of, 55–56

Beck, Abaki, xlii, 137

Beck, David, 124

Beck, Iko'tsimiskimaki, xlii, 137

Beck, Martin, 124

beef, 14, 21, 134

Below world, xl, 26–28, 31, 35–37, 72, 73, 75, 77, 95, 98, 129; and kinship relationship with Above world, 36–37, 43

Napiwa (supernatural entity), 27

Na-pos. *See* opened season

National Anthropological Archives, 112

National Museum of Natural History, 116

Natoas Kistakumaki (Holy Thunder Woman), 134

nature. *See under* Blackfeet: control of nature

navigation using stars, 43

Never Laughs band (Blackfeet), xviii, 44, 114, 134

new year, Blackfeet, 2, 88

Nicotiana quadrivalvis, 49, 52, 58, 69, 71–76, 81; cultivation of, 71–75, 76; planting, 71–74, 76; seeds, 72, 75–76

Nicotiana tabacum, 52, 72, 75–76, 83

nicotine, 76

niitóyis. *See under* Blackfeet: tipis

Niitsitapi (original people), 26–28

Nínaistɑko. *See* Mountain Chief

Nitana, 109

Ni-wax-saxs (little people), 27, 73–74

No Bear, Henry, 113

No Coat, 126

North Peigan tribe. *See* Apatohsi Pikuni tribe

North Saskatchewan River, 6

North Star. *See* Kakató'si (North Star or Star Child)

No Runner, Tim. *See* Under Mink

Not Real Beaver. *See* Kitaiksísskstaki (Not Real Beaver [supernatural entity])

Not Real Beaver Woman, xiii, xxxii, *xix*; xlii, 2, 23–24, 64, 136, 138

Not Real Beaver Woman (the author), 24

Ojibwe, 138

O'kan, 3–6, 13, 22, 50, 65, 89–91, 94,

96–97; lodge, *86*, 91, 109, 120, 130–32, 150n20

okonok. *See Amelanchier alnifolia*

Okotoks (place), *60*

Old Agency. *See under* Badger Creek: agency headquarters at

Old Chief, Irene, xlii

Old Child, 114

Old Lady Strangling Wolf, 111

Old Man. *See* Napiwa (supernatural entity)

Omahkataioaki. *See* Big Mountain Lion Woman

omahksi-kakahsiin. See *Chimaphila umbellata*

O'mɑχkskimikokàup. *See* Big Rock tipi

opened season, xli, 50, 51, 65–66, 76, 82–98

oral history, xxiii–xv, xxxvi–xxxviii, 99–118. *See also* stories; storytakers; storytellers, Blackfeet

oral tradition, xix

original people. *See* Niitsitapi (original people)

otahkoyitsi. See *Comandra umbellata*

otters, 27, 77; supernatural, 74

outhouses, 83

owls, 120; supernatural, 120–21

Owl Woman. *See* Wall, Angeline

oyster rocks. *See* rocks (supernatural entities)

Pablo, George, 113

Paie (Mistaken Morning Star), 27, 34–35, 117–18

paint, 95, 98, 117

Pakoki Lake. *See* Pɑχkå'χkeyi (Pakoki Lake)

parfleche containers, 53–55, 56, 57

Pɑχkå'χkeyi (Pakoki Lake), 54

Páyotayakχkumei. *See* Aimsback

Payottaayawaahkomi. *See* Aimsback
peacock, 98
Peigan reserve, *18*
pemmican, 53–54, 119, 128
peppermint, 53–54
Piegan Farming and Livestock Association, 122, 125–28
Piegan Institute, xvi, xvii, xxiv, 142n14
Pinus contorta, 56–57, 58
pipes, 58, 65, 83. *See also* Thunder Pipe; women's pipes
pipestems. See under *Amelanchier alnifolia*: wood
Pipestone Cliff, 58
pishkun, 38
pisstááhkaan. See *Nicotiana quadrivalvis*
place, 29
plains tribes, 52
planting sticks, 74
plants, xxxi, xli, xlii; gathering of, 2, 10, 12, 49, 50, 80, 128, 133, 135, 136, 138. *See also* berries; Blackfeet: loss of access to plants by; Blackfeet: medicinal use of plants; Blackfeet: plant knowledge; Blackfeet: plant picking by; Blackfeet: plants as food for; Blackfeet: gathering of plants by; *and individual species*
plates, 57
Pleiades. *See* Mióhpokoiksi (Lost Children or Pleiades)
Polaris. *See* Kakató'si (North Star or Star Child)
polliwogs. *See* tadpoles
Ponákiksi. *See* Cut Bank Creek
Populus deltoides, 57, 59, 91
Porcupine Hills, 96
porcupines, 99–100. *See also* quills, porcupine
Potato Woman, 106

"power of the waters," 69, 81
powwows, 141n3
Prairie People. *See* Saokiotapi (Prairie People)
prairies, 50, 63, 86, 89, 102, 121, 136
prairie turnip (supernatural entity), 36–37, 43
prairie turnips, 45–46
Prando, Father Peter, 20
prayer, 55, 71, 74, 75, 83, 137
Progressive Era, xxi, xxxviii
property ownership of women, 56
Prunus virginiana, 53, 55; 57, 128; tipi stakes, 55; use of, wood for tools, 55
puffball fungus. *See* Kakató'si (fungus)
Pulling Down Lodge, 106
punishment, 76
purification, 34–35; 83, 138

quills, porcupine, 111
quillwork, 99–100. *See also* blanket bands, quill
quirts, 56
quivers, 56

rabbits, 24
raids, 91–92. *See also under* Crow Indians: Blackfeet raids on
railroad, 4, travel by, 45–46. *See also* Great Northern Railroad
rain, xli, 38, 74, 86, 87, 88, 95, 96
Rainbow lodge, *41*
rainbows, 87
ranches, non-Indian, 15, 16
ranching, 133
rations. *See under* Blackfeet: annuity payments and rations to
Rattler, xiii
Rattler, Annie. *See* Mad Plume, Annie
Rattler, Philip, 2, *8*

traditional homelands. *See under*
   Blackfeet: aboriginal territory
transubstantiation, 159n45
travel, 44, 61–62, 64, 72, 74, 91. *See
   also* horses; mobility; seasonal
   rounds; railroad: travel by
travois, 15, 56, 57, 134
treaties: 1865, 10–12; 1868; 10–12. *See
   also* executive agreement: of 1888;
   executive agreement: of 1896; Lame
   Bull's treaty, 1855; Treaty 7 (Canada)
Treaty 7 (Canada), 11
tribal ecological knowledge. *See* traditional ecological knowledge
Turtle Mountain Chippewa tribe, xiv
turtles, 27, 77
Two Medicine River, 2, 50, 58, 64, 113
Two Medicine River valley, 64

Uhlenbeck, Cornelius C., xii, xvii, 5, 21,
   31, 47–48, 52, 62, 66, 87, 102, 113–15
Uhlenbeck, Willy, 62, 114–15
under animals. *See* Kse-ōhts-uh-pēks-
   sēks (under animals)
Under Mink, 157n3
underwater beings. *See* Soyiitapi
   (underwater beings)
Unistassamme. *See* Calf Looking
United States Marine Corps, 82
University of Lethbridge researchers,
   24, 26
Ursa Major, 79. *See also* Ihkitsíkammiksi (Seven Brothers or Big
   Dipper)

Van Gulick, R. H., xvii
vegetables, 126
Venus. *See* Iipisówaahs (Morning Star)
Vielle, James, 114
Vietnam War, 82–83

Virginia City MT, 10
visible realm, 28, 44–63, 90, 93

Wades-in-the-Water, Julia, 113
Wall, Angeline, xlii, 83, 119–21, 122
Wall, Annie. *See* Mad Plume, Annie
Wall, Bernadette, xlii
Wall, Francis, 119, 142n11
Wall, Francis (Iòkimau), xii–xiv, xviii,
   xxxiii, xxxvi–xxxvii, xl, 83, 111, 119–
   22, 127, 129, 132, 134, 135–36
Wall, Gilbert, 82–83, 99
Wall, Shirley, 142n11
Wall, Thomas Francis. *See* Wall, Francis
   (Iòkimau)
Walters, Jim, 59
war, 67, 95, 120. *See also* Vietnam War
war shields, 53
war stories, 82–83
Washington DC, 128. *See also under*
   Blackfeet: delegations to Washing-
   ton DC
water, 38, 68–69, 83, 86
Water world, xl, 26–28, 68–69, 72, 73,
   75, 77, 80, 98, 129
wealth, 95
weasel (supernatural entity), 38
weasel grass, 59
Weasel Head, 52, 53, 56–57
Weasel Tail (Kainai), 58, 92, 116
weather, 78–80, 84–89, 98; forecasting, 80. *See also under* Blackfeet:
   control of weather
Weather Dancer. *See* Weather Men
Weather Men, 90–91, 96–98
Weather Priest. *See* Weather Men
Wells, Agnes, xxxiii–xxxiv
Wells, Albert, xxxiv
west (direction), 35
wetlands, 50

wheat, 127

White Calf, 15–16, 19, 20, 52, 64, 72, 74, 108; conversion of, to Catholicism, 20, 64; death of, in Washington DC, 20, 21

White Elk, 113

White Man, Adam, 2, 63

White Quiver, 114

White Swan, Julia, 113

Wilber, Jessie, 130

wild rose. See *Rosa woodsii*

Wildschut, William, 162n59

Willow Creek, 16

Willow Creek School, 1, *7*

Willow Round (place), 58

wind, xxxv, 78, 84–85; chinook, 78, 84

Wind Maker (supernatural entity), 27, 84–85

winter, 50, 58–60, 77–78, 84, 91. *See also* closed season

winter counts, xxiii, 147n13

Wissler, Clark, xix–xx, 3, 6, 25, 28, 29, 31, 32–34, 43, 53, 55, 56, 60, 62, 66, 68–69, 70, 76, 79, 89, 91, 92–93, 95–98, 101–2, 107, 110–12, 121, 132

Wolf Calf, 108

Wolf Tail, 108

wolves, 57

Women's Buffalo Jump, *60*

women's pipes, 83

Women's Point. *See* A'kekoksistakskuyì (Women's Point)

Women's Society Left Their Lodge Pole (place). *See* Mátokeks omɑ'nis tàmoai otsítskitaχpiau (Women's Society Left their Lodgepoles)

wool robes, 56, 95

worm rocks. *See* rocks (supernatural entities)

worms, 74

Writing on Stone (place). *See* A'isinaiχpì (Writing on Stone)

Yellow Bird Woman, 106, 110–11

Yellow Calf, 113

Yellowstone River, 6, 47

Yellow Wolf, 106

Yellow Wolf, Ella Mad Plume, xxviii, 2, *8*, 106

Yellow Wolf, Louie, xxviii, 106

Yellow Wolf, Mary (Haggerty), 106, 107

Yellow Wolf, Sam, 106

Young, John, 14

Young Bear Chief, 108

yucca as medicinal, 46

In the New Visions in Native American and Indigenous Studies series

To order or obtain more information on these or other University of Nebraska Press titles, visit nebraskapress.unl.edu.